Is Physical Education in Crisis?

Leading a Much-Needed Change in Physical Education

First published in 2021 by Scholary
Suite 7, The Oval Office, Cobbler's Way, Radstock, BA3 3BX, United Kingdom

Scholary is an imprint of Scholary Ltd

Typeset in Avenir

British Library Cataloguing in Publication Data
A catalogue record for this book is available from the British Library

ISBN: 978-1-9999-0923-9 (pbk)
ISBN: 978-1-9999-0924-6 (ebk)

Table of Contents

Is Physical Education in Crisis?
Leading a Much-Needed Change in Physical Education

Acknowledgements

With grateful thanks to the following colleagues working in schools around England and internationally: All Physical Educators that shared their experiences anonymously; Eve Wagstaff, Upton Court Grammar School; Gareth Evans, Ninestiles Academy; Fiona Reynolds, Upton Court Grammar School; Grant Huddleston and Angela Whitehouse, Birmingham City University; Shaun Dowling, United Learning; Ed Lowe, St Columba's College; Paul Beeson; Taz Malhi, Wodensborough Ormiston Academy; Stewart Orton, Blessed George Napier School; Tom Brush, Nishkam High school; Matt Bowler, King Alfred's Academy; Peter Scullion; Oliver Bishop, Upton Court Grammar School; Simon Bradbury, Bulmershe School; Phil Mathe; Liam Durr, St Oscar Romero Secondary School; Natalie Rose and Sian Mason; Renee Gregerson, District Education Centre; Sean Doyle, Shenley Brook End School; Dr Rachael Jefferson-Buchanan, Charles Sturt University; Alice Curwood, Alice Smith School; Shanise Webster; Kate Thornton-Bousfield, Youth Sport Trust; Andrew Frapwell; David Worthy, Cams Hill Secondary School.

Sincere gratitude is also extended to the following colleagues for their help and support in the writing and publication of this book:

- Mark Pritchard, Principal of Upton Court Grammar School, and all colleagues at the Pioneer Educational Trust.
- The Infinite Learners, Lewis Keens and Alan Dunstan. Their pioneering work inspired me to seek change in my own.
- Danny Burton, Youth Sport Trust
- Lauren Williams, Ditton Park Academy
- Craig Bartlett, Langley Grammar School
- Will Swaithes for his time and patience. So much of my work is based upon his insight and vision.
- Dr Liz Durden-Myers for her unrivalled expertise and solution-focused approach to Physical Education. But, most of all, for her unrelenting support and belief in my work.

Finally, to my family. Kimberley, Amelia, and Theo. My true 'Why'.

Foreword

Will Swaithes

Physical Education has brought tremendous joy, opportunity, and fulfilment to my life. Sadly, I know that is not the case for all. In fact, if we look at attitudes and participation habits for children and young people or for adults (as shared annually by Sport England's Active Lives Reports), I am left wondering if PE is doing more harm than good for some. Don't get me wrong, there are some examples of truly inspired teaching within Physical Education that really does cater for the needs of all. There are even a good number of schools who have experimented with, and then embedded, a culture that ignites a lifelong passion for movement (be that sport, exercise, physical activity, or a rich combination to meet individual needs). There are some students who get a great deal from PE at school, and some of them step forward to influence the lives of the next generation by becoming physical educators themselves. However, there are still far too many schools and physical educators who continue to deliver programmes that may be fit for a young 'sport enthusiast' but fail to connect or entice most towards a physical literacy journey that offers real fulfilment or well-being benefits.

PE has long been socio-politically defined, with pressure and influence placed on it by the perceived societal needs of the time. As a subject area, it seems it has always existed on the periphery of importance and regularly campaigns for a seat at the 'grown up' table amongst the likes of English and Maths. However, its power to ensure Positive Experiences (for me, those are the important P and E of P.E) for all young people in, through and around Sport, Physical Activity and Movement (SPAM) lie not in the hands of policy makers, the nuance of curriculum writing teams, or even the communication of lobbying organisations, but in the hands of its current and future custodians – the physical educators.

What will you do to help move PE past its mere survival as a marmite subject? What will you do to secure its legitimate place in hearts, minds, and souls of all? After all, physical literacy was our first literacy…from an evolutionary perspective, it enabled us to hunt, gather, seek shelter and play, which were the foundations of survival. Later, we learnt to communicate through spoken and then written language, to pass wisdom on through the generations. But the current technological revolution tells me that developing the mind-body connection and skills to be more human are what we need most to thrive in the 21st century. Digital literacy will give us knowledge at our fingertips but what makes the human species unique is our ability to be curious, to be creative, to collaborate, and perhaps even to be competitive.

This book is written by a passionate, well-informed, critically reflective, and aspirational practitioner who aims to lead PE in a new direction. I first met Lee in 2019, at a conference I was speaking at. It was clear from the outset that he had an appetite and hunger to transform Physical Education in his setting to better meet the needs of all children, rather than continue to cater well for just a few. As a current curriculum leader, he has always asked good questions, and sought opportunities to learn from others and test ideas in his school. Lee strives to ensure PE has more value, meaning, relevance, purpose, and currency for all his students, but he also hopes this book will support you in taking the next steps in transforming your offer too. I encourage you to remove your suit of armour, to remove your defensive case for the power of PE, and to navigate this text with an open mind for change and a willingness to reflect on the impact of your own practice, leadership, or ideology.

Dr Liz Durden-Myers

At present in the primary context *"the relative value of physical activity when compared with the unquestioned value of literacy and mathematics, relegates physical education to a low status, low demand subject"* (Ennis, 2006, p.53). The challenge for the physical education community is to elevate the evaluation of physical education from a subject with a relative value, to a subject of an equal value, that is an integral part of a holistic education. The secondary context is no different, in that it has relegated core physical education with its focus on promoting engagement in physical activity, in favour of the dominant focus on examination PE and attainment grade performance (Green, 2005 and Thorburn, 2007), in or the worst case, in favour or more time in other subject areas.

Kirk (2010, 2012) argues that the ability of physical education to enthuse, engage, and promote lifelong engagement is frequently disputed, with concerns that, without a radical reform, the subject is in danger of becoming extinct. There has been an increasing amount of literature that suggests that physical education has troubled times ahead (Stier, Klienman and Milchrist, 1994; Penney and Chandler, 2000; Kirk 2010), and this leads to an increased criticality and speculation about the future of physical education.

Fairclough, Stratton and Baldwin (2002) describe how the National Curriculum for PE (NCPE) can be restrictive in its nature and can perpetuate traditional biases towards; what activities boys and girls should follow, teacher expertise and the influence of the media. All these factors conspire to affect the content and future relevance of curricular and extra-curricular programmes. As a result, many schools place a significant emphasis on team games, as opposed to lifetime activities or focussing on wider educational goals. This is still the dominant approach taken today, even with the introduction of a new, less-restrictive curriculum, physical education seems to be stuck in a game, skills-based and sport-techniques structure (Kirk, 2010).

To prepare students for a lifetime of participation in physical activity, physical educators must recognise which activities have the greatest carry-over and value into adult life and what wider educational concepts are ideally taught through the physical medium. Schools, and in particular departmental heads of physical education, should aim to provide more opportunities for all students to experience lifetime activities and explore a wide variety of educational concepts, both within and outside curriculum time. This could be achieved by reconsidering programme content, and by creating opportunities for staff (including non-specialists) to improve their subject knowledge in areas that they are less familiar in (Fairclough et al., 2002). Without the re-evaluation of what should be taught in physical education, it may continue to fail to achieve its objectives and therefore continue to become de-stabilised, with its future unclear.

This book encapsulates the journey of one head of PE in his pursuit of trying to design, implement and evaluate a more effective approach towards physical education curriculum design, promote inclusive pedagogies and a holistic approach to assessment. Lee is an inspirational practitioner who had, and continues to have, the courage to think differently in the best interests of his students. With a plethora of calls for the physical education community to adapt their approach from a game, skills-based and sport-techniques structure, but with little guidance on how this can be achieved, Lee has crafted a highly effective alternative approach. Lee provides an example here of how physical education can be re-designed to be more impactful, engaging, and meaningful in doing so it has also reinvigorated his and his student's enjoyment of physical education and physical activity.

1

What's the Problem?

My Why

PE is in a unique position in that it can directly influence the health and well-being of an individual for the rest of their lives.

Before we go any further, I must first state my reasoning for writing this book, and why I so passionately seek change in the curriculum for PE; I need to share with you my 'why'. As Simon Sinek, the Author of Start with Why puts it, 'people don't buy what you do, they buy why you do it' (Sinek, 2009, p.41).

I am a sports enthusiast and loved PE when I was at school. My PE teacher was a huge influence on why I wanted to become a PE teacher. He was passionate about sport. Beating him at badminton was one of my greatest memories from school. My family were also great role models, with both my mother and father being marathon runners. Teaching PE was the only thing I ever wanted to do. Aged 21, I volunteered in schools, became a glorified in-house cover teacher, and dreamt of being a 'real' PE teacher. It took me two attempts to gain a place on an initial teacher training (ITT) course and I genuinely loved every minute of it. I felt as if I was delivering the same lessons that I had been taught. The same skills, the same drills, the same sports, and in the same way as had worked for me over a decade earlier. It was great. I really wanted to share my passion for sport with students. However, as the years passed, this sense of enjoyment started to fade. I felt like I was losing my sense of purpose, direction, and connection with the subject I had once fallen in love with.

After many years of teaching PE and realising my ambition as a Head of Department, I recently found myself questioning my own future within education. Most teachers get into teaching for what we call the 'reward'; it's not a monetary reward, or even the reward of recognition. It's the unmatchable feeling you get when a kid does something that they couldn't do before your intervention. The reward of genuinely making a positive impact in a young person's life is unparalleled. It's a real 'money can't buy' emotion, and I found myself feeling it less and less. I was delivering sport after sport, skill after skill, and technique after technique, seeing some students thrive, but the majority trying to fade into the background. I knew they were doing PE because they had to, not because it was providing the positive experiences that would unlock a lifetime of happiness through sport in the same way that it had for me. I felt like I was trying my best to inspire the students to love sport as much as I do and was failing. Not all students, but definitely some. I was making judgements on students' ability to perform a skill whilst simultaneously passing judgment as to whether other teachers could teach the exact same thing. I was chasing perfectionism and it felt wrong. I was preaching about the importance of lifelong physical activity and then indirectly putting students off with the skill specific lesson objectives, demotivating assessments, and drive for examination results. The pressure from 'above' to deliver these aspects of PE de-railed my passion for the subject. I was in endless meetings justifying the importance of my subject or arguing why we should not take students out of PE to do more Maths or English. I was having to present GCSE exam analysis data to SLT, or embark on endless discussions about predicted grades, interventions, and disadvantaged groups. It consumed me as a Head of Department.

I was no longer student-focused. I was focused only on results, and this impacted my decision making. I planned our assessment to focus on practical ability. I removed any non-GCSE specification sports from the curriculum. I even started teaching aspects of the GCSE theory content to the lower year groups, in order to prepare them for GCSE. At the time, I felt fully justified by these decisions and, of course, my Senior Leadership Team supported them because they were designed to drive up GCSE grades. This was not why I became a Head of Department and certainly not why I became a teacher. I had lost sight of the value of PE and, following every lesson or team meeting I led, I knew it.

Feeling frustrated, I decided to complete a learning walk, not on the staff in my team, but on the students' ability to articulate why PE existed at my school; I needed some reassurance. The most common answers were, 'it's a great outlet to get away from the other stressful lessons for a bit', 'exercise is good for us' and 'we have fun with our mates'. These answers were not wrong, but they were definitely not what I was hoping for, or anything close to the potential impact PE should be having.

There has been a monumental shift towards the benefits of physical activity on the body and mind, yet I truly believed PE could be even more. I had struggled to connect with my role because the curriculum I was leading and delivering didn't correspond with my 'why'. There was a clear disconnect between my philosophy, values, and realities of my everyday practice. What motivated me to teach wasn't what I was actually delivering. I finally understood. You could say I had a 'eureka' moment, as it was as close to one as I can ever remember having.

PE could teach genuine life skills that students could apply in many aspects of their lives. It could develop them as people. PE has the power to provide you with the tools to live longer, feel happier, communicate effectively. PE has the power to lead and be led, deal with stress, embrace failure. PE has the power to create better prepared and effective employees, and so, so much more.

My 'why' is: **to prepare every child for life through Physical Education.**

The curriculum, the one I had planned, was turning some students off sport. A student voice survey showed that just under half of the students taught did not agree to strongly enjoying exercise and sports, and 39% did not understand why it was good for them. This demonstrated that students in my school did not fully understand the value of PE the way I wanted them to.

ATTITUDES TOWARDS SPORT AND PHYSICAL ACTIVITY

56%
agreed strongly that they enjoyed taking part in exercise and sports

61%
agreed strongly that they understand why exercise and sports are good for them

15%
agreed strongly that they find exercise and sports easy

PUPILS WERE ASKED ABOUT THEIR ATTITUDES TO SPORT AND PHYSICAL ACTIVITY

National figures from 2018/19 for each measure are shown in brackets.

CONFIDENCE

29%

(32%)

agreed strongly that they feel confident when exercising and playing sports

COMPETENCE

15%

(19%)

agreed strongly that they find exercise and sports easy

KNOWLEDGE

32%

(38%)

agreed strongly that they know how to get involved and improve their skills in lots of different exercise and sports

UNDERSTANDING

61%

(66%)

agreed strongly that they feel that they understand why exercise and sports are good for them

ENJOYMENT

56%

(46%)

agreed strongly that they enjoy taking part in exercise and sports

(Student Voice Results 2018)

This was not only the case in my school. Having spoken to many other local and some not so local Heads of PE, it was clear this was the picture elsewhere too. The sport-driven curriculum I observed being delivered in schools across the country was driving a wedge between me and the job I once thought I was born to do. It was driving a wedge between the children and their full potential.

Curriculum expert Mary Myatt refers to the curriculum as the 'totality of a student's experience', but student voice and quality assurance methods were painting an alarming picture. PE, the sports delivered as part of PE, and our current offering, was not connecting with some students and that was difficult to hear. I had the best of intentions to teach the more popular sports, offer as many sports as possible, run as many teams after school as we could manage, find a sport for every student, and prepare them for GCSE PE. Yet, in reality, my curriculum was aimed at the mini mes – the students that already loved sport, that enjoyed competition, and would choose to do physical activity in their own time anyway. Casey and Kirk (2021) supported my experience by confirming the research gained highlighted that those students who were benefiting most from a 'multi-sport' and technique-based Physical Education were just like their teachers.

In my experience, the students that loved PE made up a small minority of the class, and they were one of four groups of students I taught. The second group consisted of the students that would go along with it, wouldn't call PE their favourite subject, but would certainly engage. They often make good progress too. I would rely on these students to make up the numbers in my after-school teams. Group three students would comply, though would prefer to do something different if given the choice but would give it a go. They were usually good in isolated drills, but technique would drop under pressure.

Then, finally, group four, the disengaged group. These students actively didn't enjoy PE, would forget kit, do as little as possible and show minimal progression. The curriculum I was leading and the lessons that were being delivered were only targeted at maybe five students in every class, and they were the ones who liked sport already. Due to my teaching, leadership, methods of assessment, planned curriculum and applied pedagogy, we were benefiting the few as opposed to everyone.

I wasn't engaging all students and, by focusing only on skill acquisition, I certainly wasn't meeting my 'why' by preparing every student for life through physical activity. Common lesson objectives would include: 'To demonstrate the set shot in a conditioned game' or 'To understand the key techniques involved in a serve' and 'To complete the 1200m event demonstrating your understanding of pacing'. All credible lesson objectives that focus on development of sport specific skills, techniques, or tactics. The biggest issue was that, at the end of the lesson, some students were not able to meet these objectives. They had made considerable progress towards meeting them but ultimately not all students could perform a set shot at the end of the lesson, understood the techniques related to a serve, or could complete a paced 1200m race. One could argue that it was my own teaching that meant students could not meet these objectives. However, following observation feedback from peers and observing other teachers, it was obvious this was the case for nearly every practical lesson I had seen. Some students met the lesson objectives, but most did not.

Is Physical Education in Crisis?

Not only did I realise that the curriculum did not match my 'why', but it wasn't tackling any of the wider national issues either. Childhood obesity was increasing, along with mental health issues, and body confidence and activity levels were declining.

Almost 1 in 5 children are overweight or obese when they start primary school, rising to 1 in 3 when they start secondary school (RCPCH, 2020). The World Health Organisation reported that worldwide obesity has trebled since 1975, and over 340 million children and adolescents aged 5-19 were overweight or obese in 2016 (WHO, 2020). There can be no doubt that obesity is a complex problem with many contributing factors, but this is an astounding statistic nonetheless, and obesity is preventable.

The evidence is clear that movement is fundamental to the development of a young child, yet schools were prioritising literacy and numeracy, whilst the importance of physical activity was getting overlooked. There are many contributing factors to this issue though; inevitably, this will be added to the growing list of responsibilities falling on the nation's PE teachers (and no, I do not mean Joe Wicks).

We are not solely responsible for these highly complex issues, but we must be aware of the role we can play in addressing them. Government, National Governing Bodies, and other organisations have invested millions into programmes with the aim of reducing inactivity and fighting issues such as childhood obesity.

Despite the long-term benefits of physical activity regularly communicated to all and huge government investments being made to get people active, the Active Lives (Sport England, 2019) survey found only 47.7% of young people met the Chief Medical Officer's recommendation of 60 minutes' physical activity per day. In the following Active Lives (Sport England, 2021) survey, it reported that this number had fallen to 44.9% (3.2 million children and young people). Furthermore, 31.3% (2.3 million children and young people) were doing less than thirty minutes' physical activity per day. It also reported that girls were 4% less likely to be physically active than boys, though the boys' activity levels had fallen by 3.5% from the previous survey. More than a quarter of the world's population (1.4 billion adults) are insufficiently active, and levels of inactivity are twice as high in high-income countries compared to low-income countries (WHO, 2020). In fact, the World Health Organisation reports that there has been no improvement in global levels of physical activity since 2001 (WHO, 2020). Students, young people, and adults in the UK and around the world are demonstrating their lack of motivation to remain physically active outside of PE.

Not so long ago, one of the main roles of a PE teacher was to improve and maintain the current fitness levels of their students. Now, PE teachers are tasked with not only the present, but ensuring the future of the individual's engagement in physical activity too. The same Sport England survey claimed enjoyment is the biggest driver of activity. In short, the more you enjoyed physical activity, the more active you would be. That seems logical; however, only 51% of students answered that they strongly agreed to enjoying sport, which meant that 49% of students did not feel as strongly and thus were not accessing the full benefits of taking part in regular physical activity. With PE often the only time some students experience physical activity, this is certainly something that we as physical educators must consider.

As if the above is not enough to contend with, the data from the Mental Health foundation shows that 1 in 10 children suffer with a mental health disorder (MHF, 2016), which the Barnardo's children's charity equates to three students in the average class size of 30. It is also their belief that many either go undiagnosed or lack confidence and have an overarching sense of unhappiness throughout much of their school life. Mental Health problems are now one of the main causes of overall disease burden worldwide (MHF, 2016). The Active Lives survey (Sport England, 2019) also indicated a clear association between activity levels and perceived happiness. The more active a student is, the more resilient they claimed to be, and the greater the feeling of confidence and competence in sport they felt (Sport England, 2019). The following Active Lives further supported this claim, as students that indicated they were more physically active also claimed to be happier than those who were less active. Less active students also reported higher levels of loneliness, lower levels of positive thoughts and overall mental well-being when compared against their more active peers (Sport England, 2021). The link between inactivity and mental health is undeniable and should be raising alarm bells across PE departments and schools alike.

It is fair to say that the burden on physical educators has never been greater than at this moment. It is time to face the brutal reality and evaluate our effectiveness in promoting active lifestyles and consider the part we are playing in tackling these issues. Collectively, as teachers, we work with the vast majority of young people for 40% percent or more of a child's waking time and provide key curricula and programmes that can positively impact attitudes towards activity (Cale and Harris, 2019). I wish to make it clear that I do not believe that PE teachers are to blame for the current situation that PE finds itself in. In fact, I would argue the opposite. PE teachers have gone above and beyond, making the very best of what they have been given. Many PE teachers have become 'skilful operators of a hidden curriculum that uses the technique practices merely as a vehicle to communicate the values and joys of physical activity, or to facilitate for students the practice of responsibility for self and respect for others' (Kirk, 2010, p.4).

One of the most effective methods of improving the health and well-being of students is a whole school approach, incorporating cross-curricular learning with the culture and ethos. For too long, PE departments have remained some of the biggest and only in-school advocates of physical activity, with PE lesson time under threat. In 2018, the Youth Sport Trust reported that 38% of secondary schools had cut PE lesson time to allow more time for more 'academic' subjects like English and Maths.

With so much on our plate, where do we start? In truth, much of the battle could be won by adopting a physical literacy-focused approach. Physical literacy is considered to be the foundation of participating in lifelong Physical Education, and is defined as 'The motivation, confidence, physical competence, knowledge and, understanding to value and take responsibility for engagement in physical activities for life,' (IPLA, 2017). Although not limited to school years, nurturing physical literacy will have a significant impact on an individual's life. The Active Lives survey by Sport England in 2019 confirmed the importance of physical literacy in engagement as well as physical, mental, and social health. The survey found that physically literate children and young people are more likely to be active. Physical literacy has five elements: enjoyment, confidence, competence, understanding and knowledge. The more elements present, the more active a child or young person is likely to be. It also stated that 'physically literate children and young people are happier, more resilient and more trusting of other children and young people. The more elements of physical literacy present, the higher the levels of happiness, resilience and social trust.' (Sport England, 2019). Whilst physical literacy is not a new term, I have found it almost impossible to explicitly deliver all aspects of it through a sport-driven curriculum.

PE teachers work tirelessly to ignite a passion in students, to get them active and enjoying sport. It is time to question whether, with so many growing issues, we are still meeting the needs of our students with our current curriculum. Or worse, are we actually doing more harm than good?

If we are not meeting their needs, it is time to come to the realisation that our current Physical Education philosophy is failing those that we teach. Students are telling us they are not enjoying physical activity, they are voting with their feet and opting to be inactive, and they are suffering mentally like never before. It is time to ask the question: is Physical Education in crisis?

Albert Einstein is often mis-attributed with the saying, 'the definition of insanity is doing the same thing over and over again and expecting different results', but whomever coined the phrase makes a valid point. Through the pressure to achieve results, evidence progress, and be considered as academic equals, we have perhaps forgotten what's most important: putting our students first.

PE is in a unique position in that it can directly influence the health and well-being of an individual for the rest of their lives. There has never been a more important time to change how we deliver Physical Education; however, there is no need to completely discard the current system. 'Innovation requires the creative transfer of the fundamental and powerful concepts of the traditional disciplines' (Stern, 2017, p.1). In my opinion, schools can and should continue to teach sport and sport specific skills, though these should not be the sole focus of the learning. By introducing wider concepts, we can empower learners and provide lessons that allow them to transfer their learning to new contexts – surely a key aim for any teacher. It's not a complete overhaul we need, just a shift in curriculum focus, as well as a reconceptualising and broadening from sport to physical activity. Though, for meaningful change to occur, we need to face the brutal reality about the dominant but failing approach to PE and how it is delivered.

The good news is, we have an innate ability to foster individuals that have a genuine love for our subject and are motivated to engage in physical activity and develop life skills through a student-centred curriculum that supports our students way beyond the classroom (or sports field, as is more likely). The better news is it won't mean huge amounts of work, negatively impacting GCSE results, progress of the most able, or losing the sports we love!

If your why is like mine and you want to know how to better meet the needs of all students, then this book is for you. If your 'why' is nowhere near close to mine, do not put the book down just yet, for Sinek also spoke about how we are drawn to those that can communicate what they believe (Sinek, 2009). Through this book, I hope to inspire you to understand why change is needed in Physical Education, why I feel so passionately that we are currently failing our students, and what the future of PE could look like.

Some of what I discuss, particularly regarding the current failings, might seem controversial and overly harsh, but I remain resolute that there will be certain aspects which will resonate with you. It is time for us as a profession to face the brutal truth: PE needs to change in order to survive. Much research has highlighted this fact for over twenty years. David Kirk recognises this in his book *Physical Education Futures* (2010). He argues that change within PE is inevitable. He questions if this change will happen because of physical educators driving change or if it will be forced on us by governments and policy makers, who have grown tired with the lack of progress we are making in tackling many of the issues I will raise in this book. I have spoken to numerous teachers and gathered many opinions and experiences of where we are taking the lead and bringing about positive and meaningful change for PE. I will also draw on evidence and research to present the most innovative thinking in relation to PE and its past, present, and future. This book is written by a PE teacher, for PE teachers. We must ask ourselves, 'does Physical Education as we know it have a future?' (Kirk, 2010, p.9).

The All Blacks have long had a saying: 'leave the jersey in a better place'. Their task is to represent all those who have come before them, and ensure they build on what they have taken on to and leave a positive impact for those that follow. 'Understanding this responsibility creates a compelling sense of higher purpose. It's a good lesson for us all: if we play a bigger game, we play a more effective game' (Kerr, 2013).

As physical educators, and custodians of our subject, how can we leave Physical Education in a better place than we found it? What is going to be our legacy? I believe the information in the following chapters of this book and my positive and meaningful PE ideology could be it!

Take Away Reflections

- Does your current PE offer match your 'Why'?
- Does PE meet the needs of every student?
- Does a sport-driven curriculum support the needs of our society?
- Could PE be more than just Sport?
- How, as a subject, could we change for the better?

2

The Evolution of Physical Education

'Out of adversity comes opportunity' – Benjamin Franklin

As can be seen in the diagram right, created by Will Swaithes to highlight how PE in the UK has evolved, change in Physical Education is nothing new. Our subject has evolved greatly over the years in response to social, cultural, and political pressures, often adapting to the need of the nation. In this chapter, I outline some of the changes PE has been through, whilst discussing how it has remained resistant to change once more traditional sports were introduced. I also discuss how physical literacy, whilst an important emergence, has been a challenge to adopt. For clarity, it is important to understand before moving on what we mean by PE. 'Physical Education is the planned, progressive learning that takes place in curriculum timetabled time and is delivered to all pupils' (AfPE, 2015). The subject and the experiences within PE have evolved throughout the last century, and we find ourselves now in a place, following a worldwide pandemic, whereby the needs of our students have changed dramatically and reported widely. Has PE adapted effectively in the past, and will it be able to do so in the future?

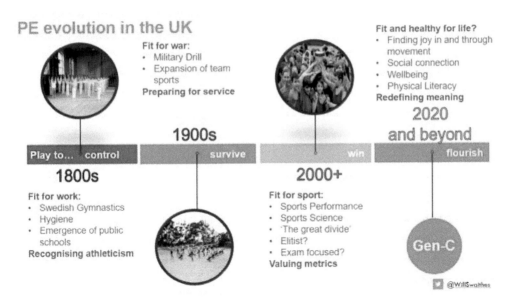

PE evolution in the UK

Fit for war:
- Military Drill
- Expansion of team sports

Preparing for service

Fit and healthy for life?
- Finding joy in and through movement
- Social connection
- Wellbeing
- Physical Literacy

Redefining meaning

2020 and beyond

1900s

| Play to... control | survive | win | flourish |

1800s

Fit for work:
- Swedish Gymnastics
- Hygiene
- Emergence of public schools

Recognising athleticism

2000+

Fit for sport:
- Sports Performance
- Sports Science
- 'The great divide'
- Elitist?
- Exam focused?

Valuing metrics

Gen-C

@WillSwalthes

PE in the Past

The principle has always been the same; physical activity improves the ability of the individual to meet the demands of our environment. In 1883, it became illegal for children under 9 years old to work, and they could only work full time if thirteen or over. Child labour was commonplace, with 12-hour shifts being the norm. This meant that opportunities for education were limited. Progress was being made towards the end of the 19th century, with key government policies being introduced and more schools opening for the middle classes.

'In 1890 the Board of Education had 'recognised' physical exercises as well as drill as legitimate parts of the school day but work then was dependent on the military handbooks and Archibald Maclaren's system based on German gymnastics' (Bailey and Vamplew, 1999, p.19). The Nation needed physically fit and productive workers and there was an intention to employ Physical Education specifically for the benefits to be gained in sharpening the responses and efficiency of the pupils: a benefit to both industrial production and military effectiveness (Bailey and Vamplew, 1999). Organised games were slowly being introduced to schools at the start of the 1900s, as it was seen as a good way to teach discipline and would be employed as an appropriate means of preventing unruly behaviour.

This was not to last for long, as the fear of war and the apparent concern regarding the physical fitness of recruits, raised in key government reports, meant that PE reverted to military drill. In 1919, a new PE syllabus was written, developing areas that had not previously been included. The use of music to encourage Swedish gymnastics was introduced, as well as the reintroduction of organised games.

A more substantial syllabus was introduced in 1933, in which organised games had more prominence; the use of outdoor education and the teaching of good posture were included, and greater emphasis was placed on the importance of regular Physical Education within schools. Despite this, schools were often ill equipped to deliver effective Physical Education, though, towards the end of and following the second world war, government proposals for a post war Britain, health and hygiene were high on the agenda.

In 1944, not only PE but education underwent one of its biggest changes, as the government declared 'secondary education for all' in the Butler Education Act. With this change brought the need for teachers qualified in delivering PE. However, PE was not mandatory, and schools only had to provide facilities for Physical Education.

Many organisations were developing, and publishing agreed rules for their sports, from tennis and netball to rounders and swimming. It was in the 1940s that 'there was more emphasis on individual movement and less on gymnastic unison. Body awareness via experience of time, weight, space and flow, and a recognition of individual differences, came to the fore in the Physical Education curriculum' (Bailey and Vampley, 1999, p.77).

Although a better understanding as to the importance of PE was emerging, the increasing range of extra subjects in schools, financial difficulties and a lack of trained teachers meant that the focus was moving away from Physical Education and towards academics. After a century of state-provided education, a government sponsored National Curriculum for children aged 5-16 was finally implemented in 1989, with Physical Education introduced as a statutorily required curriculum subject in 1992 for the first time in its history.

The National Curriculum set out 'end of Key Stage' aims and provided some consistency and clarity as to the nature of the content to be delivered. Sports- and games-focused curricula dominated, and this was reinforced by the 1996 policy document Raising the Game, to which the then Prime Minister John Major affirmed this point: 'competitive sport teaches valuable lessons which last for life. It improves health and it opens doors to new friendships. My ambition is to put sport back at the heart of weekly life in every school. To re-establish sport as one of the great pillars of education alongside the academic, the vocational and the moral' (Department of National Heritage, 1995, p.2).

The attention to the benefits of a physically active lifestyle meant that more consideration was given to PE in schools and what it was, or was not, achieving. Various organisations released reports stating the importance of PE in schools, and the impact it had on lifelong participation. Sport England launched several initiatives aimed at getting more people involved in sport, creating more places to play sport, and awarding more medals through higher standards of performance in sport. The motivation to get more people engaged in physical activity at all levels was evident, whilst improving the country's outcomes at major sporting events. It could be argued that, whilst grassroots participation was a consideration, the purpose of creating more elite athletes was more of a focus over the benefits associated with physical activity.

Despite the larger spotlight on PE and changes in legislation regarding resources and allocated time, the understanding of how to truly deliver quality PE was far less clear. The government target in England is to deliver two hours per week of physical activity, and to provide the opportunity to attend a further two to three hours outside of curriculum time; this, although desirable, usually sets a standard far lower than the recommended daily requirements (Harris and Cale, 2019).

A revamped National Curriculum was released in 1999 and, for the first-time, games were compulsory for Key Stages 1, 2 and 3, and were optional, though highly encouraged, in Key Stage 4. This overhauled National Curriculum outlined the knowledge, skills and understanding that were expected of students into four 'aspects':

-    Acquiring and developing skills.
-    Selecting and applying skills, tactics, and compositional ideas.
-    Evaluating and improving performance.
-    Knowledge and understanding of fitness and health.

Schools were encouraged to use a 'best fit' approach to assessment and required a level descriptor to judge a student's performance at the end of each Key Stage. In 2007, the secondary National Curriculum was once again revised, and four aspects were changed to five:

-    Developing skills in physical activity.
-    Making and applying decisions.
-    Developing physical and mental capacity.
-    Evaluating and improving.
-    Making informed choices about healthy and active lifestyles.

This revision also brought about a change in the range and content that could be offered to deliver a wider choice of learning:

- Outwitting opponents.
- Accurate replication.
- Exploring and communicating ideas and emotions.
- Performing at maximum levels.
- Identifying and solving problems.
- Exercising safely and effectively.

In 2013, following a report led by Professor Tim Oates, the Government produced legislation by which the use of levels, in order to assess students, would be revoked, and this would come into force in September 2014. This also included the latest revamp to the secondary PE National Curriculum and reaffirmed its aims:

- Develop competence to excel in a broad range of physical activities.
- Are physically active for sustained periods of time.
- Engage in competitive sports and activities.
- Lead healthy, active lives.

The Government continued to pledge funds (though many argued not enough), via multiple policies, to encourage engagement in physical activity and promote the positive impact that regular exercise can have on the nations' physical, and now mental health. 'Sport is one of the Department for Education's five foundations for building character and can help young people to develop skills such as confidence, self-belief, dedication and resilience. Sport also instils values and virtues such as friendship and fair play' (Department for Education, 2019).

In order to deliver the National Curriculum, most schools adopted a sport-driven curriculum that focused units of work on individual sports, ensuring the key skills in sport were delivered. Lesson objectives and assessment were also often aimed at the student's ability to successfully complete these skills. Originally, PE had been delivered to create fit and efficient workers. It shifted to building strength through German and Swedish gymnastics, and then again to improving fitness in preparation for war. Following the war, PE was aimed at improving hygiene and developing team sports.

Throughout these changes, the principle has always been the same; physical activity improves the ability of the individual to meet the demands of our environment. A strong message around the benefits of competition and traditional sports have been delivered through policy, as well as the need to provide everyone with an opportunity to participate in physical activity. Meanwhile, a growing understanding that physical activity can support the development of a person, mentally and socially, as well as physically, was widely acknowledged.

The majority of schools adopted a multi-activity approach to curriculum design, often focusing on competitive sport. Currently, this is the dominant form of Physical Education in schools and has been since the 1960s in the UK (Kirk, 2010). This method of Physical Education delivery has proven incredibly resistant to change. One reason, and in connection with a drive for more success on the global stage, is that sport is globalised and commercialised, now more than ever. Kirk (2010) considered 'if the growth of high performance in elite sport raises questions about how we define success and ability?' (p.8). This obsession with performance, and the influence of the media that covers professional sport so heavily, will most certainly have played a strong part in the current drive towards perfection in Physical Education.

PE in the past has evolved to meet the needs of the nation and, while the needs of the nation have continued to change, our curriculum has remained unchanged for some time. The significance of this is that we have a legacy of sports, and therefore shaking it off has proven difficult. Teacher training still revolves around coaching badges and skill acquisition, whilst professional development amongst PE staff is still targeted at technique or GCSE exam delivery. As the UNESCO 'Quality Physical Education' report reminds us 'Physical Education is the most effective means of providing all children and youth with the skills, attitudes, values, knowledge and understanding for lifelong participation in society,' (2015, p.6). This is an exciting and emerging theme amongst physical educators looking to collaborate.

The Emergence of Physical Literacy

Everyone, no matter prior experience, ethnicity, sexuality, religion, gender, or age can continually develop their physical literacy and engage in physical activity throughout their lifetime. The driving principle is motivation.

It's clear that PE has changed throughout the years and, although the methods have differed, the end goal of getting people active, managing hygiene, and improving health have been the same. More recently, the idea that PE focused on the immediate health of students transitioned to an appreciation of lifelong participation. Dr Margaret Whitehead presented the principle of physical literacy in 1993 and, from this research, a definition was developed. The term physical literacy describes the motivation, confidence, physical competence, knowledge and understanding that develop in order to maintain physical activity at an appropriate level throughout life (Whitehead, 2010, p.12).

This definition of physical literacy includes four interconnected elements (affective, physical, cognitive, and behavioural) that change and adapt across the lifespan. Whilst physical literacy is seen by many to be the aim of Physical Education, it is not limited to school years. It is something that can be achieved at any age and can have a significant impact on the quality of life, throughout all stages of life.

Many argue that physical literacy should be as much a part of a school's culture as literacy or numeracy. The more physically literate a person is, the more likely they are to participate in physical activity throughout their life. Everyone, no matter prior experience, ethnicity, sexuality, religion, gender, or age can continually develop their physical literacy and engage in physical activity throughout their lifetime. The driving principle is motivation. This concept has prompted considerable re-thinking by many policy makers around the world, with regards to a child's physical development and motivation to participate in physical activity throughout all stages of life. There is, however, controversy within the field of physical literacy, which has led to multiple definitions and applications, differing greatly in various publications – this has led to confusion. Some authors have used the term to focus purely on the acquisition of skill and movements, and therefore only focused on physical competence. Physical educators have therefore found it difficult to seriously consider a physical literacy informed approach, and its application within the curriculum has been more coincidental than purposeful, if achieved at all.

'Physical literacy has been described as a longed-for concept and has gained widespread global interest. This interest has also given rise to calls for physical literacy to be operationalised, providing clarity and guidance on developing physical literacy informed teaching practice. Operationalising physical literacy is crucial in moving the concept forwards by providing substance to the claims made by physical literacy advocates' (Durden-Myers, 2020). Physical literacy, and all it encompasses, is almost impossible to measure in a culture obsessed with evidence of impact through data, leading most educators in charge of PE to opt for a competence-focused assessment. We are chasing perfection that, for the overwhelming majority of our students, is unattainable. Some schools have moved the curriculum to incorporate various other pedagogical models, such as teaching games for understanding or sports education, with some success. A physically literate person is motivated to participate in physical activity and, whilst the shift in pedagogy will engage more students than a lesson taught using drills to develop skill, can we be confident that every single student is receiving the same positive experience?

The advancement in my understanding of physical literacy could not have come at a better time, with the growing issues around obesity, mental health, inactivity, and enjoyment in PE. Policy makers must ensure clarity around the true aim of Physical Education in schools, so that school leaders and physical educators can truly deliver a curriculum that meets the needs of its students.

In 2020, the Covid-19 pandemic put the nation in lockdown. From the middle of March until September, schools were closed, with the exception of key workers' children. People were asked to stay at home and advised to only leave the house for essential supplies and to exercise once a day. The inclusion of physical activity to the small list of permitted guidelines highlighted the importance that regular exercise can have on physical and emotional well-being. The government were endorsing exercise as an important part of everyday life. In preparation for schools to re-open, PE was forced to reflect on its curriculum, ensuring a Covid-secure curriculum could be delivered when schools reopened. This period of reflection caused many educators to question if the current curriculum was meeting the ever-changing needs of our students, as they were forced to consider limiting equipment, losing facilitates, and removing team and contact sports. Much of the world was plunged into a second lockdown from January 2021, further forcing students to stay home and learn remotely.

'Out of adversity comes opportunity' – Benjamin Franklin

This brings us to the present. A time where, through circumstances beyond our control, we have been forced to adapt. Although it could be considered an exciting time for PE, in which the opportunists among us can look to make improvements, make a bigger impact, matter more, and change the way we deliver PE in the country forever. Yet PE, with a sport-driven model, remains resistant to change, and the main form of PE around the world. So why are so many physical educators reluctant to create meaningful change?

PE has often been forced to evolve to meet social or political needs. Though, in more recent times, despite external pressures and changes in the needs of society, PE, or, more specifically, the delivery of PE, has remained resistant to change. Focusing on the delivery of sport and developing successful sports people, it is my belief the subject has fallen behind, and is no longer meeting the needs of its students.

Physical literacy, and the understanding that everyone can continually develop physical literacy throughout their lifetime, and reap the health benefits attached to physical activity, has provided many with a justification as to the importance of PE on school timetables. This has come about in a time when some are even reducing and questioning PE's importance on school timetables and, especially considering many educators find developing and adopting a physical literacy approach challenging, with little guidance or professional development available.

'Physical Education fails, by its own admission, to develop skills and thereby facilitate lifelong physical activity. Young people appear to be showing dissent. Physical culture is, most certainly, in constant process. And governments have expectations that appear to surpass the modest offerings of current practice' (Kirk, 2010, p.64). PE, in its current form, is not working.

Change is evidently needed, and Covid-19 has delivered this opportunity. 'Physical Education, as the only curriculum subject whose focus combines the body and physical competence with values-based learning and communication, provides a learning gateway to grow the skills required for success in the 21st century,' (UNESCO, 2015, p.6). It's time to reflect on our failings and look to the future. Despite our best intentions, what are we getting so horribly wrong? More importantly, what can we do to bring PE into the 21stcentury, and meet the needs of our students once again?

Take Away Reflections

- Has the PE you deliver changed from the PE you received at school?
- Why is PE so resistant to change?
- Why is better and more widespread understanding about physical literacy essential?
- How do we nurture physical literacy in all students?
- How does your current PE pedagogy positively or negatively impact your ability to nurture students' physical literacy?

3

A Case for Change in Physical Education

Fundamentally, all subjects seek to provide a learning experience in which students can transfer their learning to new contexts. In this chapter I outline some of the faults with the current PE curriculum. I asked teachers what we are doing wrong with regards to the PE curriculum, keeping in mind the national issues of obesity, inactivity, mental health, and enjoyment of PE. It was clear this question evoked strong feelings about the need for change, though there was some contention as to what that change would entail.

This was a far more controversial topic than I had ever imagined. Numerous teachers kindly shared their stories, and some wished to remain anonymous, as they felt speaking out could get them in trouble with their schools. Nevertheless, the responses were strikingly similar, passionate, and reassuring.

Penny et al. (2009) state that achieving quality in PE requires it to be demonstrated within and across curriculum, pedagogy, and assessment. This chapter focuses on these three areas of common and traditional PE delivery. The following evaluation of the sport-driven curriculum and subsequent archaic pedagogy and elitist assessment commonly employed might seem overly negative, problem-focused, and harsh; however, the intention is to shed as much light on our current systems failings, real teachers' experiences, and evidence-backed research as possible, to better support the need for truly meaningful change.

A Sport-Focused Curriculum

Even the most talented teachers could not achieve success for all through a sport-driven curriculum.

The 'Why' of Our Curriculum – Intent

What are we trying to achieve, and why is it so important to understand this intent? In 2019, Ofsted set out their new inspection framework, which focused much more heavily on the curriculum. Specifically, inspections would dive into a curriculum's intent (what it aims to achieve), implementation (what it is doing to achieve it), and impact (evidence to indicate whether it is achieving it).

Although, understanding and articulating the department's intent is far more important than simply an answer for the sake of Ofsted. It develops a connection between the curriculum, the teacher, and the students. A teacher should understand why they are teaching that topic, where it fits into the bigger picture of the curriculum, the impact it will have on the child if taught, or indeed not taught, and what this lesson, scheme of work, and curriculum are hoping to achieve.

Without this understanding, the teacher could lack the motivation and full appreciation of what is required to deliver the curriculum effectively and passionately. For the child, they must make the connection between this lesson and the possible need to apply its learning in life: past, present, or future.

Too often when asking a student within a lesson 'what are you learning?' they glance up and read the lesson objective off the board. Even the follow up question of 'why are you learning this?' is met with a blank look or a shrug of the shoulders. Does this mean students are just completing work to get it done, or is the learning really worthwhile? Both teachers and students need to know why this lesson is so important now, and in the future. They must feel a sense of purpose and build a relationship with the curriculum content, otherwise a true opportunity to motivate and engage students is lost.

Guidance on how to discover your team's intent, and to articulate it to everyone, is discussed in later in the book. Right now, take a moment to reflect on whether your current curriculum and your intent align. A curriculum intent should reflect the national, school and departmental objectives. This sounds reasonable, but a Head of Department is given very little chance to succeed in this task with so many mixed messages coming from everywhere about what the aim of PE actually is.

The National Curriculum provides this purpose of study for Physical Education: 'A high-quality Physical Education curriculum inspires all pupils to succeed and excel in competitive sport and other physically demanding activities. It should provide opportunities for pupils to become physically confident in a way which supports their health and fitness. Opportunities to compete in sport and other activities build character and help to embed values such as fairness and respect' (Department for Education, 2013, p.1).

From this we can ascertain that competitive sport and improving knowledge around health and fitness are the main objectives. No issues so far; a sport-driven model delivers these aims. Key government policy also emphasises the importance of physical literacy, which is creating a great deal of confusion when planning a PE curriculum. Do the policy makers want us to focus on building character, health and fitness through competitive sport, or achieve physically literate students? This does not include any mention of the need to support in the fight to tackle childhood obesity and mental health issues.

Our school leaders will state that a student's health and well-being, after safety and safeguarding, is of paramount importance to a school. Yet, PE lessons are still being cut from timetables and continue to put increasing amounts of pressure on department leads to produce progress data and examination results. Should our intent focus on passing national exams or school-based assessments? Or should it instead focus on tackling inactivity, raising attainment, evidencing progression, competitive sport, improving fitness, supporting mental health, or any of the other key issues that seem to fall on the shoulders of our nation's PE teachers?

Fundamentally, all subjects seek to provide a learning experience in which students can transfer their learning to new contexts. We should be no different, and the good news is there is a solution that will enable us to meet all these needs and articulate a clear and simple intent. In my opinion, one thing is for certain, a sport-driven model is not it. If your department's intent is to create one or, if possible, two elite athletes, then a sport-driven model is right for you. Perhaps your intent is to win a County Cup with your Year 10 football team. If so, then you are on the right track!

I have never met a PE teacher that chose teaching for those reasons, yet our curriculum is aiming for just that. Most PE teachers will cite, 'wanting to share their passion for sport' or, 'to engage all in physical activity', which seem like honourable reasons to become a PE teacher, and they are. Yet, our sport-driven curriculum is failing to meet these objectives.

The research completed for this book demonstrates that not all students are passionate about sport, and they are certainly not all engaged in physical activity. Even if the objectives mentioned above do not sound like your current curriculum intent, whatever it is, I can hazard a guess that a sport-driven model, where performance is the only indicator of success, is failing to meet it. Even the most talented teachers could not achieve success for all through a sport-driven curriculum.

The 'What' of Our Curriculum – *Implementation*

Creating and developing a curriculum is a huge task. As teachers, we undertake comprehensive training that, for the most part, does not cover curriculum design. We are left to complete this task with little guidance and mostly through trial and error. It is therefore understandable that the content taught through our PE curriculum has remained often unchanged, or received only minor tweaks from time to time. The biggest changes have been the inclusion or removal of particular sports, equality regarding the opportunities provided to each gender, and the development of games-focused models, for example: 'Teaching Games for Understanding' and 'Sports Education'.

Though the lesson objective is often focused on skill acquisition, as Cale and Harris (2006, p.28) point out, 'the promotion of active lifestyles has been a key aim of PE curricula in the United Kingdom and around the world for many decades. For example, one main aim of the National Curriculum for England is to ensure that all pupils lead healthy, active lives'.

This might be one of the main aims of PE, but our curriculum and schemes of work often miss out much of the key detail that is required to explicitly meet that goal. Health and fitness are most commonly taught via a scheme of work revolving around methods of fitness and fitness testing, hardly encouraging lifelong participation or developing an understanding of maintaining good health. The Association for PE (AfPE) released a statement in 2015 questioning the impact of fitness testing as a means of measuring and developing fitness in young people, 'AfPE strongly supports positive efforts to promote and enhance children's physical activity but is cautious against the use of some fitness tests and the overuse of fitness testing as a means of achieving this. Evidence suggests that fitness testing can be counterproductive to these goals for some children, and that some fitness testing commonly practised in schools is questionable,' (AfPE, 2015). It is worth reflecting on the curriculum you currently offer and how it promotes and measures fitness and the impact this has on the students it serves.

As previously discussed, many schools employ what could be described as a sport-driven or multi-activity curriculum. This infers that the curriculum is built around the delivery of various sports and activities with the knowledge of these activities and the acquisition of specific skills at the centre of the curriculum delivery. In terms of the day-to-day practice of this form of Physical Education, we might more accurately speak about Physical Education-as-sport-techniques (Kirk, 2009).

Below is an example of an oversimplified version of a Key Stage 3 sports-driven curriculum. The specific sports, length of delivery, and groupings might be different. During my many conversations with teachers, it became evident that this example is not that dissimilar to many of the curricula currently being employed across the country.

Term 1	Term 2	Term 3	Term 4
Boys: Football	Boys: Rugby	Boys: Athletics	Boys: Cricket
Girls: Netball	Girls: Hockey	Girls: Tennis	Girls: Rounders

The schemes of work that accompany these sports outline the various techniques that should be taught, along with suggestions for assessments, drills, and specific technique-focused lesson objectives. There is little mention of that key aim to promote active lifestyles discussed above, and any progress made over the scheme of work (other than competence) in relation to some students' physical literacy is purely coincidental. We have taken huge strides in the last few decades in understanding the importance of physical literacy, and the relationships between physical activity and physical and mental health. PE curricula both before this was understood, and now in the present, are fundamentally not that different. This sport-technique-based form of Physical Education has been spectacularly resistant to change, though this is not due to a lack of ideas or physical educators calling for change (Kirk, 2009). Therefore, in this case, we are teaching sports in PE, and not children through PE.

Relevance of Content

88% of businesses believe school leavers are not prepared for work (British Chamber of Commerce, 2014). This statistic, along with the other issues raised, suggests that PE, as well as other subjects, could do more to prepare our students for life.

'An overwhelming majority of curriculum content is aimed towards the development of sport specific techniques or specific movements, patterns or solutions that have been identified to produce a clearly identified goal within a sporting context' (Sporticus, 2020). This leads to lessons that celebrate those that can replicate these techniques, and deviate from the original aim of gaining enjoyment through physical activity. This is not relevant in the wider context of modern PE aims, as Kirk notes, 'today's Physical Education has been scarcely relevant for at least the last 30 years of the 20th century' (2009).

The argument that students do not need to learn certain topics taught in school, because they will never need to access them again in their lifetime, is something most teachers might have heard at some point. Maths teachers might relate when students complain about learning Pythagoras Theorem or English teachers when teaching Shakespeare. Without an understanding of why students need this learning, they can fail to make a meaningful connection with it. Students can struggle to find the relationship between the content and the importance it has to their lives. If they fail to understand where this learning could be applied in their futures it will be difficult for them to see any point in engaging. One thing I always felt confident about was that if a student said to me, 'Sir, why do we need to do PE?' I would have a strong answer in that, 'physical activity has many long-term physical and mental health benefits'. But, the truth is, that is a flippant statement and an easy answer. An English teacher could have a similar response as to the overall importance of literacy to the long-term success of that student, but that doesn't answer the question about whether studying Shakespeare is needed for a child to achieve success in the future.

The point is that, while teaching an over-head clear shot in badminton, should a student say, 'I am never going to need to do this again in my life,' they would be right, and I would have no comeback. It's true, unless they become a professional badminton player, that technique will never help them achieve anything. It can be considered a redundant skill. Please do not think for one second I am suggesting you remove that technique from your scheme of work; I am not. I am simply suggesting that perhaps our sport-driven curricula do not always meet the long-term needs of our students.

When discussing relevancy of common PE curricula, it would be remiss not to mention the qualifications gained in our subject. Delivering a formal qualification in PE, whilst my favourite part of the job, must also be discussed if we are identifying issues with our current relevance. For clarity, I am referring to the practical elements of the GCSE qualification in England, and equivalent qualifications provided worldwide that assess practical ability across a number of sports. In England, students are required to sit two examinations that make up 60% of the overall grade. They are also required to complete coursework (10%), and must be assessed in three separate activities (10% each). The activities are broken down into skill elements and full context.

The pressure to gain results in these qualifications could deem the changes required to improve the PE experience counterproductive and against the drive to make the subject more academic. If results are the defining feature of our education system, then shifting from a model that prepares students for their qualifications seems illogical. Offering exam specification sport- and performance-focused assessment that mirrors that of the formal qualification can be easily justified. It therefore ultimately makes our current form of dominant delivery even more resistant to the change that is so desperately needed. On one hand, we realise we are turning many students off being physically active through our sport-focused and performance-obsessed lessons, yet, on the other hand, the most common forms of qualification demand this form of delivery to ensure students can meet assessment requirements.

Therefore, I must question at this stage, though not dwell beyond this chapter for my own sanity's sake, as any changes are beyond our control, are the practical elements of the qualification still fit for purpose? Whilst the theory provides the knowledge and understanding to progress and, in my opinion, has dramatically improved the validity of the subject, the practical elements focus on high performance required for elite athletes across a few sports. Therefore, I wish to pose two further questions before moving on: what is the purpose of any qualification? Secondly, what does a PE qualification currently prepare our students for?

Surely, the purpose of any qualification is to prepare students for the next stage of their lives, whether that be further education or work. Therefore, a qualification that focuses purely on the ability to perform in a number of sports at the highest level is only preparing students to become professional athletes. The percentage of students that go on to become elite professionals must be incredibly small. I wish to make it clear that I am not proposing we lose these practical elements to the course, but shift to more relevant content. Instead of preparing students to become professional athletes, might it be more important to prepare them to coach or officiate, etc? The jobs and further education opportunities in sport are vast, yet our current specification does not prepare students for any of them, relying solely on the theoretical aspects of the course to meet these needs.

I recall once teaching a student who represented Great Britain in badminton. I should add this had very little to do with my teaching, and more to do with strict daily training schedules and years of elite coaching. Her knowledge of the theory content was strong and, of course, she gained full marks for performance in badminton. However, the specification required two further sports for which she should be assessed in. This student spent all of her free time training in Badminton. She dedicated most of her living life to this one sport. However, she needed to be assessed in two more. Despite the fact this student was in the top twenty-five in the world for her age in badminton and scored high marks in her theory exams, she came out with the second highest possible grade. This was due to the fact that her two other practically assessed sports dropped her grade down. A future professional athlete did not gain the highest grade available due to the fact she had dedicated her time to performing only one. Imagine this in another subject. A music student that could fluently play the violin and was part of the Royal Philharmonic Orchestra but lost mark because they didn't play two other instruments as well. I love teaching GCSE PE, genuinely, but aspects of the course do feed the, 'PE is only sport' and, 'PE is only for the sporty' stereotypes.

Breadth

'Multi-activity programs consist of relatively short units of lessons, sometimes as few as four to six lessons on one physical activity, before a switch is made to a new activity.

As such, the multi-activity curriculum rarely offers students opportunities to develop physical competencies and knowledge about and through physical activity in any depth' (Casey and Kirk, 2021, p.7).

Leaders have looked to offer a breadth of activities to try and engage the disengaged. Other strategies have been to offer more extra-curricular clubs, hire external coaches, to take away the competitive element of lessons and clubs, or explore alternative PE based models such as Sports Education and Teaching Games for Understanding. Whilst there is no doubt that this has likely engaged more students, these strategies could be described as plugging the leaking holes of our out-of-date curriculum.

Other physical educators might cite one of their curricula aims as supporting students to find the one sport they may wish to consider continuing after PE. It could also be argued that we are trying to do too much. Some students can experience 12 to 16 sports in one academic year through lessons alone. We are trying to keep everyone happy, when in fact not many are.

We are offering competition to the competitive, offering fitness to those that prefer no competition, and trying to build leadership through games. When reviewing the curriculum, the most common solution is not to re-evaluate what we deliver, but to add even more activities to an already busy offering. By attempting to be something to everyone, we are being nothing to most.

When discussing student disengagement, the focus has been on the teacher, the lack of sports on offer, pedagogy, or the child's sporting history (or lack thereof). Although these can all have an impact on engagement levels, have we been missing the biggest issues of all, the aim, content, and delivery of our curriculum?

Applying a Physical Literacy Informed Approach

'Physical Education when underpinned by physical literacy has the potential to raise the value of Physical Education as a worthwhile and unique subject worthy of an equal status alongside other literacies such as English (literacy) and Mathematics (numerical literacy)' (Durden-Myers, 2020, p.2).

The term 'physical literacy' gets used a lot in Physical Education, often without full understanding and accurate application. The principle of physical literacy in its entirety is complex and complicated, which can understandably lead to confusion. In truth, to add to the complexity currently surrounding this concept, there is very little guidance for educators in how to nurture and apply a physical literacy informed approach when creating, planning, and delivering Physical Education. PE curricula and teachers go some way in nurturing physical literacy, but this is a fortunate coincidence.

Physical literacy is not solely, as some discussions with PE teachers have indicated, the ability of students to perform specific techniques in sport (competence). It is so much more than that. As previously stated, physical literacy involves the individual's motivation, confidence, knowledge and understanding in relation to physical activity. As Ennis (2014) points out, the typically taught sport-based, multi-activity approach to Physical Education provides students with few opportunities to increase their skill, fitness, or understanding.

Although sport can support these elements of physical literacy for some students, for others, the emotions felt in PE lessons lead to a very different outcome. It's important to understand that everyone's physical literacy journey is unique.

The inclusion of physical literacy in government policy, specifically the School Sport and Activity Action Plan (2019), as well as a focus on competition and traditional sports within the National Curriculum, could be seen as a contradiction which incites further confusion. This does not mean that competition and traditional sports do not comply with a curriculum that aims to nurture physical literacy. The problem is that with competition as the focus, there will, by its very nature, be winners and losers.

Within a lesson or scheme of work, those already adept at a sport will succeed far more often than those with less proficiency. If physical literacy is indeed the aim, then it should be the priority in which competition and traditional sports can be used as the vehicle to support the delivery of this vision. If competition through traditional sports is the curriculum focus, then it is difficult to achieve physical literacy for all.

The mention of physical literacy by policy makers highlights its importance but does little to guide those 'on the front line' with how to apply it effectively. The complexities surrounding physical literacy are certainly enough to put off most educators from attempting to build it, more substantially, into a curriculum. This leads to a reluctance to change the current system that has been an acceptable form of delivery for many years and is most certainly the PE delivery expected by most leaders, parents, and students.

When a curriculum is obsessed with performance and proficiency, inevitably, those not in the elite group will fail, which, in the case of PE, can have disastrous long-term ramifications. When referring to individuals who show little to no motivation in later life to engage in physical activity, Margaret Whitehead (2010) stated that, 'establishing and maintaining physical literacy is highly dependent on experiences which individuals have encountered in respect of their involvement with physical activity'. Whitehead goes on to discuss how, 'it could be the case that aspects of their previous experience have been negative, and this deters them from continuing to take part. Past experiences may not have been rewarding, with individuals experiencing little success.' Dr Ekkekakis et al. (2018) agreed that memories from PE influence future engagement. Using a retrospective survey, Ekkekakis's research asked participants to rate their past experiences of PE and their current activity levels. From this research, results indicated, 'the best memories related to enjoyment of the activities in class (56%), experiencing feelings of physical competence (37%), and, interestingly, 7% were not having to take PE class any longer or skipping the class. Of the worst memories, 34% related to embarrassment, 18% to lack of enjoyment, 17% to bullying, 14% to social–physique anxiety, 16% to injury, and 2% to being punished by the PE teacher. Childhood memories of PE are associated with attitudes towards physical activity and sedentary behaviour in adulthood' (2018, p.1). Ekkekakis added, 'If improvements in PE experiences could inspire even small increases in (physical activity), millions could derive additional health benefits' (p.128). The study expresses its concerns over the vividness of the negative memories participants recalled, and how more should be done to promote positive attitudes to physical activity through enjoyment and added autonomy.

'Physical literacy informed Physical Education has the potential to improve lifelong engagement in physical activity and raise the state, status and educational value of Physical Education. Thus, if physical literacy can be operationalised in Physical Education practice, it may reform Physical Education itself and its place within the current education system,' (Durden-Myers, 2020, p.11). However, the Sport England Unity in Movement initiative (2021) recognised that, 'fewer than one in five children consider themselves to be physically literate, and this declines with age as secondary-aged children feel less confident, competent and gain less enjoyment from sport and activity. This often means they spend their time in other ways and there can be negative consequences for their well-being.'

Whilst sport can be inclusive and, admittedly, it is often the environment and culture through which sport is taught that does more to demotivate, the reality is we are unable to nurture physical literacy for all through a sport-driven curriculum, when some students feel disengaged or lack enjoyment. It is therefore incumbent on all teachers to enable all pupils to achieve and further their physical literacy (Whitehead, 2010). Durden-Myers (2020) reaffirms the part physical literacy can play in, 'transforming the aims, structure and delivery of Physical Education, shifting the focus from a 'high sports performance' culture to a more 'inclusive physical activity participation' focus with the aim of promoting lifelong engagement in physical activity' (p.53).

We must also consider the message that is given to students through the constant drive for performance. Best practice, examples of which we so readily use to demonstrate proper technique, will be linked with a feeling of inadequacy. Students will review these examples, which are often of elite or at least highly competent sports people, with their own 'incompetence' in mind, and will therefore perceive physical literacy as unattainable. This is not the case. Whitehead (2010) argues that, almost without exception, all have the potential to develop our own physical literacy, all individuals possess the capacity to develop their physical literacy.

In the book *Lifetime Contributions in Physical Education* (2021), Liz Durden-Myers, Margaret Whitehead and colleagues rightly honour the outstanding work in Physical Education of Len Almond and Joy Butler. As part of this work, Durden-Myers and Whitehead explore the unpublished work of Almond around Eudaimonia and modern psychology. Put simply, eudaimonia is the Greek word commonly translated as 'happiness' or 'welfare'; however, more accurate translations have been proposed to be 'human flourishing' and 'prosperity'. In his work, Almond draws from Ryff's (1989) six-factor model of eudaimonic well-being, which describes the aspects of positive functioning that an individual who strives to lead a fulfilled life must endorse. The six factors identified are: autonomy, personal growth, self-acceptance, purpose in life, environmental mastery and positive relations with others (Ryff, 1989). Almond explored the findings from Ryff and Keyes's (1995) study that indicated that individuals that were motivated by financial gains over affiliation with others or their communities scored lower on various measures of well-being. These individuals were aiming to fulfil their extrinsic psychological needs. However, those who valued affiliation, intimacy and community, and were attempting to fulfil their intrinsic psychological needs had more positive well-being outcomes. Almond recognised that physical literacy shared a number of constituents with human flourishing; this is further built on by Durden-Myers and Whitehead (2021, p.30-31), and summarised below:

- **Autonomy:** Students should take value and responsibility for engagement in physical activities for life. They must take ownership of their involvement in physical activity.
- **Personal growth:** Growth and accomplishment are realised in developing physical competence in physical activity. Personal growth is a very significant aspect of all work to foster physical literacy.
- **Self-acceptance:** This includes the acceptance of, and contentment with, personal potential and the awareness of strengths and weaknesses. Realistic self-perception is fostered through developing motivation and self-confidence.
- **Purpose in life:** This includes having a clear sense of direction, commitment, and perseverance. It is believed that engagement in physical

activity in the context of physical literacy can add meaning and purpose to life.

- **Environmental mastery:** In all writing about physical literacy, the need for rich and varied experience is described as lying at the heart of the enterprise.

- **Positive relationships with others:** Students should embrace good interpersonal skills of listening, understanding, and empathising. Much engagement in physical activity takes place alongside others and indeed many activities rely on the actions of others. To achieve effective participation, individuals are guided to develop mutual respect, empathy, and responsiveness in relation to others.

To fully support a student to develop their physical literacy, we must first realise the student's intrinsic motivation to participate, and aim to develop the aspects of human flourishing, as identified above. This is further explored later in this chapter.

With true intrinsic motivation comes the opportunity to engage in all elements of the physical literacy principle. It is vital that PE builds positive attitudes towards sport and physical activity. Through the new research conducted for this book, however hard it is to hear, it is clear that is not what we are doing. The issues associated with lack of enjoyment, encouragement, and success are explored later in this chapter, and these aspects can all impact motivation to participate.

Physical literacy can be the core principle which brings our profession together. It can form the common language and values as to how we respond to the growing needs of young people. Physical literacy is the uniting movement for all of us to get behind and win over the hearts and minds of everyone.

Who is the Curriculum Targeted at?

The current sports-driven curricula, as set out in the National Curriculum, encourage competition. The units of work are set out to cover a number of lessons teaching the more basic sport specific techniques, then progressing to more challenging, often more pressurised drills or competitive games.

Often, the students that participate in sport outside of school come in with a much higher level of competency, and therefore will most likely achieve the highest level. So, to reiterate, the student that already participates in the sport, and already enjoys the sport, will get rewarded by achieving higher attainment in the sport.

This is not to say that the other students may not progress with the expertise of the teacher, however, the current set-up is directed towards those who are already proficient. This could alienate those that have little experience, knowledge, or familiarity with the sport, which in turn, might lead to disengagement. PE lessons include every child, unlike extra-curricular activities and out of school clubs, which attract students who already enjoy the activity.

Harris and Cale (2019) make the point that, for many students, especially girls, school sport and PE serves as the only opportunity to participate in physical activity. The focus on sport specific and often complex skills and competition could make a child feel like they are 'no good' or even a failure. Imagine how this child feels; embarrassed or humiliated perhaps?

The current sport-driven model is elitist, aimed at the best and often forgets, though inadvertently, the rest. Those that enjoy sport will continue to enjoy sport, and those that do not will solidify their opinion and suffer the negative impact of lifelong non-participation.

Sport England's Youth Personalities (2015) research reported the complex relationships that young people have with sport and physical activity is due to their individual experiences and personalities. To fully appreciate this relationship, and to keep them active, we must recognise their differences in personality. Sport England identifies six personality types that would support leaders in their appreciation of youth engagement and to support planning a fully inclusive curriculum.

The six personality types are:
- Confident intellectuals
- Cautious introverts
- Everyday youths
- Thoughtful improvers
- Ambitious self-starts
- Sports enthusiasts

Each personality type identified with different activities, methods of motivation, expectations, and dislikes. Let's look at two of these personality types more closely. Firstly, the sports enthusiasts, these students love sport. Most of their support network is sporty, and physical activity is an important part of who they are. The sports enthusiasts are body confident and intrinsically motivated to participate in sport. They love competition and winning is important to them.

We can all picture a student like this and, honestly, they are probably one of our favourite students to teach. They might even remind us of ourselves. This is who a sport-driven curriculum is aimed at. In-fact, it suits a sports enthusiast perfectly.

They get the opportunity to compete and to win. They love sport, are confident enough to give anything a go and, most importantly, are motivated to take part for no other reason than that they enjoy it. If all students were like this, there would probably be no need for this book.

Will Swaithes, author of the *10 Steps to a World Leading PE Department* blog series for the Youth Sport Trust wrote, 'it is easy to connect with, and have job satisfaction, provided by the mini versions of yourself, who are turned on by sport and are hungry for any opportunity you provide. With limited time, as a result of increased marking pressures, intervention groups and school meetings, is it any wonder that when push comes to shove many of us focus on the easy to reach and 'the rest' fall by the wayside?' (Swaithes, 2015).

The truth is that only 10% of people aged 14-25 fall into the sport enthusiast's category. Furthermore, this makes up the smallest percentage of any of the six youth personalities. From that 10%, 73%t are male.

We should probably pause to reflect on this for a second; our sport-driven curriculum is aimed at only 10% of students, of which 73% are male, and that means just 2.7% of all students attracted by the sport-driven curriculum are girls!

At the opposite end of the personality type spectrum are cautious introverts. These young people have a lower opinion of themselves, prefer not to try new things for fear of being exposed, and certainly do not consider themselves sporty. Most alarmingly, cautious introverts don't recognise the benefits of participating in physical activity. This group makes up 17% of 14-25-year-olds, and consists 73% females; that is 12.4% of all students.

Again, we can all picture a few students that would fit these traits. Now, imagine how these students feel every time they see PE on their timetable, knowing they would most likely have to compete, could fail, and lack the confidence needed in a performance-focused environment to really engage in and enjoy PE.

The impact that our PE lessons are having on these students' ability to achieve physical literacy is devastating. Though, just because they feel this way does not mean they will never engage in PE, locate motivation, or enjoy PE; we just need to find a way to appeal to them, and the other five types, of student.

In summary, a sport-driven curriculum model is not only failing to meet the needs of our students, but actually turning many away from physical activity altogether, focusing on only the most able, and leaving those that do not value competition or traditional sports behind, often damaging motivation to pursue longer-term engagement in physical activity. This approach to curriculum design rewards ability and inadvertently discriminates against those less able. It does little to nurture physical literacy in every student.

Every student is different. They have different motivations for engaging with physical activity and for wanting to participate in PE lessons. Simply offering a breadth of activities is only stretching the workload of teachers. We are trying to keep everyone happy, when, in fact, not many are. It is time to consider how we can evolve our PE offering to involve as much physical activity as possible, whilst meeting these varied needs. It is time to finally shift from a sport-driven model to one that can truly nurture physical literacy for all. It is time for PE students to truly connect with our subject and everything it can offer them. It is time for the curriculum to fulfil the true potential of PE for all.

That being said, the curriculum is not the totality of students' PE experience. Even the best, most inclusive PE curriculum in the world will struggle to provide positive and meaningful PE for students, if those delivering it do not grasp the magnitude of the impact they can have on every individual they teach.

Take Away Reflections

- Is your 'why' for PE understood and valued by all?
- Does your 'why' align with the 'why' of others in your team?
- How is your 'why' reflected in what you deliver?
- How does your departments intent align to national and school objectives?
- Who is best catered for in your current curriculum offer?
- Who is most marginalised by your current curriculum offer?
- Who needs you most?
- What experience is your school/department currently providing students in relation to Physical Education? How do you know?

Archaic Pedagogy

'Nurturing motivation, confidence, physical competence and knowledge and understanding in a range of environments will improve likelihood of sustained engagement in physical activity for life' (Durden-Myers, 2020, p.28).

Traditional methods of teaching PE, and the ingredients of what many would have or continue to look for in a strong PE lesson, would consist of some form of warm-up, introduction to a skill, a demonstration of said skill, drills and student practice of the skill in varying degrees of challenge, and then, finally, a conditioned game that supports the development of the skill in a competitive and pressurised environment. These elements have served as the dominant form of teaching in PE with the main subject specific developmental delivery coming in the form of National Governing Bodies coaching badges.

In this chapter I outline why traditional and sport-driven PE pedagogy should be considered archaic. It is of course understandable that teachers have focused on sport-techniques, and that this has formed the dominant form of delivery. In a result-obsessed environment, PE teachers have been forced to focus on tangible skills and techniques that can be easily assessed and 'graded'. Sport-techniques are also capable of disassembly and assembly in a short period of time (Kirk, 2010), which would fit most short, sharp schemes of work. We could also consider producing a different type of teacher altogether, through altered teacher training courses. However, as discussed by Kirk on the topic of trainee teachers having a desire to change PE, 'the pedagogy of necessity and the peer pressures of workplace culture soon wash out any radical ambitions that may reside in neonate teachers' (2010, p.63). Drawing on the voices of teachers, and the research to further back up their experiences, this chapter shows the impact of our current forms of delivery on our students.

The Disengaged

It seems logical, following the researching regarding personality types, to look more deeply at the experience of a child who has become disengaged with PE. Perhaps a cautious introvert or an everyday youth; either way, this student lacks motivation to participate.

A Head of Department, from Birmingham, spoke of how one particular student really struggled with PE. They would often find her truanting during PE lessons, or coincidentally ill on days she had PE. The Head of Department spoke of how she had tried different behaviour management approaches from detentions to restorative practice, and parent phone calls to merit points for participating.

The department finally managed to get her into a lesson with correct kit. The lesson, part of an athletics scheme of work, was long distance running, specifically 1200m. Now, I know what you're thinking, a PE refuser and a long-distance run, this already spells disaster.

At the start of the lesson students were instructed to run at their own pace, jog if they had to, but to never stop running. The first students to cross the line were applauded, given more time to rest and provided endless amounts of praise. The teachers would continue to direct threats out to those students that dare to walk.

The Head of Department stood back and watched how the already disengaged girl tired and walked, whilst other students laughed (though were challenged), and teachers continued to shout. The girl managed to lightly jog around 400 metres and walk the rest, yet the focus of this lesson was on the fastest students across the line.

The teacher had even started his plenary before the girl had finished the required distance. Picture a class, all sat facing the teacher, but in the corner of their eye looking at the finish line and sniggering. The girl mumbled some profanities regarding how it was an awful lesson and quietly sloped to the back of the group as the teacher delivered the final moments of his lesson.

The Head of Department remarked how she felt awful and could now understand why this girl would go to the lengths she did to stay clear of PE. The inclusion of a long-distance running event was not the problem. The issue was the focus of the lesson, the teacher's expectations, the lesson objectives and, 99% of praise being given to specific students. Success in this lesson was judged on a student's ability to cross the line as fast as they could. Anyone seen walked had disobeyed the incredibly clear and over-communicated instructions not to stop running.

Be honest, we have all seen a lesson like this. This student then, unsurprisingly, missed the next PE lesson due to 'illness'. The girl was disengaged and demotivated before the lesson began. She left feeling even further disengaged and demotivated, but now also humiliated and shattered. Psychologist and researcher Roy Baumeister highlights that bad is stronger than good. His research indicated that bad experiences have far more impact and are processed more thoroughly than good ones. These negative impressions are quicker to form and harder to lose (Baumeister et al., 2001). Therefore, what impact has this single lesson had on her current mental state, her future mental state, and her intrinsic motivation to ever participate in physical activity again? Thus, never wanting to develop physical literacy. We can't underestimate the impact one negative experience in PE can have on a student. Much like a restaurateur will work tirelessly to encourage repeat custom, by serving tasty food or providing friendly and attentive service, the owner hopes that the next time you are looking to dine out you will remember previous experiences to eat there again. However, all it takes is one hair in the soup to tarnish all previous experiences and stop you from considering this restaurant in the future. Building a student's motivation and love for physical activity can take many lessons if not entire academic years. But, if a student has one really awful PE experience, as demonstrated by the example above, then the motivation to pursue physical activity in the future can be lost.

Enjoyment

It might seem obvious, but students want lessons that are safe, relevant, well informed, inclusive, exciting, and fun. The physical activity opportunities provided in PE are seen by many as traditional, irrelevant, boring, and far from fun (Harris and Cale, 2019).

The Sport England survey *Active Lives* in 2019 found 'enjoyment' is the biggest driver of activity. In short, the more you enjoy physical activity, the more active you will be. On the surface, this seems simple to achieve, and PE is seen as many students' favourite subject.

In reality, only 51% of students answered that they strongly agreed to enjoying sport, which means 49% of students might not feel the full benefits of taking part in regular sport. The Active Lives survey also highlights the strong correlation between enjoyment and competence. Putting it simply, the students that found sport too difficult, or perhaps experienced failure more often, enjoyed it less.

Imagine being in a sales job in which you are told you are incompetent. Your boss has not told you directly, but you are held back from pay progression in your most recent appraisal, and the appraisal before that. You receive commission for every sale that you make, and you try really hard to achieve those sales, with little success. Your boss has put you in a group with other members of staff that are struggling to sell to give you extra support, though this extra support does not seem to be helping you in your ability to convert a sale. It comes to your next appraisal and your boss looks at you and asks, 'do you think this career choice is right for you?' The likelihood is, you will decide to pursue a career elsewhere. The point being, that if we continue to assess students based on practical ability, putting students in classes based solely on ability and in-directly telling students they are not good at PE, they are less likely to pursue any form of physical activity in the future. We must consider the non-verbal messages we are sending to our students and the impact their experiences within our subject.

The Sport England *Uniting the Movement* initiative (2021) recognised the importance of creating positive experiences for children and young people in sport and physical activity. Identified as one of its five main strategies, the initiative highlighted the impact of positive experiences from an early age, and how they build the foundations for an active life. 'If children and young people have experiences that feel fun, positive and give them a sense of confidence, they're more likely to want to be active in the future.' Sport England set out their ambition, wanting every young person to experience the enjoyment and benefits that being active can bring. The initiative continued to say, 'Their needs, expectations and safety should come first in the design and delivery of activity'. A statement that, in my opinion, should be the true of all PE departments around the world. Much of the ambition from this initiative, whilst promising and exciting, is focused on sport and physical activity in the community, though it does reference the desire to influence the design and delivery of physical activity in educational settings. An understanding of the vital part that physical educators play in creating these meaningful experiences around physical activity, and the importance of nurturing physical literacy now, are at the forefront of key organisations initiatives. Though much of the power to achieve such objectives is in the hands of PE teachers and curriculum creators.

No one likes to feel like a constant failure; it's not enjoyable. Now imagine a student that you teach that might have been given that same message from PE. That message could be from a grade/level on their report, an allocated class, or even a particular lesson in which they arrived not being able to perform a technique and left still unable to fully perform that technique.

Like many subjects, the specific skills taught are often complex; unlike other subjects, students have relatively little time to master them. If we focus purely on sport related skills, some students will experience failure, often. If we measure their performance with a level or grade, they will receive the message loud and clear – they are no good at sport. Not pursuing a career in a particular field is one thing, but in PE we have a bigger responsibility; we could be turning these children away from physical activity for life.

In recent years, much work has been done on incorporating engagement and enjoyment. Student autonomy was missing for some time in the PE curriculum. Students were given a set list of sports they were to cover in the academic year, and that was that. Now, many schools are offering pathways or option blocks in which students get the opportunity to shape their own curriculum.

The Public Health England's report *What works in schools and colleges to increase physical activity?* highlights 8 principles to improve the activity levels of students. One of these principles is to 'embed in curriculum, teaching and learning – increasing the amount of time spent being physically active during PE and other lessons can improve both physical development, educational outcomes and emotional development.'

There is little argument that spending more time being active is a positive step towards getting students moving in the short-term; surely, we must reflect on the nature of the activities within these lessons if we are to ensure lifelong participation in physical activity.

Picture a child who doesn't really enjoy the taste of broccoli but is served it once a week. They have never experienced broccoli before now, as their parents had never served him to them. They eat the broccoli, because everyone else is eating it, and the chef tells them its good for their health, but, in all honesty, they don't see the benefit and feel self-conscious eating broccoli in front of others.

Sometimes, when they are eating, their peers make fun of how they chew. The chef gives rewards to all children who eat their broccoli in the quickest time, but this child is a slow eater so has never received that reward. The government has now informed all children that they, by law, should receive two portions of broccoli a week, due to the positive impact it can have on a child's long-term health.

Our child dreads turning up twice a week to eat the broccoli, but they do it, because they have to. This continues for a few years. Now however, our child is no longer considered a child and does not have to eat the chef's food any longer. Now they have the freedom to make their own choices and make their own dinners. Do you think this individual will chose to eat broccoli again?

The point being that, just because someone receives more of something, it doesn't make the experience a more positive one, or the motivation to continue that activity any stronger. Quantity is good, but quality is just as, if not more, important. Giving students that are not enjoying PE more of it will do nothing to change their enjoyment.

Lost Curriculum Time

Our PE leaders are under increasing pressure to provide examination results and progress data. The national trend regarding obesity, inactivity, and mental health is on the rise. Alarmingly, PE curriculum time is being taken away.

We are in the middle of an obesity and mental ill-health epidemic, both of which are detrimental to academic performance. Yet we are losing lesson time! It's the equivalent of telling a man in a small wooden boat to paddle upriver, against the tide to avoid the waterfall but taking away his paddle.

Sarah teaches at a secondary school in Berkshire and has been Head of PE for 6 years. Whilst the numbers in her GCSE and BTEC classes are increasing, the hours given to PE have been unofficially cut. The older year groups, moving closer to exams, are particularly vulnerable. Sarah recalls, 'often around mock exams, students will be forced to participate in intervention classes instead of attending PE lessons, leaving us with reduced numbers in class. Some of our Year 11 students, who you might argue are in most need of physical activity and the benefits it brings, have not received a practical PE lesson all year, as Maths, English and Science take priority. Students enter our sports hall, sit down in their uniform, and teachers from other subjects come in and take away their targeted students. The students used to hate it. Now, most don't even bring in a PE kit, fully aware the likelihood of them doing PE is slim. The reality is that the pressure to achieve results for the subjects that can significantly impact a school's progress data mean that time in PE is seen as expendable.'

In Sarah's school, PE has remained on the timetable, but the students are often withdrawn, the damaging impact going undetected. In many schools, it's more obvious, with lesson time being removed altogether. It seems contradictory to tell students that their health and well-being is of the utmost importance, but then eradicate the most obvious opportunity to support and improve it.

So, why is PE seen as expendable? In a culture driven by results, it's understandable that, when little value is seen in PE, the time for some students is better spent elsewhere. This has led to the questioning over whether there is a future of PE as a subject altogether.

This hugely undermines and devalues the true impact PE can have, or at least highlights the views that senior leaders have on the subject. As PE teachers, we are having to constantly justify our importance. Many decision makers in schools seem to overlook the impact their decisions are having; therefore, we must show them just how important we are. We need to make ourselves indispensable. 'In order to regain a secure future for Physical Education it must re-define its value as a worthwhile subject and an end in itself. Physical Education must look inwards to find its value rather than justify its value by serving as a means to other ends' (Durden-Myers, 2020, p.51). Not all skills we teach in PE are essential to students' lives, like the overhead clear shot in badminton or the set shot in basketball. These are not skills that students will be required to replicate in future interviews or in the world of work. With sport as our only focus, we are expendable; with changes to our curriculum focus, the right intent marketing, and a clear vision we can be essential.

Extra-curricular clubs

It is necessary, though not a part of the main curriculum, to discuss the extra-curricular opportunities and the experiences we provide. This area of our delivery forms a key part of the opportunities for physical activity we offer.

Some teachers are protective of their extra-curricular teams, so this next point may be controversial. A good extra-curricular offering should provide students with an opportunity to extend their learning, explore a new activity, do something they enjoy, and meet like-minded peers. It is worth reflecting if your extra-curricular options meet the needs of all students. Teachers give up a huge amount of time on training and fixtures, and it forms an important role within the school and wider community. The National Curriculum encourages competitive fixtures against other schools and, for many, it can form a feeling of pride and belonging when representing one's school. It is even used as a carrot to dangle in front of the naughtier children to ensure good behaviour.

This competition should not be lost. In fact, it's hugely important. However, it should not form the entirety of the PE extra-curricular offering. I have yet to meet a PE teacher who is able to enjoy a lunch break and finish at the actual end of the school day in the same day.

In order to appeal to as many students as possible, we put on as many clubs as we can in what little free time we have. Before school, break time, lunch and after school are all taken with some kind of club. The phrase of working smarter not harder is pertinent here, as we are working incredibly hard, but with little impact. Could it be that by asking students why they do not attend, what they enjoy, or what they dislike about what we offer outside of lesson time, we could achieve a more targeted approach, in which we do indeed work smarter and not harder, within lesson time and beyond?

One teacher, from a secondary school in Milton Keynes, spoke of his school's extra-curricular programme: 'whilst I enjoy the clubs I run, I only ever see the same 10-15 students every fixture. These students already play in teams outside of school anyway. Much like our actual curriculum, our extra-curricular clubs are aimed at the already engaged and competent students.' There is no denying that, as PE teachers, we are a competitive bunch. We love to win. One major influence on physical literacy is students' role models, and we must consider the part we play in this, and the message we send when getting a bit caught up in the competition.

Oliver, a teacher from Liverpool, recounted a football fixture his Year 9 team competed in: 'After a few minutes of the game, you could see one side were much better than the other. We went 3-0 up after only 10 minutes of the game. Their manager was refereeing the fixture and at 4-0, prior to the game restarting, I called him over. I told him that I was happy to stop the game, take the win, mix the teams up and just play for fun, but he insisted that we carried on. His players were openly venting their frustrations at each other, and a couple of them obviously didn't want the ball for fear of being shouted at. At half time the game was 6-0, I again offered to cut the game short to play a friendly game, but he declined saying, 'his players had to learn'; exactly what he was hoping they might learn, I had no idea. At 8-0 it was beyond embarrassing; I took 3 of my best players off as I felt the need to somehow protect the opposition.

I asked again, this time more forcefully, insisting that the game should be ended, only to be told we only had 10 minutes left anyway, so no point finishing early. It was humiliating. The game ended 11-0. After the game, I made a point to talk to the teacher and told him he needed to do a better job at protecting his students, only to be told, 'it's OK, it's character building'. This, in my opinion, is not what school-based competition should be about.'

Other teachers have recounted similar experiences to Oliver's, and we must remember at all times that we are teachers. We are not coaches. We are not elite professionals that receive bonuses for winning. We are educators. It is nice to win, but it is more important that we role model sportsmanship, etiquette, and respect. We should congratulate effort and reward contribution. Play to win and behave to educate.

As Whitehead (2010, p.161) comments, 'Practitioners working in extra-curricular contexts at school or beyond have a key role to play. It is essential that all these practitioners interact with participants as individuals and have these young people at the forefront of planning and guidance. All those involved with working with children and young people must do all they can to promote a positive attitude towards physical activity and guard against any feelings of failure on the part of the participant'.

In conclusion, if we are to truly deliver meaningful change, it is vital that every teacher flying the PE flag understands physical literacy, and the vision of creating lifelong motivation to participate in physical activity. As Dylan Williams (2011) so beautifully articulates, 'A bad curriculum well taught is invariably a better experience for students than a good curriculum badly taught: pedagogy trumps curriculum. Or, more precisely, pedagogy is curriculum, because what matters is how things are taught, rather than what is taught.' Our delivery, although well-intentioned, may have contributed to our subject's downfall. Through the experiences shared by others in this chapter, and many of my own, it would seem there are some in our profession who have forgotten we are teachers. We are not coaches. We are educators. Whether in a PE lesson, or on a pitch during an extra-curricular fixture, we are educators who should be role models of the best behaviour and strive to create an environment that can nurture and maximise physical literacy potential.

It should be no longer acceptable to continue a fixture when one team is being humiliated, or to negatively shout at a student when they are unable to continue running. We are accountable for our actions and the impact they have on a student's perception of PE and physical activity. When others are seemingly overlooking and discounting the value of our subject, we must be its loudest advocates, not by telling everyone the value of PE, but by showing them.

Take Away Reflections

- Do students enjoy PE at your school? How do you know?
- How is PE viewed by senior staff at your school?
- How is PE valued by others at your school?
- How do you create a learning environment that nurtures physical literacy?
- What is the teaching philosophy of others in your team? How does this impact the ability to nurture physical literacy?

Elitist Assessment

'The curriculum focuses too much on whether student X can do specific technique Y as opposed to developing them as a whole person.' Mr D – School in North West of England. This section focuses on common forms of performance-based summative assessment adopted by PE departments and their impact on students. We are now living in what is known as a volatile, uncertain, complex, and ambiguous (VUCA) world. Our world is constantly changing, and these changes are unpredictable, which creates uncertainty. Our current and future problems are far more complex, and the causes and repercussions harder than ever to understand. People are required to take risks, make mistakes and question 'why?' in order to understand challenges faced in our world.

So how do we predict what a student is going to need to know to prepare them for this VUCA world we are sending them out into? We can't. What we do know is the idea of developing concepts and personal skills such as communication, leadership, looking after one's health, and well-being are future-proof.

Our current sport-driven model is not meeting the needs of the nation's students now, let alone preparing them for the future. We, as a subject, must evolve and bring ourselves into the modern world, move away from a performance-obsessed assessments that judge irrelevant skills and techniques. Instead, we must establish a positive connection with PE and build the motivation to participate in physical activity away from the school context, to apply learning to unfamiliar contexts and challenge our students to own and reflect on their own personal development. If we are ever truly to nurture physical literacy and meet our intent, we must move on, adapt, and improve. So, the next big question is, how can our assessment truly support the development of the whole child, and prepare them for a better life through Physical Education?

Purpose

Before we look at the current methods of assessment being used in PE, it is important to understand what assessment is and why we need it. Myatt (2018) offers a sound definition of assessment as, 'the process of gaining insight into what our pupils know, understand and can do as a result of what we have taught them'. It can come in different forms, from formal exams to a simple conversation with a student and should be used to inform where to go next. 'Ultimately, assessment and feedback should cause thinking. It should be focused; it should relate to the learning goals that have been shared with the students; and it should be more work for the recipient than the donor. Indeed, the whole purpose of feedback should be to increase the extent to which students are owners of their own learning,' (Wiliam, 2011).

Life Without Levels

Assessment in schools has gone through its biggest change for some time, as we transitioned into life without levels. Previously, students were given a level, based on their ability to perform a skill. These levels often came with sub-levels and were complicated for teachers to understand, let alone students.

Myatt (2018) suggests that this was never the intention of levels; they were only ever meant to be best fit indicators, which would identify the knowledge and skills attained at the end of a Key Stage. They were not designed to provide information on what a child could or could not do.

Schools, in an attempt to meet the aspects outlined in the National Curriculum, were delivering roughly seven outwitting opponents, activities or games, one accurate replication activity, one maximal performance activity, and one problem solving activity (Frapwell, 2015). Therefore, students that performed better in a game situations were going to be hugely advantaged in a best fit form of assessment, over the students who performed better in other activities, due to the dominance of games in the curriculum.

Craig is a Head of Department and spoke of his earlier experiences with assessment when levels were used: 'There was a lot of pressure on us to assign a number next to each student that demonstrated progress. These were even used as teacher performance management targets. As a leader, I found it increasingly difficult to ensure consistency amongst my team, as what a level 3b might look like to one teacher was different to another's perception, despite the copious amounts of detail next to each sub-level. Levels were linked solely to physical ability and, if a student was unaware of their level, it would be highlighted in observation feedback.

It was also difficult to demonstrate progress when offering such a broad range of sports. Just because a student is a higher level in football, does not mean they would achieve the same level of competency in gymnastics. I felt as if teachers were making the summative assessment levels up to demonstrate progress. In lessons, we would actively use formative assessment, and this made the biggest impact to student progress. Through conversations with students, demonstrations, and class feedback, we were able to support learning and improve technique, yet senior leaders only cared about levels.'

Tim Oates, chair of the expert panel that reviewed the National Curriculum between 2010 and 2013, believed that the removal of 'levels' was not some arbitrary change in bureaucracy, but a fundamental shift in thinking about assessment and learning.

For many schools, the shift from levels to whatever should be replacing them was unclear. Some schools swapped levels for other numerical values or letters to indicate current attainment. Formative assessment and Assessment for Learning (AfL) were to be given more priority and while some schools employed flight paths, others used mastery statements and marking grids.

The National College for Teaching and Leadership's *Beyond Levels: Alternative Assessment Approaches Developed by Teaching Schools* report highlighted, 'inconsistencies within and across schools of existing assessment practice' (2014). Head of Department, Craig continued, 'when levels went, we were instructed we had to model GCSE grades as this would be easier for students and parents to understand and we could demonstrate progress. We were still assessing for practical performance only, although not using levels, but the same system in a different guise.' Craig's experiences were echoed in other conversations too. As much as our curriculum was having a negative impact on enjoyment levels, our assessment methods were just as archaic.

Results versus Engagement

There certainly seems to be a clear divide between those that believe PE should be about improving health and lifelong participation, and those that feel PE is in a better place now, because of its academic weighting and firmer assessment and tracking.

Clare Sealy wrote in *The Research Ed Guide to the Curriculum*, 'A few years ago, I would have found it very strange to think about the curriculum in any detail. I was much more interested in thinking about the how to teach rather than what to teach. The what, for some subjects, was dictated from on high, via the National Curriculum or, more importantly, the statutory tests that held us to account. The tests formed the curriculum and shaped what was taught' (Sealy, 2020, p.13).

When I was new to the post of Head of Department, this thinking shaped my curriculum plan; I planned to teach only GCSE PE sports. It's certainly a tough choice, on the one hand you have SLT meetings and appraisal objectives to get through, and on the other these often drill-focused, technique-intensive and -driven lessons are disengaging for most students. Is it possible to achieve both good results for practical elements of GCSE PE and enjoyment for all?

Mr D, a PE teacher in a mixed comprehensive secondary school in the Northwest, spoke of how his lesson was criticised for not focusing the entire time on a specific technique. 'I was teaching a Year 8 high ability netball class, and had planned a fun game-specific competition for the end of the lesson. My Head of Department spoke to me during my lesson about what I had planned; once I told him he gave me an 'ear full'. I was told to focus purely on drills as we were preparing them for GCSE. I felt crushed.

The girls went from being active for 75-80% of the lesson to maybe 50%, as they were waiting for their turn in the drill. It's boring even to teach, let alone be a student participating in the lesson. The girls started to associate PE with dull drills and standing around in the cold, which I can't imagine does any good for long-term engagement.

'The curriculum focuses too much on whether student X can do a specific technique as opposed to developing them as a person.'

Whilst we have sympathy for Mr D, we must also understand the pressure that the Head of Department is under, and why it may lead them to feel this way. 'Due to the achievement agenda and contribution to those all-important league tables of GCSE results, plus Ofsted scrutiny, these measures often, wrongfully, are used as the sole tangible measure of individual or PE department success. This then has associated connectivity with appraisal, pay progressions, and SLT pressure, resulting in demotivated teachers' (Swaithes, 2015). Though we must also consider our contribution to the demise of the relevance of PE. If (when being observed by a trainee teacher, SLT, Ofsted inspector, or whoever) we set lesson objectives that are 99% geared around sporting technique, and tell people correct replication of the overhead clear in badminton IS success in PE, then of course we will be judged on whether that is being developed and/or achieved.

Reliability

Craig, the Head of Department, brought up an issue he faced with consistency. He found it hard to guarantee that the marks provided by teachers were accurate, due to the pressure to demonstrate progress. Christodulou discusses the issue of reliability in her book *Making Good Progress?* (2016). She mentions how one important aspect of validity is reliability. A reliable assessment should show little inconsistency from one teacher to the next. A sport-driven curriculum often uses a quality model when assessing. This model is also used in other subjects like English and Music. This model requires students to perform a task and they are assessed on how well they have performed it.

To ensure reliability, Christodulou infers that an assessment should provide the same results no matter the time of day and if marked by ten different markers. Student performance on the day heavily impacts a quality model form of assessment. The nature of sport performance is incredibly unpredictable, even professionals have off-days. Even factors such as what a student has eaten that day, injuries, and how the opposition and teammates play can all impact performance on any given day. If you take this, and the pressures on teachers to evidence progress into account, we are left with a highly unreliable form of assessment.

Demotivated from Assessment

PE departments have chosen to publicise students' results in different forms. Some chose to put assessment grades achieved in a student planner, while others communicate attainment out to the class in a register-style approach. More recently, I have even seen assessment grades transferred to a 100-metre sprint race analogy-style notice board. The students achieving the highest grades have their pictures pinned closer to the finish line and those with lower attainment further back. Talk about rubbing salt into the wounds.

In a time where we are told that not all students find enjoyment in PE, and lack the intrinsic motivation to engage, some are, through assessment, reminding them of their shortcomings and humiliating them.

Teachers feel the need to over-communicate attainment, due to the pressure of SLT observations in which the question, 'what grade are you currently working at?' will inevitably be asked of at least a few students. Whilst it is important for a student to understand where they currently are on their learning journey, it is surely more important for a student to understand what they need to do in order to progress. We must unite and fully grasp the fact that performance-focused grades/levels, etc, and the constant indirect and inadvertent communication of inadequacies, are demotivating and doing more harm than good.

In summary, though much work has been done on assessments models within PE, the decaying physical ability driven assessment is slowly giving way to the development of a more holistic approach. However, around the country, many PE departments are still under pressure to provide GCSE-like grades, or practical performance-focused data to indicate students' ability to replicate and execute a number of sport-specific skills. This form of assessment is demotivating, unreliable, and irrelevant. It only serves the most able and reaffirms the frustrating and outdated perception that PE is only playing sport. It is directly contradicting key messages around the benefits of physical activity and forfeiting opportunities to develop physical literacy. It rewards the best and demotivates the rest.

The future of our students is uncertain. We are living in a VUCA world that is constantly changing. To prepare students for an unpredictable future requires us to highlight future-proof skills and support students to identify, observe, demonstrate, reflect, and develop these skills. A meaningful and thought-out assessment model can do this. It can prepare students for life and motivate them to be physically active.

If we are ever to truly nurture physical literacy, meet our intent, and be genuinely valued as a subject we must move on, adapt, and improve. So, the next big question is how?

Take Away Reflections

- What is the purpose of the assessment used in PE at your school?
- Does it effectively fulfil this purpose?
- What messages might the language used when assessing send to students?
- Is your assessment results or engagement driven?
- How reliable is the assessment? Are all team members using the assessment consistently? How do you know?
- How does your assessment develop skills and attributes that will be relevant to their future?
- How could you incorporate your formative assessment to inform your summative assessment?

4

An Approach to the Future of Physical Education

Shifting the focus of what we teach, how we teach it, and how we assess it will improve the experiences and meet the needs of every child. The historical perspective has laid a foundation for us to now turn our attention to establishing what the future of our subject could look like. In this chapter I discuss how conceptual learning and the tailoring of curriculum to meet students' needs can support the delivery of positive PE. I detail the change needed in teacher-mindset and delivery, in order to provide positive PE. And finally, how performance-driven assessment should make way for a holistic and progressive approach in order to deliver positive PE.

I mentioned previously that achieving quality PE involves curriculum, pedagogy, and assessment. I wish to propose a model for creating positive and meaningful PE experiences for all students. In the interest of clarity, we should consider what is meant by these three terms.

-   The *curriculum* is the totality of a student's experience (Myatt, 2018). Therefore, when discussing curriculum, we shall debate all planned components that make up the longer-term vision for learning and student experience in timetabled PE lessons.
-   *Pedagogy* can be defined as the method and practice of teaching. When considering the concept of pedagogy, we will be focusing on the lesson and the way in which learning is delivered. It is important to not only talk about the use of individual models and teaching techniques, which one might consider when thinking of pedagogy and PE, but also the relationship between the lesson, teacher, and the experiences provided.
-   Finally, *assessment* is the action of making a judgement about progress, or the level of competence demonstrated. We will be reflecting on the use and application of both formative (informal, on-going, and often

in-lesson), and summative (formal, structured, and measured) assessment, and the impact this has on student motivation.

Using a sporting analogy and simple mnemonic, I will present my vision for the future of PE. In association football, a player receives a cap if they represent their country at international level. For every appearance at this level, they receive a new cap. This process has also been applied in other sports. As physical educators, we aim to deliver world-class PE – the type of delivery that would be recognised as best practice around the world. We can represent our school at international level. Therefore, we should earn our caps. We have already identified that to deliver high quality PE we must consider our approach in the following areas:

Earn Your World Class PE Cap

Curriculum: All planned components of what is delivered

Assessment: Judgement of progress made or competence demonstrated

Pedagogy: Method and practice of teaching

Curriculum, Assessment and Pedagogy, hence the mnemonic CAP. Within each of these aspects of PE, we have opportunities to earn additional caps. In this chapter, I outline how we can earn a cap within our curriculum, assessment, and pedagogy that will enable us to deliver world class PE.

If we earn our cap by delivering world class PE, then all students will be given a better chance to receive their cap in PE.

Earn the Students' PE Cap

Connected: Students will value PE and understand the importance of the subject. They will receive relevant learning that better prepares them for life through physical activity and develop a positive attitude towards physical activity.

Appreciated: A positive and meaningful PE environment will ensure every student feels safe, respected, and heard.

Physically Literate: Students will have the opportunity to nurture their physical literacy, developing competence, confidence, knowledge, and understanding.

At this stage, I feel it pertinent to remind you that I am a current Head of PE. The reason I feel it is a good time to remind you of this is that I am not prescribing the answers or preaching from a role disconnected with the realities of teaching. I am simply outlining what I, and others, have done or are attempting to do. I am learning as I go. If, like me, you are passionate about the impact this subject can have on the lives of our students, and you are willing to be brave and try something new in the pursuit of better, then what comes next may support you in making these changes. Every school is different and, as such, the curriculum should be designed around the needs of your students. Context plays a big part in making the changes I suggest, but they can be adapted to the needs of your school. Alternative curriculum models, such as Sport Education, Teaching Games for Understanding, and Fitness for Life represent positives steps towards a more inclusive and relevant offering, and should be considered, however, they are not discussed in this book.

Our goal is to deliver a positive and meaningful experience in PE for all students or, 'positive and meaningful PE' as I call it. My Principal, Mark Pritchard, always says, 'clarity is kindness'. So, with that in mind, I will clarify what I mean by positive and meaningful in a PE context. I would however like to confirm that, in my opinion, there is no single or tangible definition for either positive or meaningful PE. However, positive PE relates to a student's feelings and emotions towards the subject, whereas meaningful PE concerns the perceived relevance and value this subject has on the life of the student.

Perceptions of what positive and meaningful PE is may alter between physical educators, and how to achieve it may differ in various schools. In fact, in his research article *Pedagogical principles that support the prioritisation of meaningful experiences in Physical Education: conceptual and practical considerations* (2021), Tim Fletcher argues that there is no single definition of meaningfulness within PE. He does however identify meaningfulness and its relationship to values and emotions connected to an experience.

My vision for positive and meaningful PE (and one that I hope will resonate with many others) is:

- Positive PE requires teachers to reward progress not perfection. Positive PE is assessment focused on development, not performance, therefore encouraging students to learn from mistakes and motivating them to engage. It is a positive and enriching environment in which all students can flourish through physical activity, thus nurturing physical literacy. It is a curriculum that students have ownership of, enabling them to shape their own pathway. Students know they will be guided by caring teachers that will challenge, support, and encourage.
- Meaningful PE is a curriculum that students truly connect with and see the value of. It delivers relevant and enriched content that can be transferred to various situations throughout an individual's life. Meaningful PE is assessment that permits students to take ownership of their learning, identify their strengths, and have opportunities to develop their weaknesses. It's building relationships with their teachers based on respect and encouragement.

Together, positive and meaningful PE can bring PE out of the crisis we find it in and take it to exactly where we know it can and should be: a vital subject that is considered as important, if not more so, than numeracy and literacy. A subject that creates the environment whereby all students can nurture their own love of physical activity, and gain the knowledge, understanding, confidence and competence for lifelong physical engagement. A subject that meets cultural needs. There is, however, no single positive and meaningful PE answer. There are in fact many. Every school is different as so are the needs of the students within them.

The following diagram shows the relationship between these three main key components (curriculum, assessment, and pedagogy) of positive and meaningful PE. Curriculum, pedagogy, and assessment must all work together to ensure positive and meaningful PE for all. A world class and innovative curriculum is unable to deliver positive and meaningful PE in isolation. If delivered poorly, or assessed purely on performance, then positive and meaningful PE is unattainable. If two of these elements work successfully together, but the final one contradicts them, this will negatively impact student experience, and therefore fail to deliver positive and meaningful PE.

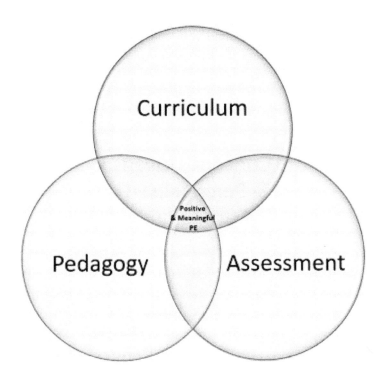

Every PE department delivers a curriculum; the way in which it is taught forms the pedagogy, and some form of assessment is used to identify progress. However, the key question is, 'do they deliver positive and meaningful PE?' Every PE department should decide how they meet each element of the framework to ensure they create positive and meaningful PE. There is no one-size fits all model. Every school is different. The needs of the students are different. However, the three main ingredients to creating a positive and meaningful PE experience remain the same.

Later in this book, other current teachers share how they are attempting to lead change in their setting. In this chapter, I outline how I have led and collaborated with others on meeting my vision for creating a positive and meaningful PE experience. What I believe to be the future of PE, my legacy, and what will save our subject.

The diagram below demonstrates how my department have attempted to create positive and meaningful PE. In the curriculum circle we are delivering a concept-driven and personalised approach to curriculum design. Our assessment is holistic and progressive, and our pedagogy is focused on inclusivity. All three will be explored in further detail, from conception and planning to implementation.

My vision is that a concept-driven and personalised curriculum will prepare students for life through Physical Education. Inclusive pedagogy whereby teachers understand and nurture physical literacy, and holistic and progressive assessment to develop the whole child, will create a positive and meaningful PE experience for all. This is how we have filled in our positive and meaningful PE framework. You should reflect on what would be included into your curriculum, assessment and pedagogy models that enable you to deliver positive and meaningful PE.

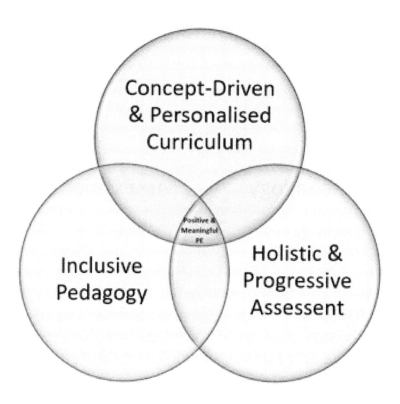

(Sullivan, 2021)

Take Away Reflections

- How does your curriculum ensure a positive and meaningful PE experience for all?
- How does your assessment ensure a positive and meaningful PE experience for all?
- How does your pedagogy ensure a positive and meaningful PE experience for all?
- What, out of these three elements, is hindering your team delivering a positive and meaningful PE experience for your students?
- What does your positive and meaningful PE model look like now? How would it ideally look?

Curriculum: Concept-Driven Approach

'We have a significant issue in Physical Education (PE) which has compounded the lack of status of our subject and our profession. It is this – it appears that PE has not claimed any threshold concepts' (Aldous and Chambers, 2021, p.151).

'Every discipline has threshold concepts. When mastered, threshold concepts are what enable students to look at problems in completely new ways' (Chambers et al., 2021). By introducing 'big ideas' into our lessons, we are able to provide meaningful learning opportunities that bring genuine value and relevancy that is currently missing. PE provides a unique environment that can influence outcomes beyond the previous skills and technique-focused results. Chambers et al. discuss the work of McQuaig et al. (2015), by identifying the three 'special characteristics' that are unique to PE. These include: 'The subject matter, the learning environments and the facilitation of caring teacher-pupil relationships' (2021, p.137). Furthermore, PE provides an environment that is able to effectively develop social and emotional learning within the affective domain, which puts our subject in a unique and important place within a school curriculum. Students are regularly provided with the opportunity to develop inter-personal skills through physical activity, though not often explicitly applied. 'These opportunities are contextualised within 'authentic' environments centred around motor skill performance and game play – which, often, involve positive interactions with peers' (Chambers et al. 2021, p.137). The learning environment, the physical activities delivered, and the relationships we build place the subject in a place to deliver learning that is unlike the learning available to students in any other subject, once again providing further evidence of the value of PE.

A concept-driven approach to curriculum design is one that moves away from subject-specific content and instead emphasises 'big ideas' that span multiple subject areas. A concept-driven approach offers an alternative to the traditional sport and skills-based approach to Physical Education curriculum design and delivery. The sport and physical activity become the vehicle for which the concept is delivered and no longer the final destination. By shifting the focus of the curriculum and the success criteria of each lesson, we are doing so much more than getting students active; we are teaching life skills and improving the experiences within PE for every child.

Myers and Land (2005) identify key characteristics of threshold concepts within learning: Transformative, Performative, Irreversible, Integrative, Bounded, Troublesome, Reconstitutive and Discursive. In summary, focusing on three of the eight characteristics, the impact of delivering threshold concepts in PE will be:

- *Transformative:* It can lead to a significant shift in the perception of a subject (Chambers et al. 2021).
- *Performative:* Students can apply their learning to new, wider contexts.
- *Irreversible:* Once threshold concepts are learned, it is not possible to unlearn them.

The impact recognised through these characteristics provides clear evidence as to the importance of the recommended shift to conceptual learning, and the power it can provide to the learners. We want students to value PE and physical activity, now and in the future; we want our learning in PE to be transferred elsewhere; and we want students to retain key life learning.

When discussing the vital topic of transfer of learning, Kirk (2010) considers two specific questions that physical educators must ask in regards to the value of their curriculum. The first is, 'how does the learning that occurs within the school relate to life beyond the school gates?' and the second is, 'how does school Physical Education during childhood and adolescence relate to the needs of adulthood?' (p.21). These questions are vital of any teacher in any subject. How does the learning in your subject transfer to other contexts, both present and future? It also leads to the question, how relevant is the learning to the learner? As presented in the previous chapter, I have argued that PE in its current multi-activity, technique-focused form does little for the relevant transfer of meaningful learning, outside of a PE or sporting context.

Cognitive scientist Daniel Willingham discusses how the brain is wired to remember stories. These stories help us remember key details and truly engage us.

He believes that teachers must create the conditions that enable us to teach concepts that come up again and again. A curriculum should not be considered as a series of singular lessons, but as a learning journey that incorporates all concepts (Willingham, 2011). When we consider the sport-driven curriculum model employed across the world, individual skill specific lessons are delivered, often designed to start out basic and get progressively more challenging.

A good example of this would be following an athletics scheme of work. Often, these lessons focus on one individual event, either track or field, per lesson. For years, I have delivered a lesson on javelin, followed by a lesson on sprint starts, etc. On their own, these are good lessons, but, as part of a learning journey, they offer little progression as the next time a student will attempt a javelin throw will be on sports day, or the following year when athletics is taught again. This means that, across the entire five years that a student attends a secondary school, they might receive five lessons on how to throw a Javelin. A curriculum should provide continuity, progression, and a meaningful connection as to what is being taught.

Feeling the frustration mounting over the lack of impact a sport-driven curriculum was providing, I decided to voice my concerns during a Heads of PE meeting, organised for our local PE schools. This network was a powerful way of collaborating with others in the same role as ourselves, though was often used to discuss extra-curricular provisions. I wanted to see if others felt the same as I did, so I put the question out, 'do you think a sport-driven model meets the needs of all students?' The question is a big one to answer off the cuff, and I didn't get much of a response. Fortunately, following the meeting, having allowed for some reflection time, two other Heads of PE got in touch. Lauren Williams and Craig Bartlett felt the same frustrations as me but had, at this time, not heard of a conceptualised learning.

I set about selling the idea to them and formulating what our threshold concepts could be:

- PE has an opportunity like never before to look at the bigger picture and fulfil the full potential of what the subject has to offer.
- 33% of students have poor body confidence issues (Youth Sport Trust, 2019), so let's teach self-esteem and self-worth.
- 92% of students suffer from exam stress, so coping skills, resilience, and mental health units are a must.
- Inactivity and childhood obesity are higher than ever, so planning and delivering units of work on diet and long-term benefits of exercise are essential.
- Competition for jobs is tougher now, so why not teach employability

skills, leadership, communication, and interpersonal skills?

- All that and more through physical activity and a concept-driven approach

I shared some of the reading I had done around the topic, and the idea of designing a curriculum journey focusing purely on concepts was born. At the start of the lockdown, around April 2020, we set about deciding what we believed to be the most important future-proof skills a student would need to prepare them for life that could be delivered through Physical Education. We wanted to develop a scheme of work that had the flexibility to be taught simply, overlapping the existing sports and physical activities being delivered. We did not want to lose sport, in fact the opposite; we wanted to celebrate everything that was great about it. We wanted to harness the power of sport to deliver meaningful and positive connections to the value of PE. We took what we perceived as being vital skills at different stages through the school journey and, from Year 7 to Year 11, devised a thorough concept-driven curriculum.

However, just identifying the concepts would be pointless if we did not know how a teacher might apply these to their lessons. I outline our approach to delivery in the next chapter on pedagogy. The value of collaborate working on this project meant we could also trial different aspects of it across three different settings, students and staff. This enabled us to fail often and learn fast. Whilst Chambers (2021) argues that PE has yet to identify threshold concepts that are exclusive to our subject, we wanted to identify the concepts that might not be exclusive to PE, but were relevant concepts that could be delivered through PE, and met the needs of our students.

The use of a wider concept provides students with a learning experience in which they can access and apply their learning to a different context when required. Ultimately, every concept and every lesson unite to achieve the aim of preparing students for life through Physical Education throughout the learning journey. Students will truly understand the importance of physical activity and will be given an opportunity to succeed that was previously only afforded to a few, which in turn will build confidence and motivation.

The diagram below outlines the full KS3 and KS4 concept-driven curriculum model created by myself, Lauren Williams, and Craig Bartlett.

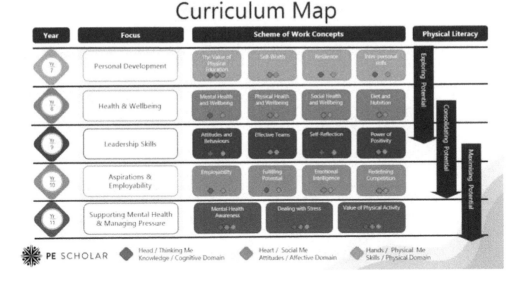

(Sullivan, Williams & Bartlett, 2021)

Each year has an overall focus; for example, Year 7 will focus on 'Personal Development', whilst Year 11 will focus on 'Supporting mental health and managing pressure'. We tried to identify concepts that would be required during this part of the student's school journey. This would hopefully provide students with more relevance to the learning content, a stronger connection to the value of PE, and permit more timely and relevant transfer of taught skills. We identified the physical literacy potential that teachers would be nurturing starting with 'Exploring potential' in Year 7 and 8, to 'Maximising Potential' in Year 11. We understood the need to add some guidance around assessment and identify the learning domains being developed during each block. We were also aware that some schools use different assessment frameworks, and therefore wanted to support departments by making these applicable to some more commonly used frameworks. The use of 'head', 'heart', or 'hand' icon would enable a user-friendly distinction as to the learning domain being developed, which would hopefully inform these assessment frameworks. Each year has four blocks or schemes of work. These blocks would focus on one big concept. Each block would consist of nine lessons that provide the knowledge and skills required to fully understand or demonstrate the big concept. As will be explained, each concept block will overlap an existing sport specific scheme of work.

The concepts identified in the curriculum plan created by Lauren Williams, Craig Bartlett and I, highlight the concepts we believe are important when delivering positive and meaningful PE, and preparing students for life through Physical Education.

Will Swaithes offered his key concepts with the following explanation: 'The thing I repeatedly find is the importance of real clarity and sharply communicated messaging to repeatedly reinforce that the education that takes place in PE is far more than just the physical.'

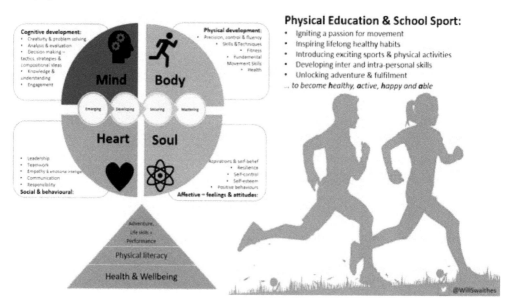

Both concept-driven models have been created to demonstrate the learning available to us through PE. It is so much more than sport. As Will articulated, it is about 'the mind, body, heart and soul.' When lessons require students to process facts through a conceptual level of thinking, they retain a greater amount of factual information, reach deeper levels of understanding, and have increased motivation for learning (Erickson, 2007).

Erickson (2007) also highlights the importance of using concepts in education in order to formulate knowledge, understand the world, and succeed in life beyond school. She argues that concepts:

- Create connections to students' prior experiences.
- Bring relevance to student learning.
- Facilitate deeper understanding of content knowledge.
- Act as springboards for students to respond to their learning.

Remember, nurturing physical literacy is an individual journey. A concept is a powerful idea that can replace a performance-focused objective, and therefore enable all to succeed in their own way.

This success, coupled with the drive towards preparation for life, will form an appreciation for the importance of PE. 'The one really competitive skill is the skill of being able to learn. It is the skill of being able not to give the right answer to questions about what you were taught in school, but to make the right response to situations that are outside the scope of what you were taught in school. We need to produce people who know how to act when they're faced with situations for which they were not specifically prepared' (Wiliam, 2011).

A shift in Focus

I reassured you at the start of this book that there would be no need to fully discard the current curriculum or the sports that we teach – they can remain. All we are doing is shifting the focus of our units of work to teach a wider concept, using sport as the vehicle to achieve this.

A concept can be defined as an abstract idea. In this case, a concept is a life skill or an important piece of learning that will support students throughout their lives. Students will acquire an understanding of this idea, develop a connection with the idea and the activity, and, finally, look to apply it to new and unfamiliar situations.

Instead of a lesson that might have previously had the objective to successfully perform a sport specific skill, that frankly only a few would be able to achieve, we teach the same skill, but without the need for the performance measure.

A concept-driven approach is vital to establishing and, for some, re-building a positive relationship with physical activity. We must clearly articulate the importance that physical activity has on a student's life in order to form the intrinsic motivation required for lifelong participation. Concepts including resilience – the ability to keep going even when faced with challenge, to remain motivated when times are hard, and to embrace and learn from failure – can now be the focus. Or, a concept such as the long-term benefits of exercise, or perhaps how to deal with stress, can become the main learning objectives.

Our own students told us through a student voice survey that, whilst many students did want to learn sport specific skills in PE lessons, the majority did not.

25. What would you like to learn in PE? (You can choose multiple answers)

More Details

- Benefits of being physically ac... 61
- How to be physically active ou... 79
- How to take part outside school 63
- Knowledge and skills I need fo... 110
- How to lead/organise a physic... 89
- Skills that will help in life 168
- Dont have a prefereance 76
- Sport specific skills 145
- Other 42

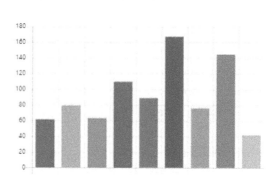

Conceptual thinking requires the ability to critically examine factual information, relate to prior knowledge, see patterns and connections, draw out significant understandings, transfer understanding across time or situation, and, often, use conceptual understanding to creatively solve a problem (Erickson, 2007).

These are all big ideas that can be delivered through sport. Shot putt, rugby, dance, and gymnastics can still be taught. If it was on your curriculum before, and you are confident the students actively engage with it, it can still be taught. We are simply overlaying a concept onto our current content.

There will be those of you reading this that think sport is already teaching various concepts: leadership, teamwork and communication, and you're not wrong – it can. However, I propose making these concepts the sole focus of the unit of work. Stern, author of *Tools for Teaching Conceptual Understanding*, and one of the world's leading advocates for conceptual learning, argues that, 'educators today seem to be faced with a choice: continue teaching centuries old ways of organising the world or throw them out in favour of innovation and creativity in order to move into the 21st century paradigm for teaching and learning' (2017, p.1). We don't have to tear up our curriculum; we are talking about adjusting our balance or stance in order to better position our students to take a shot – a shot at a better future.

Sport is not a dirty word in a concept-driven curriculum, and we do not have to lose sport specific skills from lessons. Sport is a vital aspect of a balanced and holistic curriculum. However, sport will now become the vehicle, not the final destination. 'In order to promote active lifestyles, we need to establish affective behavioural and cognitive (ABC) learning outcomes. Affective outcomes relate to feelings and attitudes (e.g.: positive attitudes towards PE). Behavioural outcomes are associate with actions (e.g.: participating in a school sports club). Whereas cognitive outcomes improve knowledge (e.g.: knowing the social health benefits of being active)' (Harris & Cale, 2019, p.31).

A concept-driven approach is an inclusive philosophy that can genuinely help every child to personally develop, which improves the affective behavioural and cognitive outcomes. Ability is no longer a key performance indicator, prior sporting experience not an advantage, nor background a barrier. PE will now truly be for everyone.

Remember the disengaged girl that was completing the 1200m athletics lesson in the previous chapter? The lesson in which the focus was to complete the running event in a good time? What if the focus of that lesson was the delivery of a concept, a bigger idea, such as persistence?

Persistence is an important life skill that every student will need at some point in their life. Time no longer matters. But that's not to say the students capable of achieving a good time would not still do so, or that the teacher could not discuss key techniques such as stride or pacing.

What if, with the lesson objective now focused on persistence, supported by a shift in the success criteria adopted by the teacher, the disengaged girl is not hounded every time she walks, but praised every time she starts running again, and therefore demonstrating the concept. Even if she does not start running again, but is able to walk the entire distance, she could be told how she is persisting, even though she finds it difficult, and is recognised for this achievement. Instead of a 'time' being used as a measure of performance, perhaps a 'Rating of Perceived Exertion' scale could be employed for students to rate how much effort they put in the lesson, or the level of intensity they consider that activity to be.

The teacher might then ask her how persistence not only helped her in that lesson, but also link it to other lessons within school, perhaps when she has demonstrated persistence before, or when it might be needed in the future. That girl would leave the lesson with a huge sense of achievement, no humiliation or embarrassment, the understanding of a key life lesson, and, most importantly, a positive connection between physical activity and reward. A concept-focused approach is an inclusive model in which all students can achieve success. Notice that the most able are still entitled to the coaching they needed to progress and receive the sport specific teaching required to advance their practical moderation grades. They are not held back in any way, and also leave with an important understanding about perseverance, which they might link to their performance differently – perhaps, what could be done to improve that finish time in the future. Also note that no sport was lost in the making of this lesson, only an outdated lesson objective.

Strategies to Deliver a Concept-Driven Curriculum

'What is the best knowledge for children to leave school with, should they discontinue their study in this subject? What is the most important knowledge for citizens? Which knowledge will bring the most meaning?' (Ashbee, 2020, p.32)

With this section, I hope to shape your future PE delivery. I believe this to be the part of the book that readers will want most, as this will be what causes a real shift in practice. I outline my devised model for conceptualised learning that could be used and applied to a PE curriculum. For this model, I have looked at a complete re-design of the curriculum by focusing only on concepts. It's important to understand that there is not a one size fits all model, and everything that follows should be adapted and applied to meet the aims of your department's intent, and, even more importantly, the biggest needs of your students this year – hence the offer will never stand still or stop being tweaked.

The diagram below illustrates a concept-driven approach to PE:

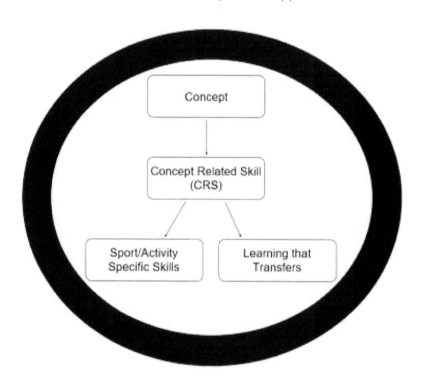

It all starts with an overall Concept; this forms the big objective of the scheme of work. To further explain this process, I will use an example:

e.g. by the end of my scheme of work, I would like the students to have knowledge of, demonstrate skills relating to, and value the concept of resilience.

I will then break this concept down into Concept Related Skills (CRS). CRSs are the micro-concepts, or smaller pieces of knowledge, required to support the overall delivery and understanding of the main concept. These will form the individual lesson objectives that will ensure students receive a full understanding of how to be resilient.

As Ruth Ashbee mentions in her contribution to *The Research Ed Guide To The Curriculum* (2020), 'what is the best knowledge for children to leave school with, should they discontinue their study in this subject? What is the most important knowledge for citizens? Which knowledge will bring the most meaning?'

I look at the CRSs I selected for our concept, resilience, in more detail later in this chapter, where I talk briefly about the flexibility of a concept-driven approach, how it can be applied to any sport and leave plenty of room for the teacher to overlap as they see fit.

Next, we have the sport or activity that the concept will be delivered through. The model refers to a sport specific skill; this could mean a specific technique, or can relate to any knowledge or practice required to participate, for example: the game, tactics, or rules.

When considering the sport you are planning to deliver, you should consider: the needs of your students and their opinion on the activities they enjoy; the expertise of your team; the resources and facilities available; and opportunity for student progression.

Finally, in my model, we have the 'how' – the way in which the concepts will be delivered – Learning that Transfers. Our concept and concept related skills will be delivered using the Learning Transfer Mental Model (Stern, Ferraro, Duncan, & Aleo, 2021). I explore how this model will inform the delivery conceptualised learning in the next chapter.

This model involves three phases of learning: Acquire, Connect and Transfer. Each phase enhances the student's ability to understand, relate and apply the concepts to previous experiences, and current and future similar and dissimilar situations. Innovators don't invent without understanding how the world works. With this foundation, they apply conceptual understanding to solve problems. We want students to not only retain ideas, but relate them to other things they encounter, using each new situation to add nuance and sophistication to their thinking (Stern, 2017).

Concept-driven Curriculum: Key Word Table

Key Concept-Driven Curriculum Term	Description
Concept	The big idea that students should understand and be able to apply to new contexts. Now the main focus of the scheme of work.
Concept Related Skill	The individual skills or required knowledge that will support the understanding of the concept. These make up our individual lesson objectives.
Sport/Activity	The physical activities used to support the learning of the concept. Can be a specific skill or development of sport related knowledge, e.g.: tactics, rules, games, etc. No longer the focus of the lesson or scheme of work, though sport specific skills are still taught.
Learning that Transfers	The Learning Transfer Model: Acquire, Connect and Transfer.

Applying the Model to Your Curriculum

In this example scheme of work, I would like my students to focus on the following 6 concept related skills (CRSs) in order to fully understand the concept of resilience.

These will now form the objectives for the each of the lessons:

Concept: Resilience

Scheme of Work Objective: for students to understand the importance of resilience and the impact that failure can have on the learning process.

Concept Related Skill	Example Lesson Objective
Embracing Failure	To understand what is meant by failure and demonstrate how it can aide learning.
Growth Mindset	To understand the differences between a fixed and growth mindset, and their impact on achieving a goal.
Persistence	To understand what persistence is and demonstrate it when faced with a challenge.
Black Box Thinking	To understand how learning from mistakes is vital to the learning process.
Marginal Gains	To gain an understanding of how marginal gains can lead to big improvements over time.
Embracing Change	To understand the mindset required to deal with, and even embrace, change.

By teaching these 6 CRSs, the students should leave the unit of work with the tools to not only understand resilience but also having had the opportunity to demonstrate it many times. Consequently, they should also develop their resilience.

Previously, our sport-driven model would have focused on a specific sport and then skills, fitness, rules, or tactics that were required for the sport. To continue my example, I shall apply the concept of resilience to basketball. A basketball scheme of work might outline the need to acquire specific skills that would be taught in a particular order, and would usually include:

- Dribbling
- Passing
- Pivoting
- Shooting (standing or jump shot)
- Shooting (lay-up shot)
- Defending

Below, I have created a diagram to highlight the mapping of this scheme of work. This is not the entire scheme of work, but will hopefully support your understanding of the concept in relation to the curriculum.

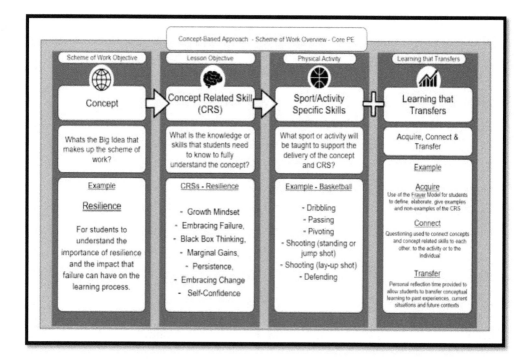

Curriculum Planning

When it comes to agreeing on the overall concepts to be delivered, the choice is limitless, from understanding mental health and dealing with stress, to diet and nutrition and employability skills. There is a vast number of important skills that will prepare students for life that can be taught through physical activity. The concepts could include, but are certainly not limited to:

- Diet and nutrition
- Employability skills
- Attitudes and behaviours of a leader
- Long-term benefits of exercise
- Self-worth
- Inter-personal skills
- Mental well-being
- Physical well-being
- Social well-being
- Effective teams
- Communication
- Power of positivity
- Career pathways

- Competition
- Fulfilling potential
- Dealing with stress

These concepts would each be broken down to include the concept related skills that would support the learners full understanding of the overall concept, as demonstrated with the concept of resilience in the previous chapter.

In summary, in this section I outline what a concept-driven curriculum is, why conceptual learning can provide meaningful connections to learning, and how it can truly prepare students for life. I have also presented the Concept-Driven PE Curriculum that Lauren Williams, Craig Bartlett and I co-created. I then focused on the 'resilience' scheme of work, demonstrating how each concept had 6 individual concept related skills that would form the lessons. These lessons are one ingredient in my positive and meaningful PE recipe, and would provide the students with the knowledge and tools to demonstrate life skills in their PE lessons, but also in a wider context. By overlapping the conceptual learning with the existing sport specific scheme of work, we are able to use sport as the vehicle to deliver vital learning, really putting the 'E' in Physical Education.

Take Away Reflections

- How does the learning that occurs within your school relate to life beyond the school gates?
- How does your school's Physical Education relate to the needs of adulthood? (Kirk, 2010)

Curriculum: Concept-Driven Pedagogy

More important than the curriculum is the way in which the curriculum is delivered. Without positive and effective teachers, the entire model fails. 'A bad curriculum well taught is invariably a better experience for students than a good curriculum taught badly: pedagogy trumps curriculum. Or more precisely, pedagogy is curriculum, because what matters is how things are taught, rather than what is taught' (Wiliam, 2011). Though it could be argued that these two aspects of positive and meaningful PE go hand in hand. Hence why pedagogy is discussed in the same chapter as curriculum.

In this section I outline the key elements required for successfully delivering a concept driven curriculum. Erickson discussed how true teaching goes beyond the presentation of information. True teachers engage students emotionally, creatively, and intellectually to instil deep passion for learning (2007).

Applying a Concept-Driven Approach to lessons

Let's return to the resilience scheme of work we were discussing in the last chapter. We now have the basis for our scheme of work. Flexibility is the real beauty of this model for any teacher planning their lessons. It can be applied to any sport or activity, and in any order the teacher wishes. The teacher has full autonomy over the delivery of this concept.

Let's remind ourselves of the concept specific skills and basketball skills required in this scheme of work.

Concept related skills:

- Embracing Failure
- Growth Mindset
- Persistence
- Black Box Thinking
- Marginal Gains
- Embracing Change

Basketball related skills:

- Dribbling
- Passing
- Pivoting
- Shooting (standing or jump shot)

- Shooting (lay-up shot)
- Defending

These basketball skills would previously have had their own lesson objective, usually based around a student's ability to complete the skill successfully. We are not losing these skills; they are still important skills to learn in order to play the game and will still support the competence aspect of physical literacy.

We are losing that skill-focused lesson objective; it is not helpful to us and what we are hoping to achieve. This is not to say there is never a place for a skill specific focus to support that of the concept lesson objective, but a shift from a sole focus on skill acquisition is the aim. I mentioned that the concept driven curriculum is flexible, and this will now be highlighted.

The teacher can apply each of the CRSs to one of the skills listed above. Some CRSs might better align themselves to a certain basketball skill than others. When looking at 'embracing failure', we really want the students to fail, learn from their failure, and then improve, which they are more likely to do with a complex skill rather than a simple skill like dribbling, which most will take less time to pick up. We could use dribbling to deliver 'marginal gains', using skill-focused games to demonstrate how very slight improvements to technique can equate to big improvements, like the use of fingertips, looking up, or shielding the ball.

Unlike other schemes of work, which are delivered in a particular order, our concept-driven curriculum has the flexibility to apply where the teacher feels fits best. Teachers should consider the order in which the sport specific skills are delivered to ensure maximum opportunity for acquisition and progression – often the most basic skill is the best place to start. Concepts can be applied as per the teacher's judgement and planning, as the model below represents an example of:

Resilience		
Concept Related Skill		*Basketball Related Skill*
Marginal Gains	→	Dribbling
Growth Mindset	→	Passing
Persistence	→	Pivoting
Black Box Thinking	→	Shooting (static)
Embracing Failure	→	Shooting (on the move)
Embracing Change	→	Defending

Learning that Transfers

This section of the chapter comes in two parts. The first part discusses how to ensure the concept is embedded, and the second part focuses on the teachable moment's element of the model, that will support learning in greater detail.

A vital process in delivering a concept-driven lesson is to seek opportunities in which to acquire, connect, and transfer key conceptual understanding.

Stern coined the phrase 'Learning that Transfers' and created the Learning Transfer Mental Model to support the delivery of a concept-driven lesson. Her work in this area is highly regarded amongst educators around the globe. She believes that the goal of all learning is transfer, and that 'we move naturally between factual instances and the conceptual rules or patterns that make up the logic of our world' (2017, p.15).

All educators hope their lessons will provide students with the knowledge to apply their learning outside of their context. The aim is that, by learning about resilience, an individual will be able to better overcome challenges in their lives, or by covering diet, when making an educated decision about dinner, they might consider nutritional value and energy consumption. Ultimately, we are not only looking to deliver a more positive experience for our learner, we are, as Stern calls it, providing learning that transfers.

To achieve this, we must look to acquire the knowledge of our key concept, connect this concept to others – for example, resilience and failure, diet and weight gain, physical activity and stress reduction – and finally transfer this knowledge to new situations.

Imagine a PE lesson in which the main focus is not on the sport-specific skill, but that of a concept, something every student will need in their lives, take embracing failure from the resilience unit of work for example. We would continue to teach our sport-specific lesson, but the sport and physical activity was no longer the destination, it would be the vehicle to deliver relevant and meaningful learning.

Students will acquire the understanding of the term embracing failure at the start of the lesson. The teacher might provide a definition and ask students to discuss examples and non-examples of embracing failure during a student-led warm up.

The class will then move into a practical activity, one that would allow them to demonstrate embracing failure, perhaps the lay-up or jump shot in basketball or a serve in Badminton. The teacher can then ask questions to connect (phase two) this concept to the PE lesson such as: *"how did you demonstrate embracing failure in that last task?"* or *"how might the concept of embracing failure enable you to make progress in this lesson?"* or *"How does embracing failure support your understanding of resilience?"*. Students will make stronger connections to the concept and the PE lesson they are in.

Finally, after further practical activities we come to the transfer phase where self-reflective questions can be posed including: *"How can you apply embracing failure to support you in another class?"*, or *"How can your understanding of this concept enable you to succeed in the future?"*. Teachers should reward attitude and progress over performance and ability. The students are still developing their skills and techniques in sport but are no-longer judged by it. They are receiving learning that will genuinely prepare them for life, in a positive and meaningful PE environment that can better nurture physical literacy. By adopting the acquire, connect and transfer phases to each lesson alongside the practical tasks we can completely change how every student experiences PE.

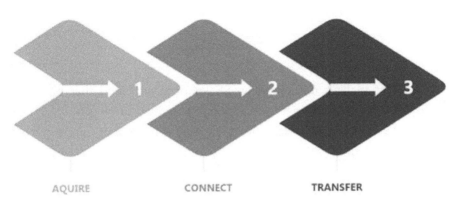

| AQUIRE | CONNECT | TRANSFER |

(Adapted from Stern, Ferraro, Duncan, & Aleo, 2021)

Acquire

One mistake we as teachers can make is assuming that all students come into our lesson with the same level of knowledge, or that common concepts, such as resilience, need little explanation. From my experience, this is not always true.

For the concept to be taught effectively, it must be acquired and fully understood by students. We are enabling students to make meaning of individual concepts. This might be through definitions, examples, and non-examples.

Strategies to support acquisition

Julie Stern recommends using the 'The Frayer Model' as a tool for concept acquisition. This can be used at the start of the lesson as a warm-up activity. The teacher can provide a brief definition of the concept or related skill. They can then ask students to elaborate, provide an illustration, an example or a non-example of the concept. This model can be seen below:

Definition:	Acquire	Example
Failure is defined as 'a lack of success.'		Provide at least one example of the concept.
Those who accept that failure is a part of life is destined to make progress.		An example of failure might be when you are attempting to score a set shot in basketball. If you do not get the correct technique or miss the target then you might
Write in your own words		decide that you are not good at shooting and stop trying.
Write the definition in your own words.		
Failure is when you give up when you have made a mistake or something is too difficult.		
Illustration		**Non-Example**
Draw an illustration of the concept. Ask them to explain this drawing to a peer or the teacher.		Provide a non-example of the concept.
		A non-example of failure is someone who is able to continue practicing something, even when things are challenging, so that they are able to eventually succeed. If a player keeps missing the set shot in basketball they might look to learn from their mistakes and find out what they are doing wrong. They can then make improvements so that they can score the
	The Frayer Model	points from the shot.

When first trialling this model in PE lessons, we found that attempting to complete the entire model in every acquisition phase took too much time. Therefore, we decided to focus on one element of the model instead of covering it all. The teacher might provide a definition and ask for discussions and class feedback around examples or non-examples. Another method that proved successful following our trials, was to provide a definition and ask students to elaborate, providing examples or non-examples during a student-led warm-up. Although not trialled by my team, as changing rooms have been closed due to the pandemic, this phase could also be delivered whilst students are changing for the lesson. This would maximise the time available for physical activity and ensure no learning opportunities are lost.

Another strategy that can be applied in the acquire phase is the State, Exemplify, Elaborate and Illustrate (SEEI) model, which enables effective acquisition. Students should state their understanding of the concept (define), give an example of the concept, elaborate their understanding (explain), and then finally illustrate (draw an example).

Whilst we could argue that the final stage of this model is not applicable or realistic to deliver in a PE lesson, the first three steps will still support effective learning and we could adapt draw to mean demonstrate. An example of this in PE, thinking back to our previous resilience lesson example, could be:

Resilience: Embracing Failure	
State	Failure is defined as 'a lack of success.' Those who accept that failure is a part of life are destined to make progress.
Exemplify	If I attempt a lay-up shot in basketball and miss, I should consider why I missed and look at this not as a failure but as a part of learning.
Elaborate	**Fail early** The belief is that if it is possible to learn from failure then the sooner the failure occurs, the sooner the learning begins. **Fail fast** We want to fail quickly so that we can begin the learning process as fast as possible. **Fail often** When the failing and learning loop has been established, we can see that the more things we try, the more failures we will have, and therefore the more chances we have to both learn and steer our project in the right direction.
Illustrate	

Connect

Once students have understood what is meant by the concept, we can then encourage them to make connections and understand the relationships between different concepts. This will enable a deeper level of thinking and learning.

Strategy to Support Connection

Strong questioning will promote the connections of concepts. See below examples of questions that will support these connections:

-       How is embracing failure and resilience connected?

- Why is embracing failure connected to resilience?
- How does the ability to embrace failure impact resilience?

More generic questions might include (though I would advocate for changing the words 'concepts' and 'concept related skills' for the actual topics you wish to question):

- How are the concept and the concept related skill connected?
- How does the concept related skill impact the concept?
- How might the concept impact your progress in today's lesson?
- What is the importance of the concept and the concept related skill to the activity you have just completed?
- Can you connect the relationship between today's concept to another concept we have covered?
- What would happen if you did not understand/apply the concept?
- What feedback could you give to a peer in order to better understand or demonstrate the concept?

Ensuring students are provided with opportunities to demonstrate and evidence these concepts will also support them in connecting concepts:

- Providing students with the opportunity to fail, practice, and improve performance.
- Record progress made.
- Peer coach and assess each other, providing feedback to improve performance.
- Discuss how they have improved from the start to the end of the lesson.
- What can they do now that they could not do before, and how does this connect with the concepts?

When trialling this phase in our lessons, we realised that students found connecting the concepts quite tricky to begin with. Therefore, my colleague, Eve Wagstaff, developed the idea of using an umbrella to highlight the overall scheme of work concept, and how the individual lessons fed into this.

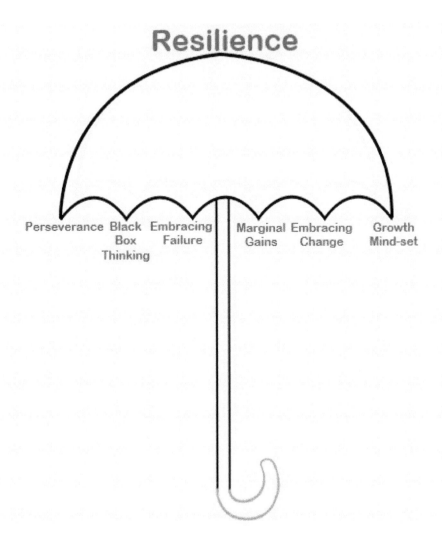

This visual representation of the overall concept and the concept related skills enabled students to make stronger links as to why each were connected. From there, we also started to incorporate concepts previously covered to see if students could make connections between a wider range of concepts.

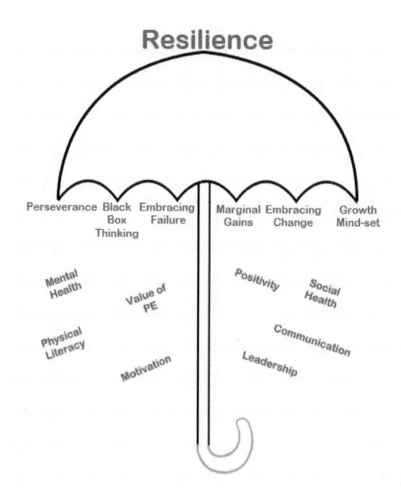

I also wanted to provide a tangible resource for teachers to access during lessons, so created the question stem bank below. Teachers could decide on the one or two questions that they felt most appropriate to ask during this phase:

Connect	
Questions stems	
How is the concept and the concept related skill connected?	How might the concept impact your progress in today's lesson?
How dies (insert concept related skill) impact (insert concept)?	Who has demonstrated the concept related skills so far in today's lesson? How?
What would happen if you did not understand/apply the concept?	What is the importance of the concept to the activity you have just completed?
Can you connect the relationship between today's concept to another concept we have covered?	What feedback could you give to a peer in order to better understand or demonstrate the concept?

(Adapted from Stern, Ferraro, Duncan, & Aleo, 2021)

Transfer

The final stage of the Learning Transfer Mental Model is transfer. Here, we encourage students to apply their understanding of a concept and transfer it to a different and more complex or unfamiliar context. Students should be given the opportunity to transfer their new learning to past experiences, where they could use it in other areas of their current lives, and when in the future their knowledge of the concept might help them.

Strategies to Support Transfer

Permitting time at the end of a lesson for personal reflection and even encouraging class feedback are great ways to promote transfer. A meaningful plenary could ask such questions as:

- When in the past have you demonstrated the ability to embrace failure?
- When have you demonstrated resilience in today's lesson?
- How did embracing failure support your progression in learning the lay-up shot?
- When, in school, might you encounter a situation in which embracing failure will be required?
- How might embracing failure and resilience impact your future success?
- How does resilience and embracing failure contribute to a successful team or individual?

More generic reflections might include:

- How can what you have learnt in PE today support you in another class?
- Give an example of a situation in your past where you have used skills discussed in today's lesson.
- How did the focus of the lesson benefit you in your PE lesson today?
- Give an example/situation of when in the future you might need to apply what we have covered in today's lesson?
- What impact would not applying or understanding the concept have on your present/future?
- How can your understanding of this concept enable you to succeed in the present/future?

When trialling the final phase of this model, we found that many students were reluctant to provide class feedback following their period of self-reflection. With some concepts, usually those surrounding mental health, we understood the need for these to be personal reflections, and that we should be empathetic to the private nature of them. However, with most other concepts, some feedback would help students transfer their learning more effectively. Therefore, we decided to create personal reflection cards and group students accordingly.

First, we trialled each member of the group receiving a different card and leading a one-minute discussion with the group to answer that question. However, we felt that six questions in six minutes did not permit the appropriate reflection time required, and often not every student was able to contribute to the discussions. So, we then trialled just one member of the group receiving only one reflection question card that the teacher felt was most appropriate to the lesson and leading a discussion. The leader could then select the best reflection to share with the class. We found this to be a better and more efficient use of time, permitting everyone to contribute and self-reflect. Once again, I would advocate the teacher being explicit about the concept or the concept related skills that should be discussed to avoid any confusion. This could also be completed in the changing rooms at the end of the lesson if preferred.

Personal Reflection How can what you have learnt in PE today support you in another class?	**Personal Reflection** Give an example of a situation in your past where you have used skills discussed in today's lesson
Personal Reflection How did the focus of the lesson benefit you in your PE lesson today?	**Personal Reflection** Give an example/situation of when in the future you might need to apply what we have covered in today's lesson?
Personal Reflection What impact would not applying or understanding the concept have on your present/future?	**Personal Reflection** How can your understanding of this concept enable you to succeed in the present/future?

Logically, some may be worried about the amount of suggested 'talking time'. Conversely, the time taken up with targeted learning and discussion points should be strictly limited. The AfPE recommends that pupils be actively moving for 50-80% of the available learning time. Deliver the concept, the task instructions, and let the students practice and play. Avoid monotonous drills with long wait times, get everyone active as much as possible with as many opportunities to practice the skill as achievable – just as a strong PE lesson would have been prior to the shift in focus.

Once again, after many failures, huge amounts of learning and adjustments to our delivery, there were still some inconsistencies with the quality or the consistency of the three phases. Some staff were getting mixed up between the connect phase and the transfer phase, often transferring the concept to other contexts during the connect phase instead of connecting the concept to the actual PE lesson. It was evident that I needed to provide some resources that would support delivery of all three phases, but, more specifically, the connect and transfer phases. Therefore, I purchased a clipboard for each teacher and outlined each phase of the model on it, meaning teachers could briefly refer to it at the appropriate times during the lesson. I placed on each whiteboard laminated sheets, which required staff to write on with board marker the brief information required for the lesson. We found that using these board dramatically reduced the teacher planning time, and anxieties around how to apply each phase to their lesson. By simply picking up the board and referring to the relevant sheet, staff could cover each phase without too much thought, and students had visual cues and teaching points. From a quality assurance perspective, this also enabled me, as a Head of Department, or indeed any member of SLT when observing lessons, to see very clearly how each element of the model supported the PE lesson, the physical tasks, and the overall learning.

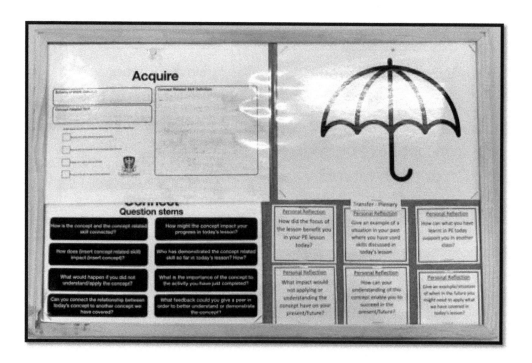

The diagram below shows each stage of the Learning Transfer Mental Model in relation to the timings of a lesson.

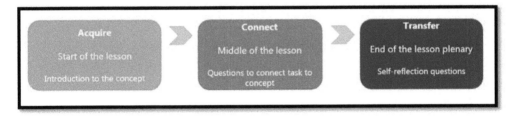

(Adapted from Stern, Ferraro, Duncan, & Aleo, 2021)

Teachable Moments

The inclusive pedagogy element of the Positive and Meaningful PE model fundamentally requires teachers to focus on the concept and to reward progression and attitude over ability and performance. We are looking to create an environment that enables teachers to effectively nurture physical literacy. However, this does not mean that teachers are unable to support the progression of physical competence. Teachable moments are times within a lesson that the concept can be embedded further, or coaching can be provided to enable practical progression. Teachable moments come in two forms:

- Targeted learning: feedback provided to an individual or small group regarding the concept, key techniques, or sport specific information.
- Discussion points: Feedback provided to a class to highlight key learning or address common misconceptions.

To demonstrate teachable moments using the embracing failure lesson through the lay-up shot in basketball, targeted learning could occur when a student who started off with the wrong technique learns from their mistakes and adjusts an element of the technique. The student does not need to be successful with the shot to be able to demonstrate the ability to embrace failure and learn from it; this could be used to demonstrate the concept to the class.

Another targeted learning example might be when a student is continuing to make the same mistake again and again – a gentle reminder to the individual of the CRS, some class feedback regarding the CRS, or even the specific skill technique support will provide the motivation to learn. By highlighting good practice, identifying ineffective attitudes, and recognising progression you are providing targeted learning.

The second element of the teachable moments within a lesson are discussion points. Through deliberations, plenaries, and a Q&A session a teacher can provide constructive discussion points related to the concept or the activity. Addressing technique, common misconceptions, or highlighting best practice to a group would be considered worthwhile discussion points. If a number of students were making the same mistake with their set shot technique, then a teacher might use a discussion point to address this.

Fundamentally, we need to provide our teachers with as much structure, support, and as many resources as we can. With supplied prompts, a teacher can truly get to grips with a shift in their habitual teaching routines, and start forming new habits that focus on concepts and rewarding progress.

Concept-Driven Lesson Planning

Leaders and teams will need to discuss and agree on the concepts and concept-related skills, as well as the knowledge, they would like students to learn. They will then need to re-plan their lessons to ensure teachable moments and opportunities for the transfer of learning take place. Already, this is a potential point of weakness in the change process.

When planning your concept-focused lessons, you should consider the content, organisation, and learning interaction. Outlined by Haydn-Davies in Physical Literacy Throughout the Life course (2010), the following should be considered in your lesson planning:

Content/selected planning:
- Has the session been planned with the participant(s) at the heart of the experience?
- Will the content meet the participant(s) expectations?
- Are the tasks set appropriate to the to the participant'(s') abilities and motivation?
- Will there be regular chances to achieve and succeed?

Organisation:
- Does the structure of the session meet the physical, social, and emotional needs of the participant(s)?
- Are timings planned to suit the participants, or have they been imposed by external factors?
- Are there a variety of resources, including media, available to support

and challenge participants?
- Have the expectations of behaviour been agreed?
- Are rules and routines negotiated, agreed and well-articulated?
- Are organisational cues understood?
- Is the learning environment safe, stimulating and challenging?

Learning/teacher interaction:
- Does the climate promote mutual respect between practitioner and participant(s), and between participants?
- Is feedback given constructively, frequently and positively?
- Is assessment for learning used to promote progress?
- Will the participants understand if they are improving?
- Are both verbal and non-verbal communication used effectively and regularly?
- Are questions used to support learning and progress?
- Are participants encouraged to ask questions?

We are essentially asking teachers to re-train their mindset about what is important within a lesson, and therefore to begin with the planning of these lessons will be vital. Collaboration is so important in this process, getting teams to openly support each other's planning, share resources and ease workloads will be the difference between the success or failure of this change. Use team meetings effectively to encourage this collaboration.

For experienced practitioners, applying the Transfer Learning Mental Model to already existing sport specific schemes of work might be relatively straightforward. Simply add an acquire phase at the start of your lesson, a connect phase after one or two tasks, and a transfer phase at the end of your lesson as a plenary. However, for newer teachers, this application might prove more challenging. The use of the clipboards should help; however, I found that collaborative planning was vital when introducing this new focus into our delivery. The following lesson plan comes from the concept curriculum and demonstrates how a concept can be applied to a sport specific skill. The lesson plan provides the key concept related information and advice on how it might be applied to the practical elements of your lesson.

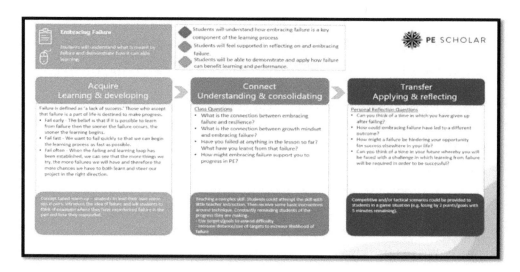

(Adapted from Stern, Ferraro, Duncan, & Aleo, 2021)

When planning collaboratively, it was important that some structure was provided. This needed to be time conscious and user-friendly. When it comes to lesson planning, the most time effective tool released in recent times is the 5-minute lesson plan devised by @TeacherToolKit. It provides brief prompts that teachers can use to help build their lesson.

Whilst this certainly proved to be a useful tool when effectively planning lessons, I wanted to take it one step further and apply some evidenced-based theory to this method of planning to really ensure and encourage 'outstanding' lessons. In my school, as in many around the country, Rosenshine's 'Principles of Instruction' have rightfully made their way into every staff training and meeting. Therefore, I incorporated the Transfer Learning Mental Model, Rosenshine's 'Principles of Instruction', and the 5-minute lesson plan for staff to use when collaboratively planning lessons.

Concept-Driven
5 Minute Lesson Plan

Acquire:
(What knowledge do students need to know?)

(Think: retrieval and direct instruction)

Connect:
(How will I enable a connections between concepts to be made?)

(Think: link concept to examples in the tasks as well as other concepts)

Sport Specific Skill:
(What sport specific skill or games will the concept related skill be taught through?)

(Think: plan the progressive tasks for the lesson, how can I keep the students as active as possible?)

Teachable Moments:
(What targeted learning and discussion points could I pre-plan?)

(Think: recognise progress, highlight attitude, always praise and encourage)

Transfer:
(How will I support students to transfer the concepts to new contexts?)

(Think: How do I know students understand what I have taught them?)

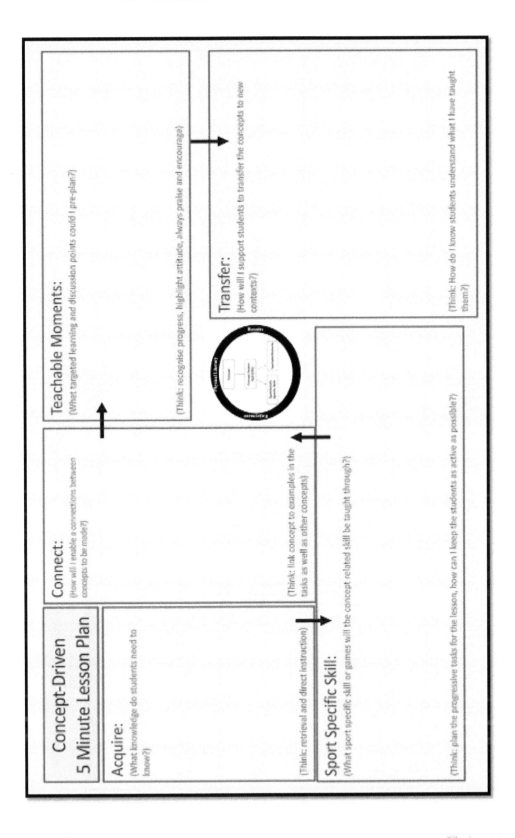

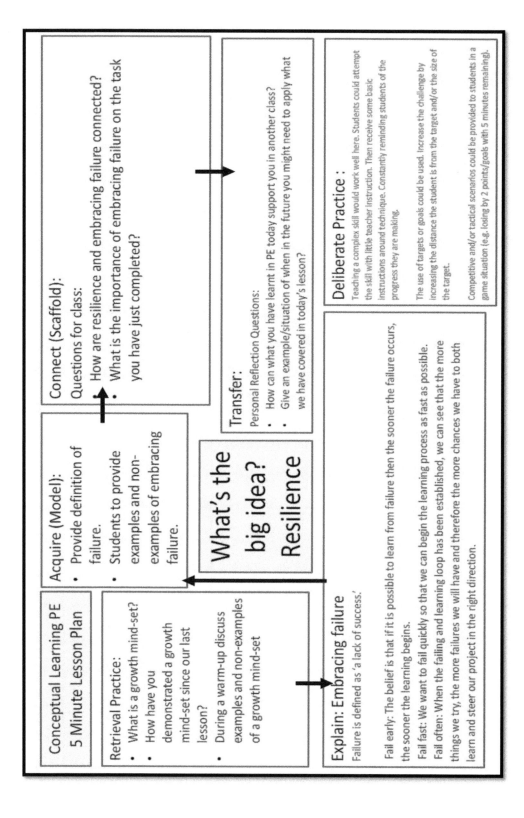

Conceptual Learning PE 5 Minute Lesson Plan

Retrieval Practice:
- What is a growth mind-set?
- How have you demonstrated a growth mind-set since our last lesson?
- During a warm-up discuss examples and non-examples of a growth mind-set

Acquire (Model):
- Provide definition of failure.
- Students to provide examples and non-examples of embracing failure.

What's the big idea? Resilience

Connect (Scaffold):
Questions for class:
- How are resilience and embracing failure connected?
- What is the importance of embracing failure on the task you have just completed?

Transfer:
Personal Reflection Questions:
- How can what you have learnt in PE today support you in another class?
- Give an example/situation of when in the future you might need to apply what we have covered in today's lesson?

Explain: Embracing failure

Failure is defined as 'a lack of success.'

Fail early: The belief is that if it is possible to learn from failure then the sooner the failure occurs, the sooner the learning begins.

Fail fast: We want to fail quickly so that we can begin the learning process as fast as possible.

Fail often: When the failing and learning loop has been established, we can see that the more things we try, the more failures we will have and therefore the more chances we have to both learn and steer our project in the right direction.

Deliberate Practice :

Teaching a complex skill would work well here. Students could attempt the skill with little teacher instruction. Then receive some basic instructions around technique. Constantly reminding students of the progress they are making.

The use of targets or goals could be used. Increase the challenge by increasing the distance the student is from the target and/or the size of the target.

Competitive and/or tactical scenarios could be provided to students in a game situation (e.g. losing by 2 points/goals with 5 minutes remaining).

Shift in Teacher Philosophy

More important than the curriculum, is the way in which the curriculum is delivered. Understandably, the habit of a PE teacher will be to continue to focus on developing the sport specific skills and, although not the focus, the teacher can still teach the skills required for the sport. The teacher should continue to sensitively correct any common misconceptions around technique and provide individual or group coaching around the skill.

Harris and Cale (2019) argue that there is a mismatch between two teaching philosophies within PE: fitness for life and fitness for performance. They state that teachers who are inclined towards delivering the fitness for performance philosophy might be influenced by sporting backgrounds, sport science-focused degrees, and 'their limited awareness of and exposure to fitness for life pedagogies' (2019, p.37). Justifiably, teachers delivering a sport-driven curriculum must try and ensure students perform the key techniques required to improve performance, or to attain fitness for performance. Though, this is not to say that through a concept-driven approach both fitness for life and fitness for performance are not both attainable.

The old lesson plan would suggest that students who were unable to perform the lay-up shot by the end of the lesson had failed to meet the objective. Now, with the focus on embracing failure, within the concept of resilience, we are celebrating those that have made progress, or that have identified a fault in their technique and made an adjustment, as in fitness for life.

Will every child be able to perform the lay-up shot? No – and this is no different from the previous system, but they will leave with a completely different feeling. They are no longer failing; they are learning. They are no longer judged by their incapability; they are commended for their attitude. We are not creating elite athletes; we are preparing students for life through physical activity. Encouragement, enthusiasm, and positivity are key to the delivery of a concept-driven approach for, without them, the opportunity to create physically literate and motivated students is lost. We must ensure that is the aim for all PE teachers who deliver a concept-driven curriculum.

A vital process in delivering a concept-driven lesson is to seek opportunities in which to acquire, connect and transfer key conceptual understanding. Though we must also consider how such an approach and any progress made can be measured, whilst still remembering to develop the movement potential of the child.

'Memory is the cognitive process of first resort. When faced with a problem, you will first search for a solution in memory and, if you find one, you will likely use it' (Willingham, 2009). Through a CDC, a new form of learning can take place and, the best part, it will happen naturally with no planning required. Many businesses are using what is known as vertical development, which refers to the advancement in an individual's thinking capability. Vertical development comes with three primary conditions: heat experiences, colliding perspectives, and elevated sense-making. We are also providing the students with all three development experiences like no other subject can.

The Centre for Creative Leadership defines a heat experience as, 'situations that help leaders discover that their current way of making sense of the world is inadequate. As a result, they seek out new and better ways to make sense of their challenge. Heat experiences are the what that initiates development' (Petrie, 2014).

By introducing a concept and then allowing students time to practice, they will often be placed in a heat experience and get to explore that concept first-hand. Once again, to look at the lay-up shot lesson focusing on embracing failure, they will get the opportunity to fail at something, and work out themselves if they will give up or learn from this to improve their technique, and potentially gain some success.

Colliding perspectives refers to providing students the opportunity to challenge and listen to the views of others. With this approach, students will learn empathy, communication and expand their own perspectives, which can be applied in wider contexts. Using the discussion points during a teachable moment, students can reflect, talk about the best and worst examples of the CRS, and examine where and how this might help then in different aspects of their lives. Key questions could be asked by the teacher to ignite these colliding perspectives, such as: 'what is more important to your learning, failure or confidence?'

Finally, elevated sense-making indicates that, as students process and make sense of these new perspectives and experiences, they enter an elevated stage of development. A larger, more advanced worldview emerges (Petrie, 2014). Opportunities to reflect on the application of the concept to them in the lesson, their school life, and the wider world will support the students to truly develop as people.

Summary

A shift is needed in pedagogy, which can be supported by the understanding and delivery of key teachable moments. Teachers must ensure positivity and encouragement take centre stage, and progress and attitude are rewarded. The concept can be delivered effectively alongside physical activity, using the Learning Transfer Mental Model (Stern et al., 2021) and the acquire, connect, and transfer phases. Collaboration is key when planning concept-driven lessons and feeding back what has worked and what has not in order to find what best suits your context. Providing teachers with appropriate structure and resources to use when planning and delivering lessons is vital, especially before new teaching habits are made, and to ensure we do not revert to previous practice.

Through Durden-Myers's research around applying a physical literacy focus to curriculum delivery, I discussed the importance that all teachers understand this concept. This will support teachers to better articulate the value of PE and change their pedagogy in order to create a more positive and meaningful PE environment. The use of meeting times and professional development can be used to introduce and reflect on key learning and keep it relevant in order to maintain intended practice.

Concepts, if delivered effectively, have the power to provide powerful learning experiences, such as colliding perspectives, elevated sense making, and heat experiences. They will be able to see the true value of PE, and transfer the skills gained from lessons to other areas of their lives. Thus, providing a more tangible value to PE, and a stronger connection to it.

Earn Your Concept-Driven Curriculum Cap

Concept-driven: move away from sport-focused and performance obsessed delivery to deliver relevant learning through physical activity.

Acquire, connect and transfer: use the Learning Transfer Mental Model (Stern et al., 2021) to ensure knowledge is obtained, linked to the PE lesson, and applied to new and unfamiliar contexts.

Point out opportunities for learning: find teachable moments in your lesson to target learning and discuss key points.

Take Away Reflections

- Does your curriculum promote fitness for life or fitness for performance?
- How might you apply the acquire, connect transfer model to your lessons?
- What impact could conceptual learning have to how PE is valued in your school?
- How does your pedagogy nurture physical literacy?

Curriculum: Personalised and Inclusive

'Just like previous generations, young people today are eager to shape their experiences. They're developing their own identities and becoming aware of how they're perceived by others. They want to challenge themselves, but they're also cautious of looking silly or failing' (Sport England, 2014, p.4).

If, like me, you have two lessons of practical PE per week, then having one concept-driven lesson per week is great but, if the second lesson of the week reverted to the sport-driven model we were trying to move away from, then all of the meaningful experiences delivered during the concept-driven lessons would be lost. Therefore, in this section, I propose a second, personalised, method of PE delivery – the 'Personality Pathway'. In chapter two, I presented the research by Sport England into the six youth personalities in their Under the Skin report. I stated that current sport-driven curriculums were aimed towards those students considered 'sport enthusiasts'. These are the students who already love sport and, as long as teachers sustain their desire to improve, they will continue to enjoy PE.

A curriculum focused on conceptual learning continues to offer this to our sport enthusiasts, but what about our other personalities? Below, I have summarised the research provided by Sport England into what would engage each of the other five personalities.

Personality	Attract Their Attention	Keep Them Coming Back
Thoughtful Improvers	- Highlight opportunities to achieve personal goals. - Offer support to set and reach these goals. - Tap into their fitness and weight-loss aspirations.	- Give them something to be proud of – recognise and reward their achievements. - Make them feel part of something. - Make any competition fun.

Cautious Introverts	- Connect keeping fit to feeling good about themselves having made the effort to take part. - Don't bring 'sport' into it. - Keep it small, familiar, and supportive.	- Recognise and reward taking part. - Open up new opportunities to develop themselves if their confidence improves long-term.
Confident Intellectuals	- Highlight opportunities where focus, dedication and creativity win out over talent. - Reassure them they don't need experience or skills to take part. - Don't bring 'sport' into it.	- Recognise and reward improvement and perseverance. - Highlight how they can enhance their CV.
Everyday Youths	- Put the spotlight on fun with friends. - Encourage them to give it a go by addressing practical barriers up front. - Throw in 'keeping in shape' as an added bonus.	- Encourage friendship. - Offer incentives and opportunities to enhance their CV.
Ambitious Self-starters	- Offer them a challenge. - Present them with opportunities to develop new sport or life skills.	- Continue to challenge them. - Help them stay committed when life changes.

(Sport England, 2014)

'Just like previous generations, young people today are eager to shape their experiences. They're developing their own identities and becoming aware of how they're perceived by others. They want to challenge themselves, but they're also cautious of looking silly or failing' (Sport England, 2014, p.4). I certainly understand those who might argue the research is dated, that not all students can be placed into one of these six categories, or that every cohort is different, and therefore will have various numbers attached to the different categories. However, the principle of identifying sports and activities that meet different needs, moving away from ability to what motivates, and taking into account various attitudes towards physical activity is, I believe, worth exploring. We therefore used this research as the foundation to create a more personalised curriculum.

Student autonomy is an important addition to PE curriculum, and there are different variations on how to achieve this. Some schools offer different pathways in which students are able to select their preferred offering, based on favoured activities rather than personality traits. Tim Fletcher, in his research article, proposes democratic approaches to PE delivery in order to help teachers intentionally and consistently prioritise meaningful experiences for students. Specifically, democratic principles support teachers fostering inclusive environments, and help students actively make authentic connections between their lived experiences inside and outside of their classroom (2021). Dr Panteleimon Ekkekakis et al. add further weight to the call for added autonomy in PE. In their 2018 study, looking at past PE memories and current activity levels, he identified student autonomy as a key driver for promoting long-term engagement in physical activity. 'Among the strongest moderators of physical activity-associated pleasure and enjoyment in studies of adults is the sense of autonomy. Although logistical constraints may preclude offering multiple options for students interested, for example, in sport-oriented activities versus non-competitive, physical activity-oriented activities, PE classes structured to accommodate individual preferences should prove advantageous over traditional one-size-fits-all approaches Providing students choice over their learning helps create a positive and meaningful connection to PE' (2018, p.127).

Personality Pathway

For our second lesson of PE each week, we wanted to offer what we affectionately named the Personality Pathway. The vision being that students would select a pathway based on their own motivations for participating in physical activity. We, on our first attempt, educated our students around the personality categories identified above, provided a survey that helped identify student personalities, and therefore assigned a pathway. We may explore the potential of offering an online (more workload con-scious) survey, assigning the pathways based on answers, without labelling the students as one of the six personality types. We are continually looking to learn and improve.

Fiona Reynolds outlines how we collaborated on the development of our

Personality Pathway in Chapter Five So, for now, I will simply outline how a Personality Pathway works. It is also important to add that this is a work in progress, which we have trialled and are running at Key Stage 4 (ages 13-16). Key Stage 3 (ages 11-12) is still in production, awaiting trial. Perhaps one for the next volume of the book.

- **Stage One:** A student voice survey is sent to all students requesting them to select or offer alternative sports or activities they would like to see on their curriculum. From these suggestions, three appropriate lists are populated that best meet the needs of the students who select one of three Personality Pathways identified in Stage Two. Our responses can be seen below:

1. Below is a list of traditional sports that we have previously included in your Core PE curriculum. Please select the sport(s) you would like to remain on the Core PE curriculum.

More Details

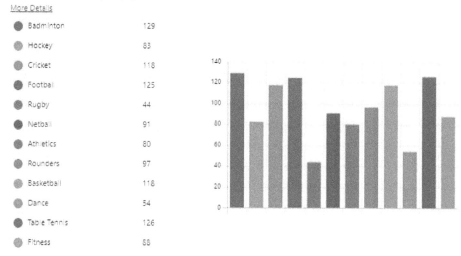

Badminton	129
Hockey	83
Cricket	118
Football	125
Rugby	44
Netball	91
Athletics	80
Rounders	97
Basketball	118
Dance	54
Table Tennis	126
Fitness	88

2. List 4 other sports/ physical activities not included in the list above that you would like to see included in your PE curriculum. (Think outside the box such yoga, dodgeball, ultimate frisbee etc)

A sample of the responses included: dodgeball, lacrosse, yoga, bench ball, street golf, fun fitness, ultimate Frisbee, tag rugby, team building games, etc.

- **Stage Two:** Students receive an online survey. The survey is inspired by the survey used by Sport England for the Under the Skin research (2014). The survey focuses on likes and dislikes, personality traits and attitudes towards physical activity. Students are given statements to which they rate themselves depending on how strongly they agree or disagree with said statement. The student statements used in the survey can be seen below:

Statement
Sport is part of who I am
My friends and I talk about sport a lot
I like to use social media to share my sporting/fitness achievements
I am good at most sports
I feel guilty if I have not exercised for a while
Sport and exercise are really good ways to reduce stress
Taking part in sport makes me feel good about myself
I am conscious of my health and fitness
My family have never encouraged me to take part in sport/exercise
I think that people my age who play sport are cool
I'm happy with my body
I worry about looking like a fool when I play sport/exercise
Winning is the most important thing to me
I am close to my family
I would rather do something that is fun and not good for me than something that is not fun but good for me
I am a confident person
Exercise is my "me" time

What motivates you in life? Staying healthy
What motivates you in life? Improving my appearance
What motivates you in life? Developing myself as a person
What motivates you in life? Competing
What motivates you in life? Being successful
What motivates you in life? Achieving goals
What motivates you in life? Doing something worthwhile
Gender
How often do you typically take part in 30 mins or more of physical activity, which is enough to raise your breathing rate

5 - Strongly agree
4 - Slightly agree
3 - Neither agree nor disagree
2 - Slightly disagree
1 - Strongly disagree

- **Stage Three:** Using the responses from the survey, students are placed into one of three pathways (automatically calculated by the survey). Our department decided to use the Sport England research as the basis for grouping the classes. We selected:

    - Pathway One: Sport Enthusiasts and Ambitious Self-starters
    - Pathway Two: Everyday Youths and Thoughtful Improvers
    - Pathway Three: Cautious Introverts and Confident Intellectuals

- **Stage Four:** At this stage, students are only aware of the pathway they have been allocated and are not aware of the corresponding sports/ activities that will be part of their pathway. This is to ensure students' responses in the survey are based purely on personality characteristics, and not on the sports on offer. Students will therefore identify as pathway one, two or three.

- **Stage Five:** Teachers and their classes are only assigned spaces or facilities for each block. They are not assigned sports or activities yet. The sports or activities will be selected by the students in the next stage. Whatever activities are chosen should be appropriate for that space. An example of this can be seen below:

KS4 PE Personality Pathway Curriculum

	Block 1	Block 2	Block 3	Block 4
Personality Pathway 1	Field	MUGA	Sports Hall	Field
	<Insert student choice>	<Insert student choice>	<Insert student choice>	<Insert student choice>
Personality Pathway 2	Sports Hall	Field	MUGA	Field/ MUGA
	<Insert student choice>	<Insert student choice>	<Insert student choice>	<Insert student choice>
Personality Pathway 3	MUGA / Main Hall	Sports Hall	Field	Sports Hall
	<Insert student choice>	<Insert student choice>	<Insert student choice>	<Insert student choice>

Personality Pathway 1 (SE+AS)	Personality Pathway 2 (EY +TI)	Personality Pathway 3 (CI +CI)
Dodgeball	Dodgeball	Yoga
Bench ball	Yoga/ Meditation	OAA
Ultimate Frisbee	Bench ball	Gymnastics
Volleyball	Ultimate Frisbee	Endurance Running/ Cross Country
Golf (Variations)	OAA	Mindful Walking
Handball	Golf (Variations)	Pilates
Tag Rugby	Gymnastics	Curling/Bowls
American Football	Endurance Running/ Cross Country	Table Tennis
Gym/ Fitness	Pilates	Aerobics
Lacrosse/ Rocket ball	Gym/ Fitness	Fun Fitness
Table Tennis	Table Tennis	Meditation/Mindfulness
Hockey	Striking/ Fielding game (Danish longball and topple ball)	Zumba
Striking/ Fielding game (Danish longball and topple ball)	Aerobics	Dance Workouts
Softball		
Indoor Football		

- **Stage Six:** Following the student survey requesting students to identify non-traditional sports they would be interested in participating in, the PE team categorise these activities into the three pathways, based on the demands and nature of the activity against the motivators of the personality types. Above, you can see the three pathways of activities, as selected by our students and organised by the PE team. At the start of the first lesson, the teacher will present a list of ten sports or activities that have been selected as most appropriate for the personality motivators. These activities are not found during the first PE lesson of the week (concept-driven), for example: if Football is a sport offered in their first lesson, it will not be an option as part of the pathway. This is to ensure a breadth of activities is offered. Students will democratically select four activities from the list, and this will make up their curriculum for the year.

- **Stage Seven:** It is worth exploring the most appropriate model-based approach that could be applied to the relevant pathways, for example: in Pathway One (Sports Enthusiasts and Ambitious Self-Starters) a Sports Education model is the chosen method of delivery for us. Whilst I do not explore what model-based practices are, and how they might be implemented in this book, this is considered in depth by Casey and Kirk in their book *Models-Based Practice in Physical Education* (2021). In their work, they explore the main ideas, critical elements, learning aspirations, and pedagogy in relation to specific models used in Physical Education. They also discuss why a models-based approach could replace the existing dominant, and failing, multi-activity, technique-focused models. They argue for employed model-based practice because 'the development of life skills and personal and social responsibility are seen as more desirable 'doings' of sport and activity-based programs than the traditional outcomes of competency and engagement inherent in multi-activity, sport technique-based Physical Education' (Casey and Kirk, 2021, p.83). This flexibility will enable the most suitable model to be applied to the relevant context. When considering which model-based practice to employ, Will Swaithes has created the below summary, which provides further information you may wish to explore:

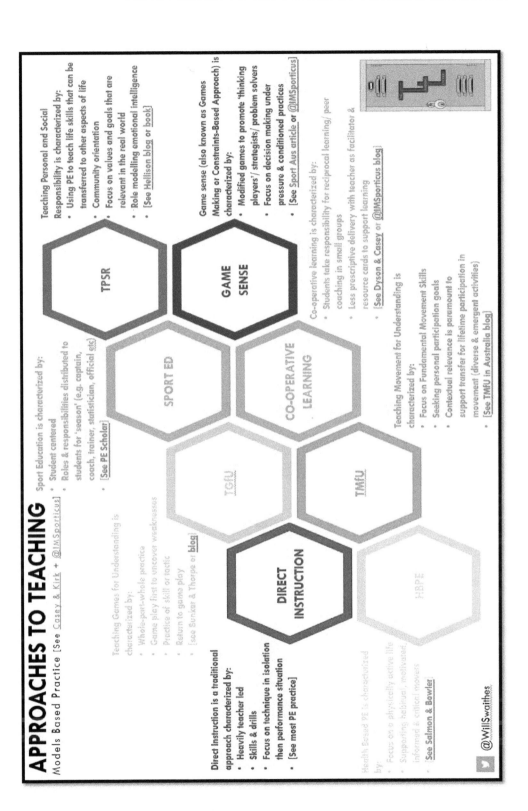

APPROACHES TO TEACHING

Models Based Practice [See Casey & Kirk + @IMSporticus]

Sport Education is characterized by:
- Student centered
- Roles & responsibilities distributed to students for 'season' (e.g. captain, coach, trainer, statistician, official etc)
- [See PE Scholar]

Teaching Personal and Social Responsibility is characterized by:
- Using PE to teach life skills that can be transferred to other aspects of life
- Community orientation
- Focus on values and goals that are relevant in the real world
- Role modelling emotional intelligence
- [See Hellison blog or book]

TPSR

Game sense (also known as Games Making or Constraints-Based Approach) is characterized by:
- Modified games to promote 'thinking players'/ strategists/ problem solvers
- Focus on decision making under pressure & conditioned practices
- [See Sport Aus article or @IMSporticus blog]

GAME SENSE

SPORT ED

CO-OPERATIVE LEARNING

Co-operative learning is characterized by:
- Students take responsibility for reciprocal learning/ peer coaching in small groups
- Less prescriptive delivery with teacher as facilitator & resource cards to support learning
- [See Dyson & Casey or @IMSporticus blog]

Teaching Games for Understanding is characterized by:
- Whole-part-whole practice
- Game play first to uncover weaknesses
- Practice of skill or tactic
- Return to game play
- [see Bunkar & Thorpe or blog]

TGfU

TMfU

Teaching Movement for Understanding is characterized by:
- Focus on Fundamental Movement Skills
- Seeking personal participation goals
- Contextual relevance is paramount to support transfer for lifetime participation in movement (diverse & emergent activities)
- [See TMfU in Australia blog]

Direct Instruction is a traditional approach characterized by:
- Heavily teacher led
- Skills & drills
- Focus on technique in isolation then performance situation
- [See most PE practice]

DIRECT INSTRUCTION

HBPE

Health Based PE is characterized by:
- Focus on a physically active life
- Supporting habitual, motivated informed & critical moves
- See Salmon & Bowler

@WillSwaithes

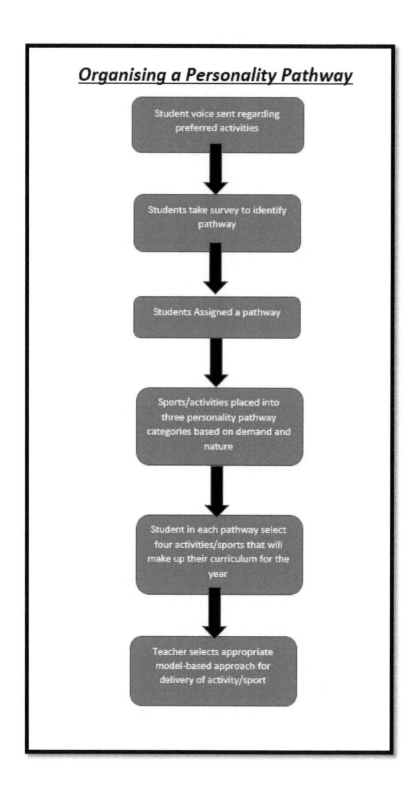

Whilst my department has opted for a pathway focused on student personalities and motivations around engagement in physical activity, I have also worked in schools that offer a similar pathway option with alternative rationale (I have included two further examples below). The main goal is consistent in that it provides students with autonomy to control their own learning experiences within PE.

Example 1 (below): Students select one of three pathways that have been designed to focus on either team, individual or expressive activities.

PE Pathway 1 Team	PE Pathway 1:	PE Pathway 1:	PE Pathway 1:
Football	Basketball	Handball/Netball	Cricket
PE Pathway 1 Individual	PE Pathway 2:	PE Pathway 2:	PE Pathway 2:
Badminton	Table Tennis	Tennis	Softball
PE Pathway 3 Expressive	PE Pathway 3:	PE Pathway 3:	PE Pathway 3:
Yoga	Dance	Fitness	Rounders

Example 2 (below): This example focuses more on the variety of activities that students indicated a preference towards. Students were more inclined to select team sports in this school, and therefore two 'teams' pathways were created. However, the sports that the different genders wanted to participate in differed and, therefore, following a student voice survey, the sports that students had indicated a stronger collective preference to engage in were selected, and the teams pathway was split by gender. The 'activity 2' pathway would focus more on the individual, and less on competitive options.

PE – Sports Education Model	Activity 1 – Boys Only (team)	Field - Football	Field - Football OR Field – Tag Rugby	Sports Hall – Basketball	Field - Cricket
	Activity 2 – Mixed	Sports Hall - Badminton	Sports Hall 1 – Table Tennis	Muga - OAA	Field - Rounders
	Activity 3 – Girls Only (team)	Muga - Netball	Sports Hall 2 - Badminton	Hall – Fitness/Dance OR Field - Football	Sports Hall - Basketball

In conclusion, offering student autonomy over the activities or structure of their lessons is an important part of creating a positive and meaningful PE experience. In my experience, it enhances engagement, enjoyment, and is actually really good fun to teach. The use of relevant model-based practices would support in the delivery of your department's chosen pathway preference. Departments should consider the logistics around student selection, identifying appropriate activities, delivery, equipment, and facility availability, as well as teacher expertise, when planning their own personalised curriculum.

Ultimately, if you have a voice in shaping what and how you learn, you will feel more ownership of it, and therefore a much stronger connection to it. This notion demonstrates that curriculums can be created with our students, rather than simply for them, and advocates student-centred educational practice Casey and Kirk, 2021).

Earn Your Personalised Curriculum Cap

Connect with students: Listening to your students is imperative when planning your curriculum. What do they want? How do you know? Understanding every student's attitude and motivations towards physical activity is vital to meet their needs.

Approaches: Consider various approaches in the delivery of PE. Model-based practices and the opportunities to engage in activities other than the traditional sports most link with PE.

Pathways: In order for students to feel connected with the subject, they must have autonomy. Allow them to choose their own curriculum and pathway. Contemplate a variety of activities that meet the nature and demands of their motivations to engage.

Take Away Reflections

- Can you identify a list of students that your curriculum is currently meeting the needs of? How?
- Can you identify a list of students that your curriculum does not meet the needs of? Why?
- How much autonomy do students have in PE at your school?
- How might increasing autonomy improve engagement?
- How might you personalise your curriculum?

Pedagogy: Personalised and Inclusive Practice

Teachers adopting the fitness for life approach will be rewarding attitude and progress instead of success and perfection.

Whilst a concept-driven and personalised curriculum will support a positive and meaningful PE experience, it is not able to deliver it entirely on its own. The way in which we teach this curriculum will have a bigger impact than the curriculum itself. There is a famous Peter Drucker quote that says, 'culture eats strategy for breakfast'. In an educational context, this implies that the culture of your department always determines success, regardless of how effective your strategy may be. Furthermore, the way in which the teachers are engaging with students and delivering learning will ultimately decide if the curriculum is effective. This section examines how you can develop a positive team that delivers the curriculum effectively and meaningfully.

Adopting a Physical Literacy Approach

To really understand the impact teachers can have on the long-term engagement of those they teach, they must understand the concept of physical literacy. I am always surprised when speaking to trainee teachers that have never heard this term before, or the experienced teachers who have heard of it but are unable to recall the main components of it. This concept, if applied effectively, could steer our subject from an SLT afterthought to the most valued subject on a student's timetable. Literacy and numeracy will always be vital, but what good are these skills if the individual who possesses them is mentally or physically unwell. The concept of nurturing physical literacy opens the door to lifelong participation in physical activity, and with that come all the long-term health benefits that will ensure literacy and numeracy skills can be put to good use.

It must therefore be considered vital to add physical literacy to the top of the PE teacher professional development list. In my experience, when asking teachers why PE is so important a common answer received is, 'a good stress-relief from the academic subjects'. This in turn raises the question of whether PE teachers are unaware of the true importance of PE. Are we devaluing ourselves?

Liz Durden-Myers, a leading advocate for physical literacy in the UK, led a research project to find the impact that physical literacy professional development can have on PE teachers (2020). She found that opinions around the value of PE shifted once professional development had taken place. One example from the research highlighted how one professional's view regarding the value of PE shifted from, 'letting off steam' to, 'to provide opportunities for children of all ages and all abilities to take part in sport and physical activity; where they can develop their motivation to take part in sport. And develop lifelong engagement in physical activity,' (p.188). Durden-Myers articulates how professionals 'not having a clear answer to the value, role and purpose of Physical Education can be just as damaging as having an answer that undermines the subject. Physical Education teachers, as educational professionals, are the custodians of the subject and they need to be able to champion and advocate the educational value of the subject in a clear and succinct way,' (p.193). Following professional development, teachers described how Physical Education can have holistic value in relation to character development, life and social skills – something that was not identified prior to the training. The training also proved to improve teacher understanding on the already dominant responses of improving health and well-being with the responses becoming 'more focused around developing holistic health, well-being and engagement in physical activity, in essence physical literacy' (p.196).

This research also concluded that not only did physical literacy develop a better understanding of the 'why' of physical literacy, but also the 'what' and the 'how'. Following professional development, PE teachers could not only better articulate what physical literacy was, but also its relationship to PE. Furthermore, they understood how to facilitate Physical Education environments that develop physical literacy. Some of the physical literacy 'how' aspects researched included:

- Encouraging students to become involved in their learning.
- Moving towards self-determined and intrinsic motivation strategies.
- Moving away from extrinsic motives and external reward strategies.
- Enforcing motivation and confidence.
- Creating a positive experience and inclusive environment.
- Holistic lessons.
- Physical competence.

One potential barrier identified is the lack of available professional development for PE teachers. Due to the perception of PE, funding and available time for professional development have been a challenge. Often, any available training is either whole school, focused on examinations, or, if sport specific, delivered by the individual sport's National Governing body and focuses on skill acquisition, though this only serves the traditional method of PE delivery that we are driving away from. Both from entry level, to teachers with experience, the opportunities for professional development, especially specific to nurturing physical literacy, must be improved. Offering physical literacy professional development would not only serve to improve teacher understanding of the concept, but would in turn provide more positive and meaningful PE experiences to students, raise the value of the subject, and better enable us to nurture physical literacy to support lifelong participation in physical activity.

As with most teacher training, to ensure teachers do not revert back to previous practice, on-going professional development is required to maintain and continue to develop understanding.

As a Head of Department, and whilst the professional development for PE teachers is limited, I must do all I can to ensure the team have every opportunity to develop their practice. Therefore, the use of meeting time is vital to the continuing understanding and development of physical literacy. Every meeting I lead follows a clear and consistent agenda.

My school, like most, has values that we live by each day. For us it is Unity, Curiosity, Growth and Service. I incorporate these values into our meeting as recurring agenda items. Below is an example of a PE team meeting agenda:

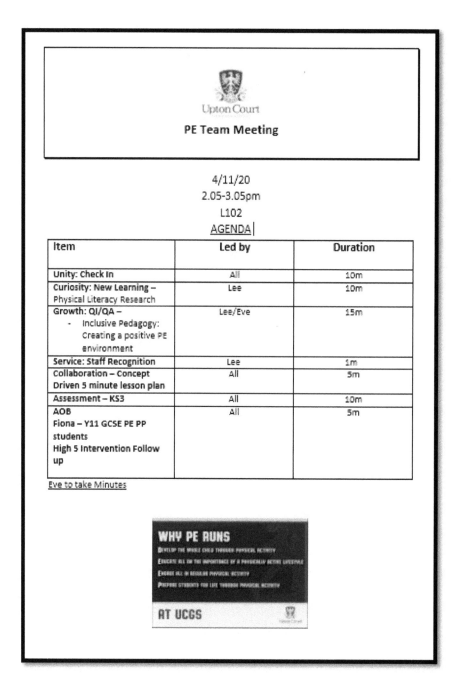

Upton Court

PE Team Meeting

4/11/20
2.05-3.05pm
L102
AGENDA|

Item	Led by	Duration
Unity: Check In	All	10m
Curiosity: New Learning – Physical Literacy Research	Lee	10m
Growth: QI/QA – - Inclusive Pedagogy: Creating a positive PE environment	Lee/Eve	15m
Service: Staff Recognition	Lee	1m
Collaboration – Concept Driven 5 minute lesson plan	All	5m
Assessment – KS3	All	10m
AOB Fiona – Y11 GCSE PE PP students High 5 Intervention Follow up	All	5m

Eve to take Minutes

WHY PE RUNS

DEVELOP THE WHOLE CHILD THROUGH PHYSICAL ACTIVITY

EDUCATE ALL ON THE IMPORTANCE OF A PHYSICALLY ACTIVE LIFESTYLE

ENGAGE ALL IN REGULAR PHYSICAL ACTIVITY

PREPARE STUDENTS FOR LIFE THROUGH PHYSICAL ACTIVITY

AT UCGS

I incorporate the school values as follows:

- **Unity:** Check In. We do this in a number of ways. One example is where each team member will state something they are grateful for, or perhaps a time in which they have failed, and therefore learnt something that week. Whatever the check-in question, the purpose is to be positive, brief, and set the tone for the rest of the meeting.

- **Curiosity:** New Learning. This is where the professional development within my meetings is hidden. Every week team members will take it in turns to deliver a piece of research, reading, or an example of best practice to inform and improve the practice of others. I often use themes upon which the new learning must focus. As is seen in the example above, I have used physical literacy as my theme, and staff must go away and read up on the topic to provide their new learning when it is their turn. I also lead the first two or three new learning meetings to introduce the key components of the theme. I have found this is a great way to ensure we keep on top of the latest research whilst applying it to our own practice.
- **Growth:** Quality Assurance/Quality Improvement. This section of the meeting often focuses on individual appraisal objectives that have usually been set around the subject improvement plan. Staff can discuss here 'what they are up to' in relation to their objective, or ask for feedback and support from the team.
- **Service:** Staff appreciation. It is important to recognise team members who have gone above and beyond to support the team. I will buy some chocolates or a bottle of wine and acknowledge someone either within our team or in the school who has supported us.
- **Collaboration:** I ensure that at least a small part of the meeting is kept for collaboration. In this example, you can see I have used it to pair staff up to complete the concept-driven 5-minute lesson plan.

The remainder of the lesson can be used to deal with the necessary tasks that inevitably come up from day to day. Structuring meetings in this way can ensure staff remain focused on key objectives and enable new learning to maintain focus and improve practice.

In her book *Physical Literacy: A Guide for Educators* (2018), Liz Durden-Myers offers teaching strategies designed to promote physical literacy. Included in her strategies, Durden-Myers highlights the importance of using a range of teaching styles, adoption of models-based practices, as well as the use of effective planning to promote motivation, confidence, knowledge, and competence. Reflective practices and observations are also encouraged, as is using one's reflections and observations to revise practice.

The Disengaged

The heart of physical literacy is this desire to take part, persist with an activity, develop physical competence, and try new activities (Whitehead, 2010).

We must consider the impact we as individual teachers have on a student's motivation, and this should form the central focus of our behaviour and interactions with students. Disengaged students must experience the positive outcomes that can be achieved through PE. The move away from judgements around performance to the new conceptual learning approach will provide some relief from previous feelings of humiliation and failure. Whilst it may take time to re-establish this desire and drive to fully engage all students, it is certainly achievable.

Teachers adopting the fitness for life approach will be rewarding attitude and progress instead of success and perfection. Conceptualised learning will enhance this teaching style and offer a form of success that is accessible to all, leading to a more positive outcome for students. 'While practitioners will need sound practical knowledge and group management skills, it is perhaps the qualities they display that will be most important. Significant among these qualities will be sensitivity, empathy, patience, appreciation of effort and an encouraging and enthusiastic approach to the work,' (Whitehead, 2010). With a collaborative departmental approach, all staff can deliver a rewarding environment for all.

Enjoyment

Lynn Erickson offers a theory as to why older secondary school students are more likely to disengage with their learning compared to younger students. Younger students in primary school and early years' secondary school are engaged with more concept-based learning, more hands-on activities, which allow them to connect and transfer concepts. As students approach formal examinations, they engage in far more factual learning and have to memorise an increasing amount of information.

Erickson believes that the less conceptual the learning a student experiences, the more disengaged they become, whilst also finding it harder to retain key facts, meaning, therefore, academic performance suffers. Conversely, by engaging students in conceptual level thinking, not only does it improve a student's ability to memorise key information, but it improves their motivation to learn too (Erickson, 2007).

If a student is motivated, it means they are engaged and feel a sense of enjoyment in what they are doing. After all, 'motivation essentially arises from the confidence and self-esteem acquired through experience; that is experience which has been perceived as successful and has been recognised as such' (Whitehead,

2010, p.31). Essentially, by offering all students the opportunity to succeed through the understanding and demonstration of a concept, we are building their confidence and self-esteem. No one likes to experience failure repeatedly, but many students have been feeling exactly that in PE. This can change with a shift in delivery and focus.

If children and young people have positive experiences of physical activity, they are more likely to remain active. Removing the judgement around performance, and replacing it with conceptual learning, can achieve this aim, as proven by Orton and his Department.

Listening to Your Students

To believe you are delivering a positive and meaningful PE experience is one thing, but how do you know for sure? Lesson observations and quality assurance procedures will give you a good indication. Listening to your staff will help too. Analysing GCSE PE uptake and overall results can also demonstrate impact. However, when creating and evaluating any curriculum offering, you must listen to the people receiving it, your students. If you really want to make informed decisions about what activities you offer on your curriculum, you must listen to your students. If you really need to understand how they feel about the delivery of your lessons, then listen to your students. Is the assessment user-friendly and fit for purpose? Listen to your students. They will always give you the best insight as to whether you are meeting your intent and their needs.

Will Swaithes, who runs the Learning Locker, offers the following leadership approach, which would certainly endorse the idea of listening to what our students are telling us, learning from their responses and leading change to improve, re-frame or re-think our offering. This is an on-going cycle that should be completed regularly to continually meet the needs and expectations of our students.

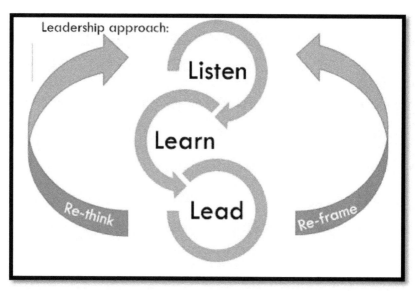

(Will Swaithes)

When conducting a student voice, there are a few ways in which you can do it, though, in my experience, online surveys have always been by far the easiest and most effective.

- **Student interviews:** A form of student voice often used in quality assurance procedures, whereby a few students are selected from a class, taken out and asked questions. In my opinion, students feel uncomfortable with this form of what they must feel is interrogation. They are also less likely to give truly honest answers to you in person.
- **Sports or Student Councils:** A great way to keep your finger on the pulse of on-going student reflections regarding a number of aspects of PE delivery is to set up a sports council. However, in my experience, the students that form a sports council are often those that love sport and PE, and are therefore likely to voice the opinions of similar students and, ultimately, not those that you really need to hear from.
- **Online surveys:** Having tried both of the above, this method of collecting student voice is by far the most time efficient and effective at reaching as many students as possible. There are many online platforms that can be used to create surveys, and even collate and analyse responses. Most recently, we have taken to using Microsoft Forms for this purpose. The students are emailed a link and can complete the survey either during a lesson or in their own time.

Once you have decided on the method you wish to employ to collect your students' opinions, you must then decide what information you are hoping to gather, and the form of answers you want to collect. Asking students to select one of a number of possible responses (multiple choice) is easy to analyse and user-friendly. Requesting longer answer responses, whilst allowing for a greater insight, can be time consuming. Below is a list of useful questions around different areas of inquiry that you may wish to consider:

Basic information
- Name (be careful as this may hinder the honesty of the answers).
- Gender (to analyse how the different genders perceive various lines of inquiry).
- Year group (to analyse how different age groups perceive various lines of inquiry).

Checking student confidence and understanding around sport and physical activity
- Outside of your PE lessons, on average, how many days per week do you do physical activity over 60 minutes per day?

How strongly do you agree or disagree with the following statements? (ratings: strongly agree, agree, neutral, disagree, strongly disagree):
- I enjoy taking part in exercise and physical activity outside of school.
- I enjoy taking part in exercise and physical activity in PE lessons.
- I feel confident when I take part in physical activity.
- I find exercise and physical activity easy.
- I understand why exercise and physical activity are good for me.
- I know how to get involved in sports and clubs at school?
- I know how to get involved in physical activity outside school?

Student opinion around PE - How strongly do you agree or disagree with the following statements? (ratings: strongly agree, agree, neutral, disagree, strongly disagree):
- I enjoy my PE lessons.
- I feel included in PE lessons.
- I like the school PE kit.
- I like the way we are grouped for PE.
- I have a choice in what we do in PE.
- What activities do you enjoy the most? (open answer).

Impact of PE - (Ratings of impact: very positive, positive, neutral, negative and very negative):

- What impact do you think PE has on your school work?
- What impact do you think PE has on behaviour?
- What impact do you think PE has on your health?
- What impact do you think PE has on your mood?
- What impact do you think PE has on your pride in our school?
- What impact do you think PE has on making friends and feeling included?

Students' motivations and barriers to participation:

- What motivates you to be physically active?)You can choose multiple answers)
  - Being healthy
  - Feeling good
  - Improving your appearance
  - Having fun
  - Being with friends
  - Being with family
  - Trying new things
  - Learning skills
  - Challenging myself
  - Competing against others
  - Leading/organising others

- What stops you being physically active? (You can choose multiple answers)
  - Lack of confidence in ability
  - Feeling self-conscious and shy
  - Have not found something I enjoy
  - No one to take part with
  - Lack of time
  - Lack of transport
  - Lack of information
  - Lack of opportunities
  - Nothing

- What would you like to learn in PE? (You can choose multiple answers)
  - Benefits of being physically active
  - How to be physically active outside of school/throughout life
  - Knowledge and skills I need for GCSEs and A-Levels
  - How to lead/organise a physical activity
  - Skills that will help me in life
  - Sport specific skills
  - Do not have a preference

- The work I am proudest of in PE is? (open answer).

- What I have most enjoyed about the curriculum since September is...? (open answer).

Student opinions around curriculum intent
- How well are we currently meeting our curriculum objective to (insert your objective(s) here):

PE runs DEEP at UCGS. How well do you think the department currently meets each of our curriculum objectives (extremely well, well, neutral, not well, not well at all):?
- Develop competence and confidence across a range of sports and activities
- Educate all to value physical activity
- Engage all in regular meaningful physical activity
- Prepare all students for success in wider life

This, of course, is not a comprehensive list of avenues you may wish to explore but will hopefully give you a strong starting point to truly understanding how your students feel about PE and physical activity in your school.

When it comes to collating and analysing responses, do not take anything personally. See every response, positive or negative, as a chance to praise and improve. You might also consider communicating the responses with students to let them know how they have helped shape your future PE delivery. The technique of 'you said, we did' is a good way to demonstrate that *this is what you told us, we listened* and therefore *made the following changes*. In my opinion, this is a fantastic way to give students a voice and allow them to feel that they really have an input into their PE lessons, what they are taught, and shaping their curriculum. It will also give you and the PE team a good insight into what is working well, what might need more communication, or what needs to be developed. It is the perfect tool to demonstrate the impact of changes, or to support you in selling why change is required to truly create a positive and meaningful PE experience for all.

Lost Curriculum Time

Ofsted's new Inspection Framework, which came into effect from September 2019, gave greater recognition to schools' work to support the personal development of pupils. This included the opportunities students have to learn about eating healthily and maintaining an active lifestyle.

The Framework also included the term 'cultural capital', which is defined as: 'the essential knowledge that children need to be educated citizens' (Ofsted, 2018, p.31). This term takes the learning gained in the classroom to new and unfamiliar contexts, which is the exact aim of conceptual learning.

Some schools and departments were worried by this inclusion, as their past results and lessons that often 'taught to the test' were no longer sufficient. They were to develop individuals' character, improve resilience, teach life-skills through their contact time, and many had not attempted this before. They taught their specification, and that was it, although many skills could be considered coincidentally transferable.

We, in PE, have been talking for some time about the ability to create leaders, good communicators, team player, and healthy individuals. The difference being that now, our contributions were being recognised by inspectors, which, of course, was of great importance to Senior Leaders.

In terms of advocacy, it is important to communicate the evidential impact our subject has on meeting the needs of our students during a time when well-being is at the forefront of impactful change in schools. The *Active Lives* Children Survey conducted by Sport England in 2019 recorded a clear correlation between those students that considered themselves more physically active engaging in 60+ minutes of exercise per day, and feelings of happiness and belonging.

For most PE teachers, this will come as no surprise; we have known the benefits of physical activity on mental well-being for some time. This report goes on to highlight that, the more active they were, the higher level of resilience respondents showed. Even better, the *Power of PE: The Future of Physical Education* report, released by the Youth Sport Trust, confirmed that active children's brains work better, giving them improved capacity to learn.

At the same time, better attitudes towards school and improvements in psychosocial health create a more conducive mindset for learning. In fact, there is no evidence to suggest that time in PE has any detrimental impact on academic performance. The most powerful statement came from the results from the Youth Sport Trusts *National PE, School Sport and Physical Activity Survey* (2014), where it was found that 70% of schools considered that sport makes a positive contribution to behaviour and reduced truancy.

In his book *Pivot, Flex, Adapt: Physical Education Through the 2020 Pandemic*, Shaun Dowling (2021), with the help of many other practitioners, assesses the impact that the Covid-19 pandemic had on Physical Education, and how the subject overcame the challenges presented. Dowling shares many examples of inspiring and pioneering physical educators, who went above and beyond to adapt their curriculum offering, ensuring students received outstanding PE. Dowling concludes this work by rightly identifying the opportunities this pandemic has provided, by identifying five suggested priority areas for the future of PE. His first, and most important priority area, was to raise the status of Physical Education within the National Curriculum. In fact, Dowling calls for the subject to be made a core subject alongside Maths and English in the UK. Highlighting the strong, evidence-backed arguments around links between regular physical activity and improved brain function and cognition, the increasing role that cognitive science is playing in teaching and learning, and the obsession with academic performance, it certainly creates a compelling case. 'Use research-based evidence to convince policy makers in government to elevate Physical Education to being a core subject in the National Curriculum, thus affording physical literacy an equivalent status to literacy and numeracy' (Dowling, 2021, p.171).

There is so much available evidence to support us, it's just about taking the time to find it. Whether it's fighting obesity, supporting mental health, raising self-esteem, reducing disease, or improving academic performance, the list goes on, we truly are vital to our schools, our students, our communities, and indeed the nation. Never forget that, and ensure others do not either. Though, as identified by Dowling, if we go back to the traditional multi-sport, technique-focused approach to PE delivery, then much of our argument is lost, and the future of the genuine need for this subject must be in question.

In this chapter, we have looked at how conceptualised learning could be incorporated into your core PE curriculum, in order to shift the focus from performance and deliver important learning for life. I introduced the concept-driven approach application to core PE model. Using reliance and basketball as an example, I highlighted how each aspect of the model can ensure that the acquisition, connection, and transfer of the concept takes place. Curriculum planning should consider the needs of the students, and this was highlighted by reviewing the youth personality types identified by Sport England.

In order to achieve enjoyment, results, and nurture physical literacy for all, we must adapt our current practices, incorporating the latest research, the needs of our students, and the understanding that sport cannot not be the sole purpose of PE. Our current curriculum approach is contributing to the downfall of PE and, despite our best intentions, doing more harm than good. Listening to your students is one of the most important aspects of implementing change. You can use their opinions to make accurate and informed decisions, whilst also providing tangible proof to stakeholders as to why change is needed.

Earn Your Inclusive Pedagogy Cap

Catch them achieving: Look for opportunities and teachable moments. Build positive relationships with all students, looking to praise and encourage in every lesson.

Attitude and progress-focused: Reward for attitude and progress, and not for performance and ability.

Physical literacy informed approach: Use the principle of physical literacy to create a positive and meaningful PE environment that promotes positive attitudes towards physical activity, which can create lifelong engagement.

Take Away Reflections

- What strategies could you employ to employ a physical literacy informed approach to PE delivery?
- What PE non-sport specific professional development have you and your team received?
- How can you utilise meeting time to maximise professional development?
- How can you ensure new learning and practice is relevant and maintained?
- How do students feel about PE at your school? How do you know?

Assessment: Holistic and Progressive

There can be no doubt that assessment has been an area of contention and challenge for physical educators for some time. The need for standardisation, accountability, and evidence has driven many assessment models that are not fit for purpose.

Schools and departments are reflecting on all aspects of their offering, following the updated Ofsted Education Inspection Framework (2019), which included curriculum intent, implementation and impact as major parts of the judgements made.

'At the intended level, curriculum is that which is planned. At the implemented level, curriculum is that which is taught. At the achieved level, curriculum is that which is learnt. The alignment of these three curriculum components is therefore essential to curriculum coherence. What unites these components is assessment' (Frapwell, 2015, p.30).

A bespoke concept-driven PE assessment model has yet to be created. However, many PE leaders have produced some fantastic models that move away from assessing only physical performance. They have created a more student-focused developmental model that looks to develop the whole child.

In this section, I present the key thinking required to create a concept-driven assessment model and in the next chapter provide examples of those doing something similar. There can be no doubt that assessment has been an area of contention and challenge for physical educators for some time. The need for standardisation, accountability, and evidence has driven many assessment models that are not fit for purpose.

The AIESEP Position Statement on Physical Education Assessment describes assessment as, 'a process by which information on student learning is obtained, interpreted and communicated, relative to one or more predefined learning outcomes. It serves several educational purposes, such as:

- Guiding and supporting the learning process of students,
- Informing teachers about the effectiveness of their teaching and curriculum,
- Deciding whether students may progress to a following phase in their learning process
- Providing evidence of student learning for relevant stakeholders (accountability).'

(AIESEP, 2020).

Assessment is often referred to in two different forms: summative and formative. However, assessment guru Wiliam argues, in *The Research Ed Guide to Assessment*, that summative and formative assessment should not be separated as different forms of assessment, as assessment can be used both summatively and formatively. He claims that it is not the forms of assessment that are different, but what a teacher infers from the results that separates them.

A PE example of this would be an assessment in which students must demonstrate the correct technique in the triple jump. A summative use of this assessment would inform the teacher how often the student managed a valid jump, the length achieved in the furthest attempt, or an average achieved across all jumps. Conversely, a formative inference would be to consider what the student might need to do in order to improve the frequency of valid jumps, or the overall length and consistency achieved. In this simple example of assessment, a teacher can make two uses of the information provided from it.

This point is further supported by Christodoulou (2016) in her suggestion of combining both summative and formative assessment in a 'descriptor-based assessment'. By using descriptors of performance, teachers can assess student performance throughout the entire scheme of work, and use these observations to provide a summative grade once completed. Descriptors also provide a more holistic focus, rather than placing all attention on more specific skills.

The descriptors can be applied to different contexts, content, tasks, and sports in order for students to demonstrate the appropriate skills to meet the criteria. The generic descriptors eliminate the need for different assessment criteria in every sport delivered. Christodoulou does outline some limitations to this model, including teacher bias, and the inability of the model to identify why students are unable to perform a task. She also suggests the use of a 'progression model' in order to fully communicate what a student needs to do to get from one stage to the next.

A progression model offers a more specific description of what is required to move to the next stage, and should highlight what students should be able to demonstrate. Providing an amalgamation of the two models will truly support the delivery of a concept-driven curriculum.

We must be honest and say that devising a model that assesses concepts is a much more complex task than one that assesses purely skill acquisition. This is one of the reasons so many continue to assess physical ability only. Leaders and teachers need to clearly communicate the model and the criteria required to progress. This is where a rubric can support us. 'A descriptive and clear rubric can transform learning by providing students with information about where they are and what the need to do to grow' (Stern, 2017, p.110).

Stern outlines examples that an effective rubric might contain in order to successfully demonstrate conceptual understanding: ability to articulate and explain conceptual relationships; analysis and synthesis of the conceptual statement in connection to multiple examples; and evaluation of the transferability of the concept. The rubric should move from basic to more complex skills, in order for students to demonstrate progression, and understand higher level learning.

This can be incorporated in with the concepts, attitudes, and skills you would like to develop over the course of the curriculum. Once the aims of the curriculum and the learning that will take place are decided, an assessment success criterion should be established. These criteria form the basis of all formative assessment and provide a clear framework in which students and teachers can understand what is required to progress. A progression model should start by considering what the best attaining students should be able to demonstrate, and then work backwards (Odell, 2020). We must consider the knowledge, skills, and concepts that a student should be able to demonstrate at each stage. The stage descriptors should be student-friendly and concise.

The Curriculum for Excellence Benchmarks for Physical Education in Scotland offer a clear example of an assessment rubric. 'Their purpose is to make clear what learners need to know and be able to do to progress through the levels, and to support consistency in teachers' and other practitioners' professional judgements,' (Education Scotland, 2017, p.2). These benchmarks were created to aide professional dialogue as part of the moderation process to assess where young people are in their learning. They were also designed to support holistic assessment approaches across learning.

The Benchmark outlines (p.2) where suitable evidence of progress and achievement might be obtained:

- Observing day-to-day learning within the classroom, playroom or working area.
- Observation and feedback from learning activities that takes place in other environments, for example: outdoors, on work placements.
- Learning conversations.
- Planned periodic holistic assessment.

The benchmarks also avoid excessive teacher workload and irrelevant and unnecessary assessment for students; another key component of strong assessment in PE.

The benchmark covers 4 main areas of assessment:

Assessment Area	Holistic Concepts
Physical Competencies	- Kinaesthetic Awareness - Balance and Control - Coordination and Fluency - Rhythm and Timing - Gross and Fine Motor Skills
Cognitive Skills	- Focus and Concentration - Cue Recognition - Sequential Thinking - Prioritising - Decision Making - Multi-Processing - Problem Solving - Creativity
Personal Qualities	- Motivation - Confidence and Self-Esteem - Determination and Resilience - Responsibility and Leadership - Respect and Tolerance - Communication
Physical Fitness	- Stamina - Speed - Core Stability and Strength - Flexibility

It goes on to include columns on 'Experiences and Outcomes for Planning Learning, Teaching and Assessment' and 'Benchmarks to Support Practitioners Professional Judgement'.

The Curriculum for Excellence offers staff a clear understanding of what students are required to do in order to progress, and sets clear guidance when assessing a student's current 'level'. The language is both staff and student-friendly and would allow schools an opportunity to create their own bespoke assessment, with this holistic benchmark as a strong starting point.

When creating your own rubric, labelling forms an important part of the message you are communicating to students. Avoid the use of numerical levels or grades. 'As soon as students get a grade, learning stops. We may not like it, but the research reviewed here shows that this is a relatively stable feature of how human minds work' (Wiliam, 2011). This method only serves to demotivate and demoralise.

It does not promote learning and the progress that can be made. Many schools have opted for a label that establishes each stage of the learning process from 'emerging' or 'developing' to 'mastery'. This provides students will a better understanding of their own learning pathway and, whilst ambitious, also enables the opportunity for reflection. A level or grade seems final; however, a stage feels more representative of what learning actually is – a journey.

One practitioner whose work has influenced the thinking and practice of many in our subject is PE practical assessment guru Andy Frapwell. Widely known for the creation of the Head-Heart-Hands assessment framework, Frapwell is a key driver in linking theory to practice. Clear motivations in Frapwell's work centre around putting the student first, understanding how students learn, and creating a learning environment in which mastery can be achieved. In his book, *In Deep: Learning to Learn* (2011), Frapwell presents his extensively researched idea of 'learning to learn'. 'The concept of Learning to Learn moves our thinking to a process of discovery about learning. If we understand learning and its various forms, then competencies and skills can be developed and used to help learners learn more effectively, and so become learners for life' (p.6). In conversation with Frapwell, he provided the following summary of mastery learning:

- **Mastery learning ensures learners obtain mastery in related aspects (H-H-H) of Physical Education, using a selected activity before moving on to the next unit.** It has at its core the research-informed approach that each and every learner (unless they are SEND) can master the standards expected for each Key Stage, given sufficient instruction, time, and perseverance. This has implications for how we sequence and combine learning – it cannot be the way of a 'one skill per week' approach.
- Bloom's Learning for Mastery (1968) and the work of Biggs and Collis (1982) both emphasise that, while learning is linked to factors like student aptitude and quality of instruction, **all learners can achieve mastery, if they are provided ample opportunity and allowed to learn content at their own pace.**
- One of the most important elements regarding the quality of instruction is to **differentiate learning to allow all learners access to the same learning content.** This will involve combining differentiation by task and differentiation by process. It is not differentiation by outcome.
- Over 50 years of research suggests that **mastery-based learning is linked with higher learner achievement (attainment and progress) rates and**

positive learner attitudes towards Physical Education, when a mastery approach is implemented from a young age.

- **Teaching for mastery involves metacognition.** Learners know why they need to learn a particular skill, concept, or behaviour; they learn what skill, concept, and behaviour content are related; and they learn how to apply the skills, concepts, and behaviours of PE to improve (the why, the what, and the how).

- **Teaching for mastery encourages physical activity behaviours and lifelong learning.** When learners are given time to learn and succeed, they're more likely to feel competent and have confidence in their abilities, and therefore enjoy the activity; they will learn to value resilience and perseverance, and understand their own learning needs; learners learn to learn – they become learners for life.

(Frapwell, 2021)

This philosophy of 'learning to learn' is further supported by the Education Endowment Foundations *Metacognition and Self-Regulated Learning* Guidance Report (Updated 2019), which identifies 7 recommendations for which teachers can deliver 'mastery teaching', two of which include:

- Explicitly teach pupils metacognitive strategies, including how to plan, monitor, and evaluate their learning (p.14).
- Set an appropriate level of challenge to develop pupils' self-regulation and metacognition (p.20).

Self-regulation is the key to unlocking the true value of assessment in PE. Students will be aware of their strengths, areas for development, and the strategies they can use to learn and develop further. The focus of assessment should be on developing, and not about proving. The value students place on the form of assessment being used is also important. Ensuring students understand what they are learning, why they are learning it, and how to improve are vital in students creating a meaningful connection to assessment and development.

Frapwell and the Association for Physical Education (AfPE) released *A Practical Guide to Assessing Without levels* (2015). This book presents the aforementioned Head-Heart-Hands framework for organising content and criteria. The content represents the 'key skills' (Hands), 'essential knowledge and concepts' (Head), and 'vital behaviours' (Heart) expected of all learners by the end of their respective Key Stages:

- Physical, referring to the changes in the body, growth, movement, and environment perception (**psychomotor domain**).
- Cognitive development addresses the mental processes including memory, language, and problem solving (**cognitive domain**).
- Social/emotional development, pertaining to how children handle relationships and their own emotions (**affective domain**).

Frapwell also identified the connection between each aspect of development and their connections to physical activity, and what each individual should be or be able to do (though originally applied to what students should be able to be/do at the end of ages 10-11, it can be applied to older learners):

Head (cognitive domain). The thinking physical being:
- Decision maker
- Analytical – deep understanding
- Confident
- Tactician

Heart (affective domain). The feeling physical being:
- Social and emotional
- Involvement and engagement
- Attitude
- Character and values
- Healthy active lifestyle

Hands (psychomotor domain). The doing physical being:
- Physically competent
- Growth and development
- Physically active
- Competitive

Many schools have adopted this, or similar frameworks, when planning their curriculum and assessments, in order to focus on these three aspects of development. It should also be said that this approach to assessment should not be considered as relaxing expectations for students, or as making it easier. It instead makes it more personal, inclusive, and relevant to the students' needs.

Oliver Bishop and I worked on developing our own form of practical assessment, taking into account as much of the research and best practice as we could get our hands on. The truth is, I do not think a perfect model currently exists. There are many good frameworks, and the shift from performance to holistic is certainly welcome and needed, though assessment had us stumped on many occasions. We decided to go back to basics and agree what was important to our context, and what we wanted the students to leave with, following their time with us. We wanted students to own their assessment and truly use it to highlight their strengths and develop their areas for improvement. We also wanted it to motivate students to improve, and be used as a tool in lessons to challenge. Of course, we aimed to focus on the development of the whole child, and meet our curriculum objectives. As will be outlined later in this book, the department's curriculum objectives are to:

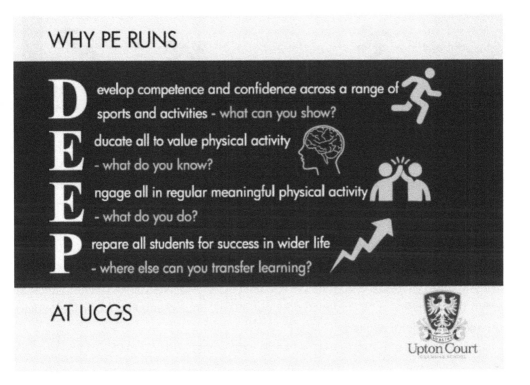

It was important to us that this was reflected in the assessment rubric. Using the already established DEEP acronym that was used to embed our objectives, we established the areas/themes we wanted to develop most.

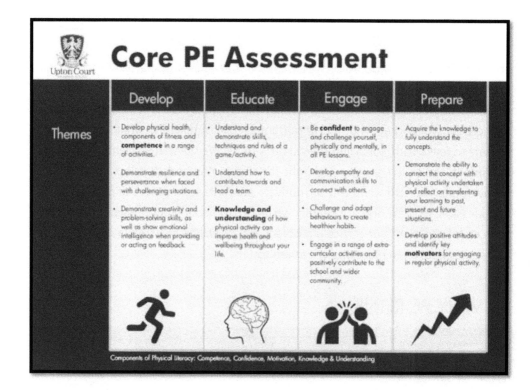

From there, and after many discussions with the team, Oliver set about writing what the stages of learning might look like against each theme, starting with a basic level of competency/understanding to a mastery level. This was then incorporated into an assessment rubric. This went through a number of drafts, took hours of meeting time, and, to be honest, will no doubt continue to be tweaked further. In order to better demonstrate how students can meet each aspect of our curriculum intent, we added icons to each and simple sentences such as, 'What do you know?' and, 'What can you show?'. The icons were placed next to the relevant intent sentences and within our assessment to evidence how our intent, implementation (curriculum), and impact (assessment) aligned.

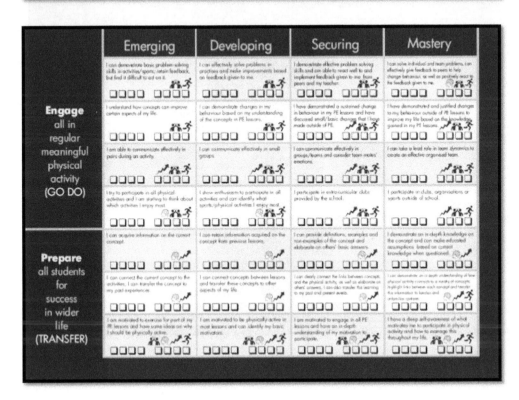

It was intended that students would tick off each assessment criteria as they achieve it; however, Oliver rightly wanted to explore a more accessible and user-friendly form of reflection. One that better demonstrated progress and areas for development. We also wanted it placed into the student planners, which would save on PE printing costs and be more accessible to students. Therefore, with support from the department and advice from Will Swaithes, Oliver produced an assessment wheel that students could colour in, depending on the stage of assessment they were currently working at. The example below shows one page in their planner, focusing on the mind aspect of our assessment. Each wheel focuses on a curriculum objective and incorporates the stages on learning within our assessment. If students achieve emerging (everyone should), then they would colour that section in. Over the course of the year the wheel should be completed accordingly and will hopefully demonstrate the progress made through different aspects of the assessment model, but would also highlight the areas (other than just physical competence) that students may wish to develop further.

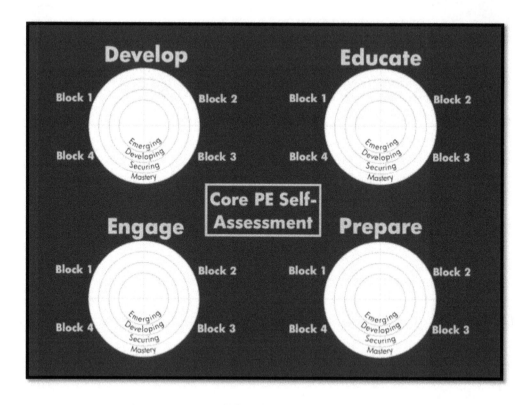

The above work was completed over the course of a year, and went through many changes and adaptations. It would be an understatement to call this project a challenge, but one that we truly believed in. As with the curriculum, this is a working model, and is subject to constant review and change.

Summary

As the final element of the 'Positive and Meaningful PE' model, I looked at assessment, and the need to re-focus it. To deliver a concept-driven curriculum effectively, our assessment should follow suit. No longer should we assess chasing perfection, but a more holistic and development model should be adopted. One that incorporates a formative approach to reach a summative conclusion.

Earlier in the chapter, I introduced Len Almond's work around human flourishing. I discussed the 6 factors as discussed by Almond from Ryff's (1989) work. I wish to revisit this now to highlight how the ideas presented in this chapter support this model:

- **Autonomy:** Students have the opportunity to understand what motivated them to engage in physical activity and actively have a choice about the sports and activities on their curriculum as part of the personality pathway options. The responsibility is placed on the students and, therefore, they must take ownership of their own engagement.

- **Personal growth:** A concept-driven approach to curriculum design provides life skills and a genuine connection between PE and the value it has in students' lives.

- **Self-acceptance:** Through holistic assessment, reflection, and directed schemes of work on this very topic, students are challenged on the ways they see themselves, their perceived limitations, and provided with the tools to overcome obstacles.

- **Purpose in life:** A positive and meaningful environment is created that enables teachers and students to nurture physical literacy. Students learn as part of the concept-driven curriculum, and the tailored curriculum within the personality pathway fully supports students to connect positive experiences, benefits of regular physical activity, and a desire to engage in the future.

- **Environmental mastery:** Students are exposed to different learning opportunities. They acquire key knowledge and understanding of concepts, connect them to their PE lessons, and transfer them to familiar and unfamiliar contexts. Thus, feeling more secure and confident in various environments.

- **Positive relationships with others:** Through specific schemes of work and lessons and social health, teamwork, conflict resolution, etc, as part of the concept-driven curriculum, as well as the models-based approaches employed as part of the personality pathway, students are provided with numerous opportunities to build and maintain meaningful relationships with others.

In order to nurture physical literacy for all, we must adapt our current practices, incorporating the latest research, the needs of our students, and the understanding that sport cannot not be the sole purpose of PE. Now we better understand the 'why' and the 'how', it's time to focus on the 'who'. In order to make the required changes, we need leaders. So, what makes a good leader? A leader is someone who is experienced, has been in education for years, and in a position of responsibility, right? Wrong! Amongst many other things, a leader is someone who can see how things can be improved, and who rallies people to move toward that better vision. If you have read this far, you obviously believe in a better future for our subject. PE needs leaders. PE needs You! In the next chapter, I explore how leaders like yourself can lead change within PE and beyond.

Earn Your Holistic Assessment Cap

Challenging: Assessment should be challenging and provide opportunities for the students to reflect on what they have done, the progress they have made, and how they can develop further.

All-inclusive and student-friendly: Everyone should understand how to, and have the opportunity to develop. Consider the message that your model sends to students.

Progressive and holistic: Provide a clear framework that moves through phases of learning and develops the whole child, and not solely practical ability.

Take Away Reflections

- When considering autonomy, personal growth, self-acceptance, purpose in life, environmental mastery, and positive relationship with others, how is your department enabling your students to flourish?
- What makes up your teams 'Positive and Meaningful PE' model?

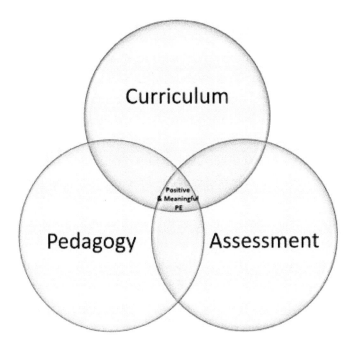

5

Leading The Change

We must recognise that, for some, change means taking a risk, stepping out of our comfort zone, and doing something different to what has been done before.

We have looked at why change is needed, what change looks like, and the impact it could have. In this chapter, I draw on the experiences of teachers around the country who are leading the way in improving their PE curriculum, pedagogy and assessment, which demonstrates the impact our changes could have. I want to re-emphasise how a concept-driven approach, holistic assessment model, and supportive teaching can meet the needs of our students and provide a more positive and meaningful learning experience.

This chapter may come across as if it were written for Heads of Department only – it isn't. We are all leaders. If you are in charge of people, then you are a leader. If you teach, then you are a leader. This chapter is written to support all leaders in leading the change needed in Physical Education. I have spoken to many PE leaders who have kindly shared some of the work they have done to implement meaningful change. Some of these examples may resonate with you, and others may not fit your context or vision. PE leaders are going above and beyond to overcome the challenges currently facing us, and my hope is that you find something of value based on the work of others.

Implementing change is one of the biggest challenges a leader can undertake. Success will require a significant shift in mindset and goes against the training we have received and the habitual practice we are so accustomed to. There may well be staff who do not agree with the change, SLT that are reluctant to support it, and parents who desperately want their students to play sport to a higher level, which they still can with this approach. In reality, whilst making the changes within my own department, and then by writing this book, I have been on a roller coaster of emotions. I have experienced frustration when staff do not feel as strongly as I do, or do not implement aspects of the delivery, despite numerous conversations. I have also experienced pure joy when students speak of their new found enjoyment in PE, and when a teachers deliver amazing concept-driven lessons. This learning journey, and the successes I have experienced, would not have been possible without the numerous failures. Whilst I, and others, present to you their work, it is vital to remember that this is the result of many ups and downs. I am absolutely aware that, by the time this reaches print, I will hopefully have adapted or improved some of what my department delivers. Curriculum, pedagogy, and assessment should always be evolving and improving. Only then can we continually attempt to meet the needs of our students. Embrace failure, celebrate small wins, and remain committed to your values.

My assumption is that, if you are still reading, you agree with me, at least to some extent, and you're invested enough to find out how you can go about implementing this change. We must recognise that, for some, change means taking a risk, stepping out of our comfort zone, and doing something different to what has been done before.

In the book *The Art of Being Brilliant*, Cope asks, 'what would you do if you knew you couldn't fail?' I do not believe for a second that this approach will fail, but, my point is, imagine the impact we could have on the lives of these young people if we go for it!

One of the greatest sports people to ever live, Michael Jordan, once said, 'Some people want it to happen, some wish it would happen, others make it happen.' This quote makes me think of two things: firstly, we sincerely are the pioneers of change that will improve the lives of young people forever; and secondly, I really wish I'd said that.

When faced with change, we can all react differently; some seek and embrace change, others are wary of it and need some convincing, or some totally reject it altogether. This is exhibited in *Who Stole My Cheese* by Dr Spencer Johnson (1998). The allegory features four characters: two mice 'Sniff' and 'Scurry', and two little people 'Hem' and 'Haw', each representing a different reaction to change.

The characters all live in a maze (representing the real world) and are always seeking cheese– whatever it is we want in life. Every day, Hem, Haw, Sniff and Scurry visit Cheese Station C, a place they have visited for a long time for their satisfying and nourishing cheese. One morning, Sniff and Scurry arrived at Cheese Station C to discover there was no cheese; it had all gone. They weren't surprised, since they had noticed the supply of cheese had been getting smaller every day. They were prepared for the inevitable and knew instinctively what to do. So, they were quickly off in search of new cheese.

Later that same day, Hem and Haw arrived. 'What! No Cheese? Who moved my Cheese? It's not fair!' Hem yelled. They went home that night hungry and discouraged.

The next day, Hem and Haw left their homes and returned to Cheese Station C once again. But the situation hadn't changed, still no cheese. Haw suggested, 'Maybe we should stop analysing the situation so much and just get going and find some new cheese. Haw decided to leave Cheese Station C, while Hem was more comfortable staying in the cheese-less Station and wait.

Meanwhile, mice Sniff and Scurry went farther into the maze until they found Cheese Station N. They found what they had been looking for – a great supply of new cheese. Haw set out alone, not knowing which direction to head in. Eventually, he too finds the magnificent Cheese Station N and reflects on his learning along the way:

- Change happens and they will keep moving the cheese.
- Anticipate change and get ready for the cheese to move.
- Monitor change and smell the cheese often so you know when it is getting old.
- Adapt to change quickly, the quicker you let go of old cheese, the sooner you can enjoy new cheese.
- Change – move with the cheese.
- Enjoy change and savour the adventure and enjoy the taste of new cheese.
- Be ready to change quickly and enjoy it again and again

(Johnson, 1998)

Although it is a fable, the messages delivered are true of most teams; we all deal with change differently. Some teachers will be on board straight away and completely buy into your vision, like Sniff and Scurry. Others might take time to see the benefits of change, rather like Haw. There might even be some that are against change and moving away from a sport-driven approach, more like Hem.

In this chapter, I hope to provide the guidance required to make a meaningful change with your team. It is important to understand that the suggestions in this chapter will not happen overnight. Meaningful change takes time. It cannot be done alone, and first you will need to create and share your vision.

Your 'Why'

I spoke at the start of my book about my 'why'. It is the one thing that motivates me to do what I do; without it, my work would lack direction and passion. My 'why' is to prepare students for life through physical activity. I share this passion with anyone and everyone, and it forms the foundation of everything I stand for in my professional career.

Very few people can articulate their 'why'. It is your cause or belief: why you do what you do. Ask yourself, 'why do you get out of bed every morning? And why should anyone care?' (Sinek, 2011, p.39). I wish I could offer you some meaningful advice as to how to establish or discover your 'why', but I can't. Only you know what drives you, or why you became a teacher and have remained one. What I want is to demonstrate how impactful knowing your why can be.

One of the most inspirational Head Teachers I have been fortunate enough to work with is a man called Mark Pritchard. He is emotionally intelligent, knowledgeable, but, most importantly, driven to achieve his 'why'. Mark Pritchard's 'why': 'To inspire students and staff to be better than they imagined.'

Every conversation he has and every decision he makes comes back to this statement. You leave every meeting with him inspired to take a risk, leave your comfort zone, and seek professional and personal development. His 'why' inspired me to do something I never would have dreamt possible – write this book.

The power of your 'why' is unquantifiable and priceless. It truly is the difference between failure and success. Once you know why you do what you do, you hold your own destiny in your hands.

Your Team's 'Why'

It's one thing to explore your own 'why'; it's a completely different thing to share this with others and hope they will share it too. One of the biggest concerns Heads of Department have shared with me was getting their teams on board with changing the curriculum. There were real and understandable concerns that moving away from a sport specific focus and to a concept-driven approach would be a difficult sell.

Ask your team to explore their own 'why' and share this with each other. No teacher that I have ever met does this job to 'produce an elite athlete' or 'win a county competition with their Year 10 football team', and if that is their 'why' then they have missed the point of being an educator.

Most will say they want to share their love of sport, or get students to understand the importance of physical activity. This is your opportunity to highlight how the current curriculum is not aligned to their 'why'. If what really drives them is to share their love of sport, then ask them to write a list of those students that the teacher has helped fulfil that aim, and a list of students that perhaps they have not.

Some interesting questions could be used at the start of a meeting to ignite discussion around what they hope to achieve in their professional lives. Examples of these are:

- At the end of your career, if you were to write an autobiography about your life, what would it be called?
- Picture yourself at your retirement party. Three ex-students stand up and say one thing each about how you. What would you like them to say?

Once you have agreed on your individual 'whys', you can agree on your department mission statement. Your department mission statement will form your team's values. All decisions you make and everything you do should reflect these values. Your mission statement should reflect what your department hopes to achieve. An example of how a mission statement might look:

> The PE department are dedicated to helping each student exceed their personal expectations in academic and physical PE. Commitment, resilience, and persistence are celebrated, and the importance of a healthy, active lifestyle is fully embraced by all.

'It is increasingly important that we remember, recognise and make explicit, the learning that goes beyond improving sporting performance, so that we can make the PE offer meaningful and relevant to all students' (Swaithes, 2017).

Students and other stakeholders are unlikely to remember your mission statement or build any true connection with it. This is where your curriculum intent comes in. The students that will embark on their learning journey in your subject will experience this curriculum intent first-hand. Though they might not always be able to articulate it.

In the past, leaders wanted their students to be able to communicate their subject's intent in case Ofsted or SLT visited. It certainly made the department look good if the student could say why that subject was so important to their lives. Whilst on the topic of Ofsted, in the *Inspection Framework* (2019), PE departments should consider if their vision and purpose of PE is clear and understood, and if it is relevant and meaningful to students. Though, for us in PE, and for the provision of the knowledge and understanding elements of physical literacy, it is vital that students fully appreciate why PE is so important to them. Therefore, we need to market ourselves as clearly as possible. A catchy phrase or mnemonic can help achieve this. See the following example of curriculum intent from Upton Court Grammar School in Slough. We have used the word D.E.E.P to outline each of their main curriculum objectives. Now, when students are asked why PE exists at their school, they can remember this mnemonic and it will support them to clearly articulate the purpose of PE.

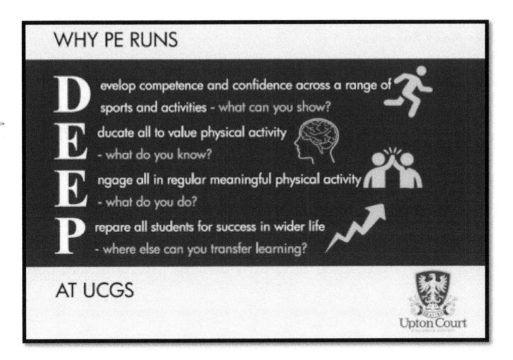

WHY PE RUNS

D evelop competence and confidence across a range of sports and activities - what can you show?

E ducate all to value physical activity - what do you know?

E ngage all in regular meaningful physical activity - what do you do?

P repare all students for success in wider life - where else can you transfer learning?

AT UCGS

Upton Court

It is important to over-communicate your intent. Add it to email signatures, hang it up on walls, refer to it in every lesson and team meeting. Do not just communicate your intent, live it.

In summary, recognising, knowing, and communicating your own 'why' is vital to maintain your own drive and motivation. It will also help when making key decisions and realising your vision. Supporting your team to do the same, and to combine these to create a team 'why', will give them direction and purpose. Reminding them of this shared vision during challenges, and celebrating success, will continue to motivate them as you drive the team to meeting the objectives you have collaboratively set. It is ultimately this vision that can be the difference between getting others to buy into what you hope to achieve and collaborating with you to achieve it. In short, knowing why you do what you do, could be the deciding factor between achieving your individual and team goals or not.

Take Away Reflections

- What would you do if you knew you couldn't fail?
- How can you better share your 'why'?
- Do the department's curriculum objectives reflect individual members 'why'?
- What would students say if asked, 'Why does PE exist at this school'?
- How does your delivery meet the values of your school?

Curriculum, Assessment and Pedagogy

Remember your team's 'why' and the likelihood that it includes learning for all students and not the exceptional few.

The 'What' of Our Curriculum

'Staff expertise, equipment, facilities and timetabling all play their part in decision making about the nature and content of the curriculum. The overriding influence, however, should be the learner's needs' (Frapwell, 2015, p.34). I spoke previously about Shaun Dowling's book *Pivot, Flex, Adapt: Physical Education Through the 2020 Pandemic* (2021), whereby he shares the innovative work of physical educators as they look to provide meaningful PE through a pandemic. A strong case is also made for the concern that it will be easier for PE to return to its previous dominant and failing form of delivery, than to seek innovative and meaningful change. The pandemic has highlighted some of the failings of the multi-activity approach to PE delivery, specifically the statistic raised earlier that only 17% of students achieved the Chief Medical Officers recommended 60 minutes of physical activity a day during the first lockdown, highlighting a distinct lack of motivation to engage in physical activity, or a true understanding of the benefits it has to the body and mind. Thus, demonstrating the current inability to truly nurture physical literacy through that form of delivery. However, and more important to focus on, the pandemic also provided a real opportunity for change, and demonstrated the true desire around the world for PE teachers to seek alternatives that better met their students' needs. Dowling identifies a new and improved Physical Education curriculum as a priority moving forward, off the back of a lot of impressive work trialled during the pandemic. He suggests PE teachers should, 'use learning from 2020 to devise progressive, modern curriculum models which provide greater choice, variety and gender equality. Based on more holistic, health and well-being models rather than sport-focused models' (Dowling, 2021, p.176). The concept-driven model presented in this book is one such example.

It is important to remember that, even by shifting to a new curriculum, we are still teaching sport and physical activity; we now just have a different focus. The inclusion of a concept, and the shift in attention, will now form the 'what' of our curriculum. Let's look in more detail about the impact that this new 'what' can have on the learning and lives of our students.

I spoke previously about learning that transfers, and Stern's concept of acquire, connect, and transfer; now we can go further and consider how a concept-driven curriculum can support this process.

Eve Wagstaff and I have trialled a concept-driven approach to curriculum design and the delivery of said curriculum through the Learning Transfer Mental model (acquire, connect and transfer). Eve outlines in the following (figure/table) how this has been delivered at Upton Court Grammar School KS3 and KS4 PE lessons.

'We start every lesson off with the 'acquire' phase and we are explicit when teaching each phase. This phase should take no longer than two minutes and can be incorporated into the physical activity. We would often provide the students with a simple definition of the concept and then ask the students to discuss examples and non-examples of the concept during a warm-up. Students would then feedback from their discussions to the class. I would then introduce the practical (often sport specific) element to the lesson, though it is important to say that I would have planned this with the concept in mind. If I were teaching a concept in which students are able to demonstrate their learning, perhaps, for example, if I were teaching resilience, then I would plan an activity whereby this can be seen. If it is a concept that is more around knowledge, for example, diet, then this does not need as much application to the practical activity at this stage.

The next phase is that of 'connect'. Here we are using our bank of questions with the aim of connecting the activity that the students have just completed with the concept. If I had planned to see the concept demonstrated within the activity (such as resilience) then my questions would focus on examples of where these had been seen and how they impacted one's ability to learn or overcome an obstacle. If the concept is around learning (diet) then I would focus my questioning on how this concept might have positively or negatively impacted one's ability to progress in that activity. As I said, you are making a connection between your PE lesson and the concept you are delivering. Once again, this phase may only take a few minutes, with the majority of the lesson time saved for physical activity.

Finally, and delivered as the lesson plenary, we have the 'transfer' phase. In this phase we are taking the conceptual learning and applying it to a different context away from PE. We try and link it to the students' past, present or futures. We do this using personal reflection questions. Depending on the concept, students may or may not feel comfortable feeding back their reflections.

Overall, I have seen an overwhelmingly positive response to PE lessons in terms of engagement, behaviour, and overall progress. The responses from our student voice surveys have echoed this. Students are now creating a connection between PE and the importance it has in their lives, they see a reason for it existing, and understand how it can help them develop and prepare them for the future. At first, I was nervous that this approach would take too much time away from physical activity and turn off those that really enjoyed their sport. However, having trialled and refined how we deliver our new curriculum, I believe I am now an advocate for this delivery, and could not recommend it highly enough. For the first time, I feel like a teacher that is really making a difference'.

Having worked with Eve on implementing the delivery of a concept-driven curriculum, I can confirm that, throughout the entire process, it was important to collaborate, trial, learn and listen. We knew what we wanted to deliver and had the framework of how we felt it would work; what we needed to learn was the reality of its application to a lesson. Only through trial and error was this possible. Thousands of conversations following every lesson took place, as we dissected in granular detail the impact of each phase. It was important that Eve and I created an open-door culture, where every member of the team felt comfortable to have others in their lessons. One way in which we achieved this was by leading by example and always being happy for others to come in and watch and provide honest and constructive feedback. If the team witnessed us taking nothing personally, sharing failures and a need to learn, then they would be more comfortable with the process. The second method used to create this culture was to remove any individual responsibility. If something didn't work, it was not the teacher's fault – we focused purely on the process. A solution-focused approach to any issues encountered quickly switched the focus from the teacher/issue encountered to what we could all do differently next time. In fact, failure was not only discussed, it was actively encouraged, even celebrated. We made sure that if something worked, we celebrated it as one step towards our main objective and realising our individual and team 'why'.

Creating a concept-driven curriculum is something Danny Burton knows a lot about. In his current role with the Youth Sport Trust, Burton is responsible for the development and improvement of PE and School Sport at a national level within secondary schools. His role includes leading national projects, providing professional development to schools and teachers, as well as working with practitioners to review and develop their PE provisions. Having worked in the PE and sport environment for over 15 years, Burton was formerly a secondary school PE teacher and senior leader and is the author of *Teach Now! Physical Education*.

Burton's views on the state of PE echo many other current physical educators concerned about the falling levels of physical activity within young people, the increasing time spent in front of screens, and reduction in PE time, to name just a few.

Raising the important question of, 'is now the time to re-position Physical Education within our secondary schools?' Burton said, 'With mental health and obesity-related illnesses remaining frequent issues within our schools, it has never been a more important time to keep PE and Physical Activity embedded within taught curriculums. PE can help solve a number of these issues, if the PE curriculum has real purpose and relevance to the learners. The most recent Ofsted Education Inspection Framework (2019) places emphasis on a young person's personal development, at what must be, the perfect time when Physical Education is in need of being refreshed and 'future-proofed'.

Values and characteristics within this proposed framework include:

- A curriculum which extends beyond the academic.
- Develop and discover interests and talents.
- Developing a young person's character: Resilience, confidence, independence, etc.
- Instil knowledge of how keep physically and mentally healthy.
- Preparing young people adequately for their futures – including, Physical, Social and Emotional development, as well as meta-cognition.

'Taking this into consideration, could a well-designed, student-centred PE curriculum approach be well positioned within a school to meet these outcomes? Making these outcomes explicit within the PE curriculum's 'impact' will now be an important consideration for schools, as well as ensuring we actively contribute to improving health and well-being, as well as a student's attainment'.

During his time as a PE teacher, Burton was given the opportunity to re-develop how PE was taught at Key Stage 3 (ages 11-14). 'Our school had adapted a traditional model to PE, which included a breadth of study consisting of traditional sports (E.g.: football, rugby, netball, hockey, athletics, etc . . .), and students were mainly assessed using sport specific outcomes (skills, knowledge, and application). And so, a refresh was required, ensuring our school has an effective, and appropriate curriculum – other factors needed to be considered; this included a review of our department, answering the following questions:

- Were we offering sufficient breadth in the activities and content we were delivering?
- Is our curricula effectively sequenced? And do we show progression across Key Stage/Stages?
- Are our most able students successfully stretched and challenged within their PE?
- Does our curriculum adopt an inclusive approach to ensure all young

people can effectively access the content being delivered?
- What do we measure/assess/report on to demonstrate progress in PE? And do our students truly understand where they are currently – and how they can improve within the subject?

'This review led to an introduction of a concept-led curriculum, where the activity which was being taught was a secondary outcome – and the focus of the lessons/units were centred around 5 key concepts, all of which the PE department had contributed too when reflecting what we wanted our students to achieve through our subject'.

1. Skills and knowledge – we wanted to maintain some of the traditional approaches that had been in place but reduce the emphasis. We also considered that some students (e.g.: the most able and committed students) enjoyed sport specific outcomes.

2. Creativity/problem solving – this concept included application of tactics and strategies, as well as students overcoming complex tasks, creating tasks/set pieces/motifs, as well as opportunities for students to express themselves (this concept transformed how we delivered dance and gymnastics to male students).

3. Evaluate and Improve – we wanted to add emphasis on this skill/knowledge, and to reposition outcomes, particularly for any students who may have struggled to perform a task practically. That knowledge of how and what was just as important. This concept was also linked to employability skills (judgement and decision making), which allowed us to promote and advocate the relevance of tasks to a wider group of students.

4. Physical capacity/effort/attitude – we wanted to include some assessments which measured a student's physical capacity (without the obvious use of fitness testing) to track physical progress. But we also wanted the focus to not be on 'fitness', but to position effort and positive attitudes highly. We built in regular continuous runs (e.g.: 10 minutes at the start of each lesson) to encourage and develop physical fitness, after seeing a significant decline in health from our Year 7 students, and saw rapid improvement of students' fitness, as well as higher levels of resilience.

5. Leadership – we felt one of our key strengths as a department was developing leadership skills, so, to ensure this was well-positioned, included it within our assessment framework. Every student was given regular opportunities to focus on fundamental leadership skills, such as com-

munication, decision making, leading others, adapting plans, changing activities to suit needs of others, inclusion, etc . . .

'Within each unit of work, staff would be allocated a teaching space, rather than be dictated by an activity. Staff would select an appropriate activity/activities to teach, with the focus being shifted towards one or two of the above concepts. Ensuring that all concepts were at least covered twice throughout an academic year.

The change was not without obstacles for Burton and his team: 'I was fortunate to be placed in a senior position to lead staff, which made the decision/rationale to change much easier. However, with some members of the department being significantly more experienced, and used to the traditional format of PE, there were a number of challenges to overcome.

1. Adopting the new assessment concepts – this took time. Full implementation of my new curriculum took the best part of an academic year, where I focused my efforts on individual teaching staff, whilst allowing them to maintain high amounts of autonomy to teach activities in a way they perceived was best for their students. The focus was completely shifted to 'what do your students' need?', rather than the traditional structures.

Teacher resources were developed to support staff, which included:

- The use of department meetings to 'moderate' assessments for Key Stage 3 students, using video footage of lessons and applying the concepts together within discussion.
- A resource pack – example lesson plans to make explicit focus of the key concepts, assessment descriptors for each concept, etc.
- A pocket-sized version of the level descriptors – to overcome teachers not having information to-hand during lessons when conducting assessments. Some staff developed the use of these, and integrated them as a student self-assessment tool during lessons.

2. Learning walks – subject leaders within the school were actively encouraged to do this regularly. As a department, we all agreed to cover each other for small amounts of time to conduct learning walks in pairs. This allowed staff to see first-hand how other colleagues were applying the

new curriculum, whilst acting as a CPD platform and regularly sharing good practice. We created a culture of 'open-door' teaching.

3. Promoting to students – a introduction lesson was added at the start of each academic year, to position the aim and vision of PE, and to explain and promote to students that PE was not about being good at 'sport'. Reporting/assessments were explicitly written to reference the Key Concepts we had identified. A display was created outside both our boys' and girls' changing areas, to promote the Key Concepts, but also to act as a teaching tool. Students were able to self-assess using the display boards and set individual targets to improve their attainment in PE'.

Burton reflected, 'Students' perceptions about what PE is, and what the focus of the lessons was, began to change. No longer would the question: 'What are you doing in your lesson today?' be followed by a response: 'Football'. Student voice analysis also identified an increase in students who reported enjoying the subject. What was also evident was an increase in the activities we used within our teaching – rather than being dictated by a traditional curriculum map'.

Through the vision Burton implemented, students could better articulate the learning they were gaining from PE, see the value of PE, and, more importantly, develop character, confidence, and competence. Further examples of the power of conceptual learning. No other subject has a better opportunity to do what we are able to do, if delivered correctly: truly prepare students for a healthy and successful life.

David Worthy works as a curriculum leader at Cams Hills Secondary School in Fareham, Hampshire, and he has planned his curriculum and assessment around Frapwell's Head, Heart, Hands framework, and the pursuit of mastery. Worthy's aspiration was to, 'maintain and reinforce Physical Education remaining 'at the heart of school life'. Social, emotional, and physical development have been at the heart of his team's delivery, as they look to develop the 'whole child'.

Following an OFSTED 'deep dive' in 2019, Worthy reflected on his curriculum and if what was being delivered was providing the learning his team had hoped to provide. Speaking of his reflections, Worthy said, 'We delivered isolated units of work that had no clear sequence or clarity, blurred success criteria which were not fully embedded into our learning outcomes, and, most importantly, our pupils were accessing a high quality Physical Education curriculum or put simply not just accessing 'sport''.

These reflections led to a 'desire to implement significant change'. Worthy and his team considered the following questions:

1. What do we want our pupils to be able to know at the end of Key Stages 3 and 4?
2. What key skills, essential knowledge and concepts, and vital behaviours do we expect by the end of the Key Stages?
3. Do we have a clear start and end points, and what does the 'pupil journey' look like between the two?
4. How can we as a PE department further embed the social and emotional development of our pupils into our curriculum?

Inspired by Andrew Frapwell, and the Head-Heart-Hands assessment framework, Worthy said, 'This framework clearly used the social and emotional aspects of learning that I wanted to incorporate in a more formal way. I believed strongly that if these domains could be effectively integrated into our PE curriculum, then the pupils' learning experiences and progress would be enhanced with the Head, Heart, Hands principles at its core'.

Worthy understood the need for the clear and simplified communication of his vision to enable this change to succeed. He spoke to his team and SLT individually in order to 'sell' his vision, focusing on 'why we do what we do'. The major changes Worthy proposed were:

- A shift to a Key Stage curriculum and not individual year groups – pupils would not study isolated units of work and potentially have to wait 10-12 months before they would study them again, culminating in skills/knowledge being lost. Normally, time would have to be spent on recapping the same material, thus resulting in no progress being made and mastery of skills low.
- Simplifying learning outcomes for pupils – pupils would only have 7 learning outcomes to achieve during Key Stage 3 rather than extensive amounts of learning outcomes per unit of work under the old system.

Worthy and his team identified the 7 learning outcomes that they wanted to students to learn by the end of each Key Stage. Worthy commented 'Using only 7 learning outcomes would allow all teachers in the department to spend undefined periods of time delivering the planned learning outcomes to the pupils. Due to the time spent teaching not being prescribed, pupils would experience mastery driven learning, allowing content to be thoroughly embedded and understood before moving on'. In fact, the curriculum can be accelerated or slowed down based on the needs, competency, and progression of students. Teachers have the freedom to deliver whichever activities they wish in order to meet each of the 7 learning objectives. As can be seen in the diagram below, these 7 learning objectives require students to meet a lesson objective before moving on. Worthy and his team planned everything with the Head, Heart, Hands framework in mind.

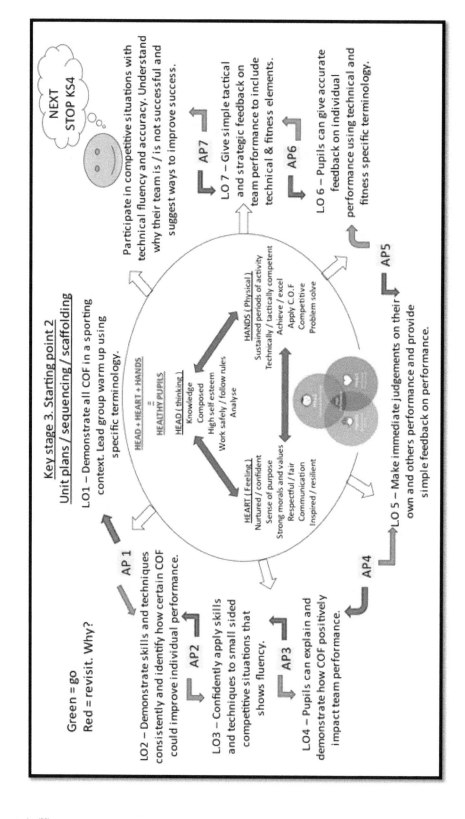

NEXT STOP KS4

Key stage 3. Starting point 2
Unit plans / sequencing / scaffolding

Green = go
Red = revisit. Why?

LO1 – Demonstrate all COF in a sporting context. Lead group warm up using specific terminology.

AP 1

LO2 – Demonstrate skills and techniques consistently and identify how certain COF could improve individual performance.

AP2

LO3 – Confidently apply skills and techniques to small sided competitive situations that shows fluency.

AP3

LO4 – Pupils can explain and demonstrate how COF positively impact team performance.

AP4

Participate in competitive situations with technical fluency and accuracy. Understand why their team is / is not successful and suggest ways to improve success.

AP7

LO 7 – Give simple tactical and strategic feedback on team performance to include technical & fitness elements.

AP6

LO 6 – Pupils can give accurate feedback on individual performance using technical and fitness specific terminology.

AP5

LO 5 – Make immediate judgements on their own and others performance and provide simple feedback on performance.

HEAD + HEART + HANDS
=
HEALTHY PUPILS

HEAD (thinking)
Knowledge
Composed
High self esteem
Work safely / follow rules
Analyse

HEART (Feeling)
Nurtured / confident
Sense of purpose
Strong morals and values
Respectful / fair
Communication
Inspired / resilient

HANDS (Physical)
Sustained periods of activity
Technically / tactically competent
Achieve / excel
Apply C.O.F
Competitive
Problem solve

When explaining how to assess the new curriculum, Worthy said, 'Each learning outcome is divided into 6 mastery statements. Pupil holistic progress is judged by the teacher and assessed accordingly. There is no time limit, or designated data drops, therefore giving substantial time periods to embed learning and revisit topics until pupils become secure in their learning'. The following diagram shows how teachers are able to deliver learning objective 1, highlighting the intent, implementation and intended impact.

STEP 1 CLEAR LEARNING OUTCOMES INTENT	STEP 2 CONTENT EXPANSION IMPLEMENTATION	STEP 3 ASSESS / EVALUATE MEASURING IMPACT
LEARNING OUTCOME	CONTENT EXPANSION Summary of module content What do pupils need to do to achieve the Learning outcome? (e.g Head - game scenario / routine, problem solve, select / apply skills, tactics, composition, competition. Heart – Discuss, debate, sustained activity level, inclusive, respect, apply all 6 health components to later life health and how they apply. Hands – Individual /pair / group / teamwork challenges, physical challenge practice, applied to an authentic game context.	ASSESSMENT / EVALUATION Incorporate inspire, nurture, excel, achieve & HHH Designed to allow students to demonstrate what they can do in order to meet the Learning outcome. (e.g adopt different role, timings, talk to pupil, question, observe performance / behaviour, presentation, unit summary from pupil)
1. Pupils can explain and demonstrate how COF positively impact team performance.	• Identify how each COF is used and impacts upon success in a game. Both in attack and defence. • Use a variety of sporting activities to enforce how transferrable COF are. • Identify weaker COF and apply a small training programme in groups to target overall improvement in game situation. Understand SPORT. • Ensure activities require long periods of physical activity.	• Identify if there has been improvement in COF? If so, why? • Identify ways of improving COF out of the PE setting. Can they identify links to local clubs? • Is respectful throughout and displays resilience. • Respond appropriately to questions to show COF are impacting upon performance. • The training programme applies SPORT and can they explain it successful. • Sustain long periods of physical activity.

Worthy applied the school's name (Cams) to the Solo framework (Structure of the Observed Learning Outcome), one that is well known to many educators, to support the development of learning, starting with a lower level of complexity through to mastery. He renamed the four stages of the Solo framework, and teachers use this terminology when assessing students based on the standard of the work demonstrated. The terminology used to assess students can be seen below.

	PUPILS PHASE OF LEARNING / UNDERSTANDING (SOLO)	Quality of work displayed (student response)
C	CAUTIOUS LEARNER (UNI)	Basic, Identify, Name, Define, Follow simple instruction
A	ASPIRATIONAL LEARNER (MULTI)	Describe, Combine, Complete, Develop
M	MASTERFUL LEARNER (RELATIONAL)	Sequence, Explain, Compare, Contrast, Analyse, Question, Organise
S	SURPASSING LEARNER (EXTENDED ABSTRACT)	Evaluate, Predict, Design, Reflect, Justify, Perform, Create, Compose, Argue

Worthy's determination to succeed and provide a meaningful PE experience for all students, in which relevant learning is delivered, is another example of how some outstanding physical educators are leading change. Though only at the start of the journey, Worthy commented, 'We have a real sense of purpose and belief in what we are trying to achieve. As we begin to implement our new curriculum and reflect on its impact, we are recognising it is a work in progress that we all, as a department and SLT, see as an effective way of developing the whole child. Instilling positive personality traits and preparing pupils for life after school are vital in today's world, and Physical Education at Cams Hill is playing an integral part in this'. The beauty of this curriculum is the ability to meet the needs of the students and the trust given to teachers in order to meet the learning objectives. Sport truly is the vehicle by which meaningful learning is delivered.

One PE leader has even re-branded PE at his school to be more reflective of what the subject actually delivers. Gareth Evans is Head of Healthy Active Lifestyles at Ninestiles, an Academy in Birmingham. This large secondary school has 1500 student of which 50% are considered disadvantaged. Evans was appointed Head of PE in 2015 but decided to change the subjects name to Healthy Active Lifestyles.

Evans wanted to explore the limitations the current perception of PE brought. 'While we would probably all agree that lifelong participation is a long-term goal, I feel that the majority of PE curriculums are not very inclusive and turn students away from physical activity as opposed to giving them the confidence and motivation to be active for life. We might think it is inclusive because we differentiate lessons, but inclusion should run deeper than that. How can we ensure every student has the confidence, competence, and motivation to be active for life? To find out more, we decided to find out why some adults and young people don't engage in physical activity, and why there are so many negative perceptions of PE. We found it is engrained in the history of the subject. Parents or staff recall being forced to do PE in socks and pants or having to do cross country while the teacher holds an umbrella in one hand and a coffee in the other. Responses from adults included, 'I wasn't one of the sporty ones', 'PE wasn't for me' and, 'I couldn't wait to never have to do PE again'. This has a knock-on effect to children today, as these negative perceptions and experiences are passed down from parent to child and from staff in school who belittle the subject by perceiving it to be dispensable'.

Like many schools, the focus on younger students was to prepare for GCSE PE. Evans reflected, 'A few years back, we were instructed to redesign our trust KS3 curriculum with a focus on 'GCSE ready'. I was part of a planning team that used GCSE PE criteria to assess students' practical ability from Year 7. The more we planned, the more disillusioned I became. How is assessing a Year 7 child against near impossible criteria going to instil confidence? Will it motivate or demotivate them? By being a part of this process, I was becoming part of the problem, and was never going to stop the negative perceptions of the subject.'

Frustrated at the view many had about PE, Evans asked his team two questions: 'What do people think we teach in PE? Answers included fitness, sport skills etc. What do we know that we teach in PE? Answers included so much more to the above. E.g.: leadership, teamwork, how to look after bodies and minds, resilience, independence, relationship building etc.' This frustration grew. 'We thought that the 'physical' in Physical Education had actually become a limitation. PE is so much more than what people think. If we truly wanted to change perceptions of PE, then we needed to change the name and change the conversation surrounding the subject. We played with lots of words and combinations and came up with Healthy Active Lifestyles because it encompasses our intent for the subject. We wanted to take a health-based approach, focusing on physical, mental and social well-being, so students know how to look after their health well-being for the rest of their lives, all taught through physical activity.'

Evans and his team set about re-branding the subject to focus on what they believed PE was truly about, moving away from the negative connotations associated with the traditional form of PE, and creating their new Healthy Active Lifestyles subject. 'I didn't want the rebrand to be the same offer with a different name. It had to look different, not just sound different. The focus is on developing physical, mental, and social well-being.

- Year 7 the focus is physical well-being.
- Year 8 the focus is mental well-being.
- Year 9 the focus is social well-being.

In truth, all years concentrate on all 3 types of well-being, but we emphasise those mentioned above in our delivery. Each year is split into different knowledge topics, linking to the assigned well-being, and paired to a physical activity or sport. The knowledge topic is taught through the activity or sport. For example, one Year 8 unit titled, 'the psychology of winners' may be linked to basketball. Students are taught how psychology can impact their performance in sport, but with links to everyday life by improving mental health and enabling us to be successful in all areas of life. This has required lots of staff CPD and sharing of experiences to support each other to teach in this new way.

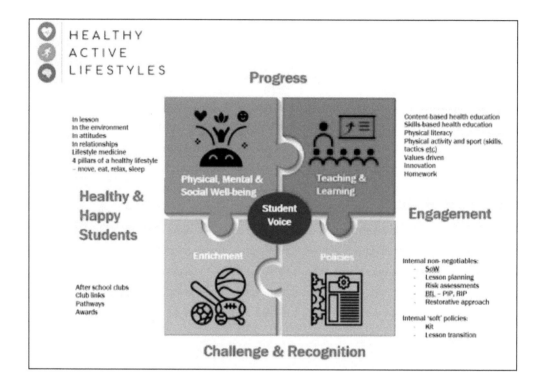

Evans continues, 'At the time of the rebrand to Healthy Active Lifestyles, I oversaw a whole school project to promote Healthy Active Lifestyles across the curriculum. I shared a vision and need for all staff to promote health and well-being. We are teachers of literacy and numeracy, but we are also all teachers of life, and have a responsibility to support students to be happy, as well as to achieve academic success. I led a group of teachers from other subjects to include health and well-being in some capacity. This helped raise the profile of Healthy Active Lifestyles, as students would hear about it on a daily basis.'

NINESTILES, AN ACADEMY

HEALTHY ACTIVE LIFESTYLES

What is Healthy Active Lifestyles?

Healthy Active Lifestyles is our brand new subject at Ninestiles, An Academy. The aim of the subject is to use physical activity to develop physical, mental and social well-being, and to teach students how to live long, healthy and happy lives.

Cases of obesity and diabetes are on the rise and for the first time in history, children have a lower life expectancy than than their parents. Healthy Active Lifestyles aims to teach students how to look after their health and well-being effectively. We will teach students the importance of exercise to improve:

- Physical well-being (e.g fitness, exercise, sports skills etc)

- Mental well-being (e.g. independence, resilience, stress relief, challenge)

- Social well-being (e.g. teamwork, leadership, developing friendships, communication)

Students will also learn the importance of diet and how to combine diet with exercise to fully lead a healthy lifestyle.

We will also support you, the parents and guardians of our students, to live healthy lives at home.

This is a really exciting initiative which has been recognised by Sport England and the Youth Sport Trust. We look forward to working with you and your children.

Healthy Active Lifestyles vs PE

Healthy Active Lifestyles is an inclusive and modern PE department. While we still focus on sporting excellence, we ensure our lessons are fun and engaging for all students, regardless of ability, so every child can have a positive experience of sport and exercise.

At Ninestiles, An Academy, we believe in health and well-being and the impact this can have on attainment. Across all years, we teach students how to live long, healthy and happy lives, rather than just how to improve performance in sport. Even at KS4, when students are under pressure from exams, we will still provide opportunities for students to be active as this is a valuable way to relieve stress.

When reflecting of the impact this subject re-brand has had, Evans said 'A whole school approach to health and well-being supported an increase in attendance, behaviour and happiness. Increases in extra-curricular attendance (84% to be precise). A focus on healthy active lifestyles has improved attainment and attitudes in all subjects who participated in the whole school project, especially boys with behavioural issues. Students are more active outside of lessons and school staff, students, and parents have a greater understanding about how important this subject is. I'm still working on making it bigger and better – but one step at a time.'

There is no doubt that re-branding the subject entirely is a drastic change; however, the logic behind this move is completely sound. As Evans identified, many key stake holders had negative views on the subject, and this was impacting the subject's ability to make a meaningful impact. Evans was frustrated, like so many are, that PE is linked with sport alone, and, in reality, the 'what' of PE is so much more than just that. Therefore, as with Ninestiles Academy, a move away from the tarnished label of PE and towards a more all-encompassing title is a beneficial one.

Whether it's changing the focus of your lessons, or re-branding the subject completely, the opportunity for change is undeniable. Shanise Webster, Head of PE in Central London, recognised the prospect of a brighter future for all connected to our subject: 'I feel that, due to Covid-19, not only are schools/students/parents and the government finally paying attention to the vital part that physical activity plays in our overall health as a nation, but that there is a need (now more than ever) for Physical Education to do what it says on the tin – educate our young people on how to stay healthy, active and happy. Physical Education practitioners should be ensuring students leave school having had positive experiences so that they go on to lead active lifestyles beyond their educational journey. For this reason, I think PE and school sport is changing so that students can 'find' their preference, and experience a range of ways of keeping fit in the outside world – not just traditional games'.

Realising the impact of Covid-19 on the fitness levels of students, and the desire to improve engagement, Webster looked to her extra-curricular offering and how this could better meet the needs of her students, introducing a number of extra-curricular initiatives to change attitudes towards PE and physical activity. 'We try to increase participation levels, in particular for girls, by including an element of choice in our after-school clubs. An example of this is the Girls Active Club, where students decide on the day what activity they would like to do – anything from benchball to cardio-trampolining. This increases enjoyment for the students and, in my opinion, replicates life after school. It hopefully strengthens the positive bond that they build with exercise, and promotes the understanding that keeping active isn't just achieved by joining a sports team. I have also introduced a student leadership programme into the PE department. Students have to complete an application form and then, if selected, go through to interview. We have a PE Ambassador for each PE class Year 7-Year 10 (4 girls, 4 boys per year group). They complete leadership training 2-3 times a year, take part/volunteer their help within the local community, and are role models within the school. They get to wear a PE Ambassador badge on their school blazer, and also have a PE Ambassador PE kit which is different to the main PE kit. We also run an annual PE Ambassador 'Olympic Legacy' trip to the London Stadium as a reward'.

Like Webster, leaders are now reflecting on their extra-curricular programmes and how to engage more students with sport and physical activity outside of school. Whilst school fixtures form an important part of a majority of extra-curricular offerings, schools are considering how many students these benefit, and how to ensure more students participate in physical activity outside of lesson time.

Personalising the Curriculum

The sports and activities that are on offer in our curriculums are as important as the concepts we decide to deliver. Even with the inclusion of conceptual learning, if a student hates a particular sport, it will have no positive impact to their enjoyment of PE.

From the findings in Sport England's report *Under the Skin*, it is fair to say that sport is not for everyone. Departments should look to offer a range of activities that meet the requirements of the National Curriculum, but also engage every personality type. This is not an easy task. A varied range of activities from sport to social fitness and goal setting to personal development will need to form your offering.

Use the Sport England report in a team meeting and ask staff to select which personality they are and reflect on students that might meet the criteria of each category. Brainstorm as to what activities and teaching approach would best suit each personality, and what is feasible for your team to deliver. One thing is for certain – we must move away from delivering only traditional sports. Those days are gone, and we must adapt and bring our curriculum into the times in which we live and work.

Whilst traditional sports work for some, we must be flexible and innovative when accommodating to the needs of all students. Remember your team's 'why', and the likelihood that it includes learning for all students and not just the exceptional few.

Fiona Reynolds and I spent a few months researching, presenting, discussing, tweaking, finalising and then tweaking some more what we called our 'Personality Pathway'. We wanted to provide some autonomy to students by which they could select their own curriculum, based on their own personal motivations for engaging in physical activity. We were aware, not only through Sport England research, but from our own student voice as well, that not everyone was motivated to engage in physical activity for the same reasons, as the responses from our student survey demonstrate below:

23. What motivates you to be physically active? (You can choose multiple answers)

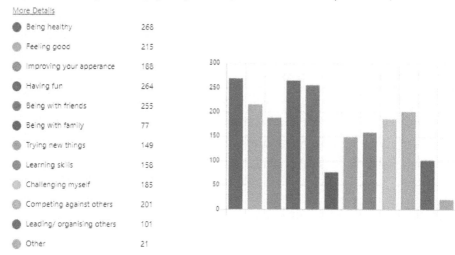

More Details

Being healthy	268
Feeling good	215
Improving your apperance	188
Having fun	264
Being with friends	255
Being with family	77
Trying new things	149
Learning skills	158
Challenging myself	185
Competing against others	201
Leading/ organising others	101
Other	21

Whilst Fiona and I led on this part of our curriculum, more specifically the second practical lesson of the week, it was important that the rest of the team had numerous opportunities to get involved. Fiona discusses how we went about creating and implementing our Personality Pathway below:

'Before we could do anything, it was really important that I fully understood what Lee had in mind when he spoke about personalising our curriculum. Having read the research and talked it through with Lee, he asked me to present it to the team. This was something I had not done before and felt nervous, as I knew I would receive questions and therefore had to become an expert. I now look back and realise how important this step was in consolidating my own understanding about how students are motivated differently to want to engage in PE lessons, and the importance of this step in getting the rest of the team to buy into our vision. I prepared a presentation and placed the key characteristics of each of the 6 youth personalities around the room and asked the teachers to stand by the personality that best matched their own. Not surprisingly, we had PE teachers stood next to 'sport enthusiast' and 'everyday youth', as they represented the characteristics one might expect from people that have chosen a sport-focused career. I then asked the team to write down the name of students in our classes that might demonstrate the characteristics of each personality. Fortunately for me, the team had already done a lot of strategic work around a concept-driven approach, so I did not need to sell the idea that a sport-driven model was not meeting every student's needs.

Once the team had understood the different motivators for participation, and identified students that they could associate with these motivators, we could start planning our curriculum. There was no doubt that despite, all our best intentions, the biggest challenges were always around logistics. We spent most of our time not discussing the most suitable activities to offer, as you might expect, but how students would select them, what we could realistically offer with facilities, the equipment we owned or would need to buy (or that our budget could afford), and timetabling. We decided to start with our highest priority students, or those mostly likely to become disengaged in PE, our Key Stage 4 (ages 13-16) students.

In Key Stage 4, we have three teachers on at a time, giving us the scope to offer three pathways. Therefore, we decided to partner the youth personalities with another that best shared common characteristics. We were aware that this model was not perfect; however, it would still provide autonomy, and allow us to better shape the delivery, depending on some, if not all characteristics. We partnered the following personalities together:

- Sports Enthusiasts with Ambitious Self-Starters
- Everyday Youths and Confident Intellectuals
- Cautious Introverts and Thoughtful Improvers

From here, taking into account our own logistical constraints, such as facility availability (we lose some teaching space due to exams), seasonal aspects of activities (weather), and any other barriers we thought of, we started placing activities we felt best matched the personalities. We had a list of activities for each three categories. We then used a similar survey to that used by Sport England when gaining their data. We decided not to inform the students of their personality type, as we also understood the limits to this research. Students were only informed on completion of this survey of the pathway they had been allocated.

We also had to decide on how each pathway was delivered. Therefore, we decided to research model-based approaches that we felt might be suited to each pathway. For our sports enthusiasts that are motivated by competition, and the ambitious self-starters that enjoy socialising, we settled on a Sports Education model. Students would be placed into teams and would be awarded points for successfully fulfilling certain roles within that team. A more health and well-being-focused model was considered for our cautious introverts and thoughtful improvers.

Students were given another student voice survey, for which they could identify activities and sports that they might be interested in pursuing. We took these suggestions and placed them into categories we felt matched each pathway. These categories were presented to each pathway, and they selected their preferred four options, which then created their year curriculum. This method ultimately meant that the team had to remain flexible with their planning, and to try not to influence student choice based on teaching preference. It also meant that for one-year group their pathway one might look completely different to the pathway one of another year group.

At first, we wanted the students to remain on the same pathway chosen at the start of the year throughout the year, though we did find that some students wanted to change at the start of a new term. So far, as of writing, we have asked students to remain on the pathway they have chosen. We believe that the pathway should be selected based on what motivates them, and not because of a particular activity that they might enjoy. I certainly understand the arguments for and against, but this is the decision we made on this occasion.

Overall, I am really proud of what we have achieved in creating this part of our curriculum offering. Whilst it is not perfect, and will always change due to the requirements of the various cohorts, the reasoning behind it is sound. I look forward to finding out the student feedback when we send out our next round of student voice surveys".

Whilst Fiona and I accept that what we have presented to you above is not the finished article, it is very much an exciting and rewarding work in progress. At the time of writing, we are working on implementing the trial of a personality pathway at Key Stage 3 (ages 10-12), which of course comes with its own logistical challenges. We have observed student engagement and enjoyment increase, and off-record conversations with students would echo these sentiments. It is our hope that through constant trial, error, feedback, and improvements we will eventually have a Personality Pathway that supports the delivery of a positive and meaningful PE experience, far more than a sport-driven model ever could.

After teaching in state schools in outer London for seven years, Alice Curwood made the jump and moved to Kuala Lumpur, Malaysia, to teach in the Alice Smith School. A year after joining, Curwood was promoted to Head of Curriculum PE.

Echoing the thoughts of many regarding the impact PE is having, Curwood said, 'In both my own experience as a child, and my early years of teaching, I have seen many students disengage with the subject, especially teenage girls. When PE is delivered as sport, and attainment focuses on performance, often students of lower ability switch off. If a student's PE experience evolves from enjoyment, challenge, variety, and opportunity, they are more likely to have a positive learning experience and attitude towards the subject. PE is bigger than physical competence and confidence. We are a subject in which core values are part of our daily practice. Within lessons, in addition to the role of a participant, students also coach, lead, officiate, problem solve, develop literacy and numeracy skills, and self and peer reflect'.

Curwood realised that PE can be so much more than its dominant form of delivery: 'Transferable skills students learn through PE, such as decision making, collaboration, communication, and independent thinking are vital to any career path our students choose to take. It is our job to make them see this and its importance. PE plays a massive role in working alongside sport in developing students' personal and social skills, which can inspire physical skills, not necessarily just the other way around. The focus of a lesson needs to move away from the quality of performance and perfecting a skill; instead, it should create an environment where students feel confident enough to try something new. Suppose a student leaves each lesson, having tried something challenging or learned something new, whether physical, personal, or social. In that case, they can begin to identify how our subject can have a positive, individualised impact, regardless of physical ability'.

Following concerns that students were not particularly engaging with the prescribed activities in Key Stage 4 (age 13-16), Curwood sought change. Wanting to provide autonomy and a more student-focused approach, the team created pathways to provide more choice. Curwood spoke about how she implemented this change and incorporate three pathways (performance, participation and aesthetic pathways) into the curriculum: 'Before launching the pathways, we finalised together as a team across several meetings, where we discussed what to offer where, how many per term and balance of facilities, avoiding clashes across pathways, etc. Students make a choice for a term at a time, and can move across pathways dependent on the activities on offer. For example, a GCSE student who is a netball player may choose the performance pathway in Term 2, having previously followed the aesthetic pathway in Term 1. Naturally, our GCSE students are pulled towards the performance pathways, though it is not forced on them. We found our top sportsmen and women enjoyed using their CORE PE lesson as downtime and to try something new. One of our students, who was representing the Welsh international football team, commented on how the yoga, stretching and mobility option helped her rest and recovery following a busy weekly schedule of high intensity training. The Performance Pathway suits students who want to access competitive activities, focusing on improving performance and skill development, essentially physical competence and confidence. This pathway is often accessed by students that have established a very positive relationship with PE already, for example, GCSE PE students. The Participation Pathway focuses on different ways of being active and healthy, while creating positive exercise and activity habits. Students have the opportunity to try alternative sports and activities not previously offered in lessons at Key Stage 3 (KS3). Finally, the Aesthetic Pathway is for learners who wish to be challenged through personal and more creative forms of movement while trying to create positive exercise and activity habits'.

KS4 PHYSICAL EDUCATION - CURRICULUM MAP - PATHWAYS

	PERFORMANCE PATHWAY	PARTICIPATION/ ALTERNATIVE PATHWAY	AESTHETIC/ CREATIVE PATHWAY
THE ALICE SMITH SCHOOL KUALA LUMPUR MALAYSIA EST 1946	Predominantly GCSE PE students and OEAON competitors. Those who want competitive activities with the focus on performance improvement.	Those wanting to remain physically active without competition or a focus on quality of performance but rather a focus on remaining active and healthy, going on to acquire habit for life. Want to try other sports/activities not previously offered in lessons at KS3	Those who wish to be challenged through aesthetic activities. Students who enjoy individual activities with an emphasis on health and fitness/exercise for life.
Term 1 (August - December)	RUGBY TOUCH FOOTBALL VOLLEYBALL	CROSSFIT BADMINTON FUTSAL HANDBALL	DANCE YOGA SYNCHRONIZED SWIMMING WATER AEROBICS
Term 2 (January - March)	BASKETBALL NETBALL SOFTBALL/CRICKET TENNIS/BADMINTON	CROSSFIT WATER VOLLEYBALL/KAYAKING WATER POLO SHORT TENNIS/TABLE TENNIS	BOXERCISE SPINNING TRAMPOLINING AEROBICS
Term 3 (April - July)	SWIMMING TRAMPOLINING ATHLETICS FITNESS	CROSSFIT BASKETBALL/NETBALL BADMINTON/SQUASH MINI TEAM	ZUMBA CHEERLEADING GYMNASTICS DANCE FIT

In order to facilitate this offering, Curwood considered staff expertise: 'I asked staff to give their first and second preference of pathways they would like to facilitate. I encouraged the team to consider both their speciality and a personal challenge to lead on an activity they have little or no previous experience with. I found staff were excited by this if opportunity was provided to support. For example, I delivered the performance pathway in Term 1 with our rugby specialist, and was able to take away several drills and practices to use in my KS3 girls' lessons when delivering touch for the first time. If staff can see the benefits of this transfer, and are provided with time to develop their own confidence in its delivery, I find them much more responsive than sending them on a course in their own time. Making the changes tangible for the team is key to gaining their 'buy in''.

Discussing the impact of this personalised shift in PE delivery, Curwood said: 'Students feel listened to and are more comfortable in the PE environment. Students in Year 10 and 11 either excusing themselves from PE or not bringing their kit has become a rarity, rather than a weekly occurrence. We have seen students enjoy an activity and take it up in their own time. For example, following a six week Zumba and aerobics unit, a Year 10 student signed up to fitness classes at the gym with her Mum and attends twice a week'. Students also provided their feedback:

- Student 1: 'There was little pressure from teachers, I didn't have the stress of trying to perform to attain a certain level, and we as students could decide as a majority what sport we'd like to do, so it was nice to have that choice. I also enjoyed the fact that we were grouped based on our preferences and not our skill levels as it gave me the chance to play against a variety of players'.
- Student 2: 'The fact that we had a choice about what sports we got to play. Compared to other years where I felt forced to do things I didn't like and it made me not like PE much. This year I genuinely look forward to it.'
- Student 3: 'They introduced sports such as crossfit and dance, which were not on offer last year and there was a wider variety of activities to choose.'

There is no doubt that offering a personalised curriculum takes planning and constant tweaking but, if done effectively, it can have a huge impact on engagement, enjoyment and attitudes towards physical activity.

Designing Your Curriculum

PE has the unique opportunity to offer so much more than simply competitive and performance-driven lessons. We have the capacity to be the most important subject on the school timetable. Physical literacy is already deemed by many to be as important as literacy and numeracy. Students must feel and see first-hand the connections between PE, enjoyment, and personal development. They need to understand its place in their lives now, and for the future, and it is down to us communicate this message...which leads on nicely to the 'why' of our curriculum.

Grant Huddleston and colleague Angela Whitehouse from Birmingham City University have developed a model that supports leaders when planning their curriculum; they call it the SPACE model. This stands for: specifics, pedagogy, assessment, curriculum and extra-curricular.

'Firstly, we believe there is no such thing as a 'perfect' curriculum. Whilst Ofsted has created these indicators, what one school does can be very different to another, for a number of reasons. Staffing, facilities, resources, location, pupils and personal philosophy are just some of the factors that can influence what curriculum a school offers; a school must create a curriculum that is effective specifically for itself.'

Their SPACE model poses reflective questions that enable departments to fully reflect on all that they offer in relation to PE. The SPACE model can be seen below:

SPECIFICS – Specific to your school, your staff, your pupils, your facilities, your ethos/philosophy.

- What PE, sport or play facilities do you have access to? How are you using them?
- What is the PE ethos of the school?
- What is the confidence, competence and experience of the staff who teach PE?
- What are the specific needs of the pupils in PE?
- How does what you are offering meet pupils' PE learning needs? How do you know?
- How does your PE curriculum allow all pupils to access the content and make progress?
- Do PE subject leaders have clear roles and responsibilities for curriculum design and delivery? What does this look like?
- How is your PE curriculum delivery equitable and appropriate for all groups?
- When and where do subject leaders ensure PE interventions are appropriately delivered to enhance pupils' capacity to access the full curriculum?
- How does the PE curriculum provide parity for all groups of pupils?

PEDAGOGY – Your approach to delivering your offer and the associated knowledge and understanding behind it.

- What PE pedagogical approaches will you attach to your curriculum?
- Are all staff who teach PE confident and competent in delivering PE lessons with a range of PE pedagogical approaches?
- What value do you place on providing a variety of approaches when teaching PE?

- How do your approaches promote learning in PE lessons?
- How do your approaches promote lifelong learning and are they inclusive?
- How do you know if PE subject leaders have the knowledge, expertise and practical skill to design and implement an effective PE curriculum?
- How and when do school leaders ensure ongoing professional development is available for staff to ensure that PE curriculum requirements can be met?

ASSESSMENT – Your assessment of pupils, staff and the effectiveness of your approach

- Do you promote a holistic model of assessment within PE?
- Does it promote the whole child learning across all domains of learning (cognitive, social, affective, and psychomotor)?
- How do you ensure progression in PE is being made across all areas of the PE curriculum?
- How much input will pupils have in their own learning?
- When do leaders (at all levels, including governors) regularly review and quality assure the subject to ensure it is implemented sufficiently well? What measures are put in place to support subject leaders if it isn't?
- Is your assessment in PE excessive or onerous, or is it manageable?
- How do you know if your assessments in PE are reliable?
- What impact is your assessment model having on your pupils' motivation in PE lessons?
- What impact is your assessment model having on your pupils' progress in PE lessons?

CURRICULUM – Your offer of PE at your school.

- What activities will you offer and how do you rationalise this? Do all staff understand this rationale?
- Does your curriculum cover all areas of PE and how broad a range of activities and learning are you offering?
- How will you ensure progress across year groups/Key Stages and does your mapping support this?
- How do curriculum leaders understand important concepts related to

curriculum design, such as knowledge progression and sequencing of concepts?

- How, when, and where do you incorporate resources into planning and teaching, and for what effect?
- Is your curriculum ambitious and does it have sufficient depth and coverage of knowledge and skills, including centrally prescribed aims?
- How do you know that your curriculum offer delivery is the same as that which is planned?
- How will you ensure the curriculum is successfully implemented to ensure pupils' progression in knowledge and skills?
- If secondary, will you include links to qualification PE (e.g.: GCSE PE) during PE, and how will you justify this?

EXTRA-CURRICULAR – Your offer of sport and physical activity at your school.

- What physical activity and sport do you offer outside of your timetabled PE lessons?
- If primary, what unstructured physical play opportunities do you offer outside of your PE lessons?
- Does your extra-curricular offer align with your curriculum activities?
- What other ways do you promote physical activity and sport outside of lesson learning?
- Do you link to any local clubs, allowing pupils to move on to the next step?
- What school sport do you offer? How do you select who plays/represents the school?
- Does your curriculum offer align with school sport and wider participation opportunities, e.g.: School Games and leagues?
- Who takes responsibility for promoting your extra-curricular offer?
- (Huddleston and Whitehouse, 2020).

Erickson (Curriculum and Instruction for the Thinking Classroom, 2007) looks more specifically at how to support your team once the curriculum has been designed and implemented. She offers the following guidance to leaders:

- Create a community of learner's climate.
- Listen to what teachers have to say about implementing the curriculum

(support, resources, time, etc.).

- Brainstorm and discuss ideas as to what a concept-driven classroom (or practical lesson, in our case) looks like.
- Identify team members who can assist others in the implementation of a concept-driven lesson plan.
- Plan ways for teachers to support each other (peer observations, coaching, meetings, additional training, etc.).
- Allow time in meetings for collaborative planning and discussions. Offer as many opportunities to collaborate as possible.
- Encourage reflective problem solving to address problems with implementations.
- Provide weekly bulletins to recognise achievement and support for future planning.
- Inform the community regarding best practice and learning opportunities.

(Erickson, 2007).

Shaun Dowling kindly shared the planning that went into the design of United Learning's PE delivery, and is a prime example of keeping your team, school, or Trust's values at the heart of your vision. Dowling is Head of Sport at United Learning, a group of over 80 academy and independent schools across England. His role is to support the subject leaders in each of those schools in delivering the best possible physical education, school sport and physical activity (PESSPA) provision they can for their students, whilst also enabling departments to collaborate, share, and learn from each other. The Group has extensively reviewed and updated their PE offering to better meet the needs of their students and deliver positive and meaningful PE experiences for all.

Dowling, and the PE leaders across the Group, understood the need to be clear about their vision for PE when starting out in the creation of their curriculum and assessment models in 2015. Dowling explains, 'We had two main starting points: firstly, what are the Group values that we can drive through Physical Education; and secondly, what is our vision for Physical Education? At the time, we heard from respected partners such as AfPE and Youth Sport Trust (YST), and read about the models they were forming. In particular, we studied AfPE's 'Head, Hands, Heart' model and YST's 'Thinking Me, Social Me, Healthy Me' approach within their My Personal Best resource. Both aligned with our determination to produce a curriculum framework that was outcomes driven. In doing so, PE departments could adapt the framework to meet their school's specific culture, history, facilities, and teacher strengths, and all of the other variables which determine any one PE department's unique offer.'

Dowling shares the thought processes he and his team went through when designing their provision: 'United Learning has 6 core values, so we began by exploring what they would look like in PE. The ambition was that United Learning's values would be brought to life through high-quality Physical Education, sport, and health-promoting physical activity, so that every young person is:

- Ambitious – to excel: to be the best they can be in and through PE and sport.
- Confident – to participate, perform and lead.
- Creative – in their decision making and in finding solutions to increasingly complex challenges.
- Respectful – of themselves, of all their peers and all adults involved in their sporting life, whether they be teachers, coaches, officials, medical staff, etc.
- Enthusiastic – about engaging in physical activity and sport in school, out of school and beyond school life.
- Determined – to persist in overcoming obstacles, to lead healthy lifestyles, and to achieve their best.

Having been clear that we wanted the curriculum to be outcome driven, we had to be clear about what those more tangible outcomes would be. In doing so, the Working Group settled upon a three-strand approach: performance, health and leadership.

1. Our KS3 Physical Education (PE) and Health curriculum will bring out 'the best in everyone' by developing physically skilful young people who have developed the skills, knowledge, understanding, character, and confidence to prepare them for KS4 PE.
2. Our PE and Health curriculum will enable our young people to forge a positive lifelong relationship with physical activity and sport.
3. Our PE and Health curriculum will prepare students thoroughly for the rigours of accredited courses in KS4 and beyond, through a knowledge and understanding of relevant and appropriate elements of sport science.
4. Such is our commitment to developing generic leadership/employability

skills in young people through PE and sport, our ambition is to enable achievement of our KPIs in Years 7, 8 and 9 to be recognised with a bronze, silver, and gold 'Fit to Lead' award. Furthermore, students in Year 9 who opt to undertake a further assessment can achieve a 'Fit to Lead' qualification.

'Outcome 1 became the 'Fit to Perform' strand; Outcomes 2 and 3 became the 'Fit for Life' strand; and Outcome 4 became the 'Fit to Lead' strand. These are probably best summarised through this diagram:'

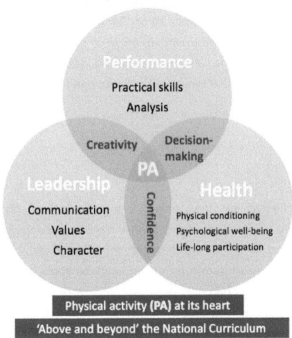

The final outcome provides a common, unique United Learning curriculum framework, but one with sufficient flexibility for the traditions and cultures of each school to be retained and celebrated. The simplicity and flexibility of the framework was important for United Learning, as they knew each school was unique and would have to apply it to their own context.

Dowling also understood the need to listen to the students. He explained, 'As departments implemented this through the first three years, they constantly revised their provision and how they interpreted the framework to best fit the needs of their students. During this time, nearly 40 secondary academies were invited to participate in Sport England's Secondary Teacher Training (STT) programme. This enabled a large Group-wide survey of over 6,500 students in 2019 to inform both the network as a whole, and specific schools, of what students thought of their experiences in PE, school sport, and physical activity throughout the school day. Three main themes emerged that PE departments needed to improve further:

1.   Students wanted more choice in PE.
2.   Students wanted more variety in PE and school sport.
3.   Students wanted greater gender equality in PE, school sport, and physical activity.

Although Covid-19 interrupted a lot of planned CPD, sufficient training was able to take place to enable PE departments to improve the quality of their teaching and breadth of provision. When the survey was repeated in 2020, the following percentage of students reported that those three priority areas had improved respectively:

1.   72%
2.   74%
3.   77%

Dowling reflected on the 'activities that had been particularly popular additions, including orienteering, table tennis, handball, trampolining, and Parkour. PE departments and students reported that the more health-promoting activities, which had been prioritised during lockdown, such as yoga, exercise to music and fitness/exercise challenges had also been well received. Some PE departments are planning to include these activities in curriculum time and/or in their co-curricular provision as schools return to normal in 2021. In addition, several PE departments made effective use of digital solutions, especially using gamification tools, apps, and online competitions, all of which could have a role to play as PE departments design their new curricula.'

Dowling continued, 'In doing so, more schools are having to re-consider how they provide for students throughout the school day, and also support them in being active outside of school. Again, this is where the lessons learned about digital solutions could have a part to play. Previously, apart from 'pick-up' games in the playground, physical activity sessions before, during or after the school day, largely required adult supervision – not always possible or desirable. In future, however, physical activity could be taking place and logged/evidenced without the need for such supervision, getting changed or specialist facilities. With so many children not meeting the CMO's recommended levels of daily physical activity, PE departments can be providing students with activity timetables with a menu of options for them on every day of the week. Links to YouTube channels or schools' own shared areas can enable children, especially those not attracted to team games, to be more active on more days of the week.

'The need to develop skilled individuals who have mastered key learning remains a critical component of PE. These foundations are crucial for confidence, progression, and lifelong participation – none of which are mutually exclusive. Standards in the fundamental movement skills have to be high in order for young people to be able to access sports and activities which require the application of those skills to more complex situations. Deliberate practice to ensure that schema are stored securely in long-term memory remains a core part of the learning process in PE. What we are learning, however, is that sport-driven curricula appeal to only part of the student population. If PE has the ambition of enabling young people to be truly Fit for Life, then the needs of all children need to be met, not just those for whom formal sport is part of their identity. Health and well-being activities, personal exercise and fitness activities, street sports, online competitions and a host of other modern and exciting activities can be skilfully added to students' experiences of PE – some more easily than others, and most requiring additional training needs, but, if the profession wants to reach all children, and enable all children to benefit from enjoyable, relevant and purposeful Physical Education, then change is needed'.

'At United Learning, we have been delighted with the results of the 2020 survey, but the progress made is still not sufficient. Those three priority areas remain areas for development, and new ones have emerged, especially around physical activity levels. We are beginning to revise our PE and Health Curriculum framework for September 2021, but the implementation of it in each school will be the critical variable in its success. Will our framework need to be more prescriptive? To what extent will the lessons learned during Covid-19 be formally included in the new framework? Will the three strands still be the driving forces of the new curriculum, or has a different or additional strand emerged? It will be fascinating to lead the Working Group on this new iteration of the United Learning PE and Health Curriculum, and to see how the 2021-2024 model impacts upon young people.'

The outstanding work of Dowling and his team have demonstrated real measurable impact. The collaborative nature of the planning and implementation, the simplicity and flexibility of the frameworks to permit bespoke application and ability to learn and adapt delivery continue to ensure that United Learning are able to better meet the needs of their students through Physical Education. The ability of the framework to deliver positive and meaningful PE, whilst keeping the traditions and values of sport, and the life lessons that can be delivered through it, is one example of the innovative thinking that is taking place around PE.

Application of Physical Literacy

By applying concepts to the sports and activities you had previously taught, and offering student autonomy, you will be able to better meet the conditions that would support the ability for students to develop their physical literacy. Physical literacy includes your emotional, physical, and mental engagement or, more simply, how you behave, think, and take part (IPLA, 2020).

At the heart of physical literacy is the motivation and commitment to be active. We are fundamentally offering a far more positive experience, in which student attitude, progress, and the transfer of conceptual learning is now the rewarded outcome. Student self-confidence and self-esteem are enhanced when appreciation is shown for effort and improvement (Whitehead, 2010).

The concept provides the knowledge and understanding, the sport provides the competence, the shift of focus and new success criteria provide the confidence, and all of these together ensure enjoyment. With enjoyment, as the evidence suggest, students are more likely to be motivated to participate in physical activity, thus, physical literacy is achieved. All because we changed the focus of our curriculum. We are enabling the highest possible quality of PE and school sport experiences, in order to motivate students and encourage them to be active in their own time (Harris & Cale, 2011).

Ed Lowe is a Director of Sport at St Columba's College in St Albans. Like many leaders, the enforced break, due to the pandemic, afforded him the time to consider his current curriculum and reconnect with his purpose and 'why'. 'Reflecting on how students responded to remote learning gave us – and hopefully them – a snapshot into the future as to whether they were suitably educated to cope with certain situations, as well as review the motivation of students to maintain physical activity.'

Lowe was hoping to shift the focus of the whole 'sporting' provision. The proposed shift included re-branding PE to, PE and Well-being, as he looked to develop a more positive education experience, focusing on concepts and personal qualities in order to achieve physical literacy. 'Ultimately, we are looking to achieve a better sports option that appeals to the greatest number of students, and equips them with a combination of physical intelligence and personal skills that are transferable within and outside of the subject.'

Lowe discusses some of the challenges he faced when leading this change: 'Whilst we have moved away from judging ourselves on results in competitive sport, there is still a misunderstanding with some parents (and members of the SLT) as to what constitutes 'success' in sport. Therefore, we have adapted what we offer and ensured our primary focus and aims are promoted more than ever.'

The geographic area in which the school is located is heavily focused toward competition, and Lowe recognised this pressure to perform: 'Whilst the experience of the pupils is the primary driver, there does need to be something we can hang our hat on in this very competitive market and influential area.' Despite these pressures, Lowe continued to deliver his vision and during the lockdown he and his team planned the shift from a performance to concept-driven approach to curriculum design.

Through virtual meetings, they made great progress and established an action plan: 'I am lucky that I have a couple of established staff that are avid podcast listeners who have been adopting and adapting their practice constantly through coaching specific forums, so they are attuned to change and self-improvement. There are also a couple of younger teachers who are keen to develop themselves. Therefore, I gave suggested reading, watching and listening, as well as summarising the main themes that are emerging and that I wanted to be considered.'

Lowe used the additional responsibilities held by some of his team to his advantage, with three Heads of House in major pastoral positions and two deputy Heads of House who were very much aligned with holistic development and personal qualities, the culture he was aiming to create.

Finally, Lowe reflected on the desired impact this will have on his department's ability to achieve physical literacy 'Lockdown demonstrated the often lack of motivation from a majority of students to exercise regularly. Through this shift in our delivery, we hope to instil a greater understanding and motivation surrounding lifelong engagement.'

As Ed Lowe and numerous educators experienced post first lockdown in 2020, activity levels amongst young people dropped dramatically. The number of children meeting the Chief Medical Officer's guidelines (of taking part in sport or physical activity for an average of 60 minutes or more every day) dropped from 47% to 19%. 43% were doing less than half an hour of activity, and a worrying 7% did nothing (Youth Sport Trust, 2020). To any physical educator that truly feels the traditional PE delivery supports the ability to nurture physical literacy, then surely these statistics say otherwise. As Lowe and his team identified, something had to change.

Another PE curriculum pioneer, and someone who understands the long-term impact that PE can have, is Sean Doyle. Starting as an unqualified PE technician in

2010 at Shenley Brook End School, Doyle progressed and gained Qualified Teacher Status and subsequently became the PE Team Leader in 2017.

Doyle said, when considering the current state of PE, 'There is a sea-change coming in the sector. The Covid-19 crisis has put a Health and well-being approach in the forefront of the minds of the public and, encouragingly, the UK Government. We absolutely must build on this in education to give some hope of developing a more active nation. The most recent 'rebuilds' of our education system – the 2019 OFSTED Inspection Framework and the 2020 Relationships and Sexual Health Education (RSHE) curriculum – all move in this direction, but the dots are yet to be fully joined up outside of the PE bubble: that High Quality Physical Education will contribute to students' cognitive, social and emotional well-being, just as much as the physical'.

During his time in Physical Education, Doyle has developed two points of clear understanding about our subject:

1. 'The pitches, courts and playgrounds of this country can be the most powerful environments for the holistic development of young people.
2. Not enough of these young people leave school feeling equipped to lead the healthy, active lives they are entitled to'.

Doyle reflected on a moment that troubled him and inspired him to seek change, 'Two students ran a 1500m race. A club runner barely breaks a sweat and puts in a mediocre time for their standard. Their often-sedentary peer takes 4 minutes longer, but covers the highest distance they ever had, and has clearly being working at a high intensity level throughout. We used to be obliged to assess that the lazy club runner had demonstrated high levels of progress because of the outcome achieved. This is not an acceptable model of assessment and can have a significant impact on the student and their family who rely on feedback to guide their children. Not being a 'PE person' can no longer be a tolerable justification for inactivity, and schools have a significant part to play in this'.

Doyle and his team went about 'tearing up the Key Stage 3 curriculum and started again. The first job was to empower our student voice. This experience isn't designed for the adults, so why should it be designed solely by the adults? We asked every one of our students from years 7 to 11 which attitudes, skills and knowledge they would want to leave school having acquired from their ideal PE curriculum. Overwhelmingly, and with an objective approach to the survey, it was the employability, psychological and transferable life-skills that featured most heavily. Confidence, determination, motivation, resilience, teamwork all outweighed sport specific skills.

In the more practically driven responses, health-related fitness concepts were more prevalent than those involved in invasion games and other sports. It became clear to us that our young people are instinctively driven to succeed in their environment, and will make positive choices if they feel part of the process'. The Happy, Healthy, Success curriculum was created with the aim of delivering clear learning outcomes and assessment points linked to the concepts identified by students.

	Commitment	Activity Levels	Effort	Heart Rate	Decision Making	Preparedness
YEAR 7	Motivation	Resilience	Expression	Nutrition	Empathy	Teamwork
	Sports Hall	Sports Hall 2	Gym	Fitness Suite	Astro	Hard Courts

	Integrity	Body Health	Enthusiasm	MVPA	Independence	Social
YEAR 8	Self Management	Individuality	Inspiring	Perserverance	Respect	Leadership
	Sports Hall	Sports Hall 2	Gym	Fitness Suite	Astro	Hard Courts

Clear routines were established: 'Our students know that when they enter the changing rooms, they are about to learn far more than how to shoot hoops or score goals. Reflection on the activities through plenaries is now a far more inclusive process, with even those who have struggled having a voice understanding how their effort and application has had an impact on them in more varied ways'.

Doyle offered an example of how his curriculum was delivered, and the power it possesses. The concept being taught was 'social benefits of sport' being delivered through Badminton. 'A looked-after Year 8 boy, relatively new to the school, but already with a reputation for causing disruption, becomes frustrated at a less able peer on his court. They are attempting to move into cooperative rallies. Having vented his frustration to the perplexed peer, he approaches the board: 'how can I enjoy this socially if he can't even play'. My response: 'wouldn't you both enjoy it more if you could help him to play?' seemed to resonate. He asked to go into the store cupboard and pulled out a plastic tennis racket for himself and his peer. 'Let's try this before we try badminton, it's much easier'. At the end of the lesson, the previously frustrated young man asked me to allow them to demonstrate to the group, making a big fuss over what he had taught his new mate.'

With this example, the power that concepts provide when delivering relevant and meaningful learning can be seen. Doyle listened to his students and shaped the curriculum around the learning they wanted, providing holistic development and equipping students to lead healthy and active lives.

A Fully Inclusive Curriculum

Those students that were already experienced and competent in sport continued to flourish in a sport-driven curriculum, whilst the majority of remaining students became disengaged. I argued previously that this curriculum model suited the 'elite'. With the addition of a concept driven approach, our remaining students are now able to access success not previously available to them. There is learning, progress and enjoyment to be had for all. This is further supported by our understanding of the different youth personalities and how to engage each of them.

In the last chapter, I presented the research from Sport England's Under the Skin report (2014) and identified an opportunity to use this information to support the planning of our curriculum or the groups in which the students are assigned.

I believe there to be two obvious ways in which to plan a curriculum, keeping youth personality and the research from Sport England in mind. First, departments can develop and distribute a survey to students, which would identify their personality and place them into a designated group. Based on their groupings, the activities best suited to their personality would be delivered. However, this would be complex and time consuming, as well as not giving students the autonomy that a world class curriculum should include.

The second and more viable option is for the department to plan pathways, focused to the needs of the personality types. These pathways would include activities suited to the categories, and students could select the pathway most suited to them. This would enable students to identify their own personality type and permit them the opportunity to select the activities they most enjoy. This would work best with Key Stage 4 students, for whom this research is designed.

When it comes to making PE inclusive for all, Dr Rachael Jefferson-Buchanan, currently lecturing at Charles Sturt University in Australia, took steps to ensure that girls received meaningful PE. Jefferson-Buchanan set out to 'feminise Physical Education', to ensure that girls were not put off physical activity through Physical Education.

Raising an important discussion surrounding concerns about girls' participation levels, which are in steep decline, Jefferson-Buchanan said, 'evidence shows that adolescent girls are far less likely to lead active lifestyles than their contemporary males'. Whilst discussing issues around the negative impact on health, Jefferson-Buchanan mentions, 'it can also affect the development of feminine self-confidence and self-esteem. If we continue to be unsuccessful in our attempts to inspire the majority of female students to participate in physical activity outside school (and beyond their scholastic years), then a review of what we teach must take place'.

Understanding the important role that teachers play, Jefferson-Buchanan argues that 'our responsibility as physical educators weighs heavily on our shoulders, since it is no exaggeration to say that we can positively or negatively influence a young woman's lifelong attitude towards physical activity. Physical Education experiences for some adolescent girls can become irrelevant, frustrating, and indeed prevent them from wanting to participate in sports activities beyond school'.

Whist realising that there was no perfect solution to meet each student's physical needs, Jefferson-Buchanan believes it is possible to raise the level of female participation through well-considered curriculum design. Whilst teaching at the International School of Geneva, Jefferson-Buchanan worked hard to 'feminise PE' by ensuring her curriculum was 'non-sexist, co-educational, and also flexible enough to enable female students from 14 years upwards to select physical activities with or without distinct gender bias'. By maintaining equal access to male-dominated sports at a younger age, Jefferson-Buchanan acknowledged the individual preferences towards certain activities that girls of 14 years and older displayed. Therefore, in order to cater for all abilities and gender interests, the following programme was developed:

Dates	Module A	Module B	Module C
Sept - Oct:	EITHER: Golf	OR: Aerobics & Steps	OR: Soccer
Oct - Dec:	EITHER: Squash	OR: Table Tennis	OR: Volleyball
Dec - Feb:	EITHER: Taekwondo	OR: Badminton	OR: Basketball
Feb - March:	EITHER: 10 Pin Bowling	OR: Stretching & Yoga	OR: Tchoukball
March - May:	EITHER: Golf	OR: Handball	OR: Track & Field
May - June:	EITHER: Tennis	OR: Softball	OR: Trampoline

'Students must choose one module (A, B or C) for each period given, to create their individual programmes of PE. Through choice, all students seem to gain a greater sense of ownership, and, more importantly, female motivation and attendance have greatly improved since implementing this type of curriculum'. Jefferson-Buchanan concludes, 'Physical Education should be inclusive and facilitate all students in their learning, be they female or male. We should consider the repercussions of excluding young women from male-dominated sports, and simultaneously offer them 'feminine' alternatives to a traditional games-orientated curriculum'.

Whilst inclusivity is a complex issue, and involves a wide range of factors, listening to our students and tailoring our curriculum accordingly is an important step to meeting the needs of all students. As Jefferson-Buchanan has demonstrated through her work, inequalities exist, and they must be addressed now before more students are turned off physical activity for life.

A vital component to creating positive and meaningful PE experiences for our students is inclusive pedagogy and the relationships we build with students. One teacher that is fully aware of the impact teachers can have on how students feel about physical activity and PE is Renee Gregerson, Physical Health and Education (PHE) Coordinator for the Surrey School District in British Columbia, Canada. Gregerson is an advocate for creating authentic and caring environments for students.

'Each student is unique, and recognising this as value and of importance strengthens the learning environment. This can be accomplished and supported by the educator's words, actions, enthusiasm, and through sharing their own personal challenges and accomplishments. But it's not enough just to tell a story or to encourage through words of affirmation. The student has to feel they matter, not only in the presence of the educator and their peers, but individually on their own. Building a sense of worth can be difficult, but it's not impossible.'

Moving beyond simple praise and encouragement, Gregerson believes that sharing our own vulnerabilities and struggles can enhance the student's connection to the subject. 'When the teacher offers small gestures, in the moments where the student makes a challenging decision that seemed out of reach days or weeks ago, this can have a big impact. Though I believe it's moments of authentic and wholehearted shared experiences of poor decisions, struggles and failures with expression of growth, and a new knowing of oneself that students connect with most. I share stories of how it felt being in high school, struggles I encountered, and how it changed my view on who I was. I allow my students to get a glimpse of what went on in my head and how I made sense of the moments.'

An important consideration is how our interactions with students support or hinder their ability to create meaningful connections with the subject, and therefore their longer-term attitudes towards physical activity. 'Words are not enough; it's the everyday interactions and connections that support and develop the intrinsic understanding of the 'why' of PHE'. To be genuinely inclusive, teachers should consider normalising all feelings and emotions, and promote positive habits and behaviours during class discussions. By role modelling openness towards these components of delivery, students will feel more comfortable and confident to engage in these aspects of learning.

Listen to Your Students

The statistical evidence regarding enjoyment and engagement levels, as well as the research presented regarding youth personalities and performance-focused assessment, might be surprising to some of us.

Have we been unaware of the changes, or in this case student opinions, evolving before our eyes? To create a truly bespoke curriculum, a department must listen to the opinions of its students. What do they love about PE? What do they dislike about PE? What would they want to improve? Or what would they like more of? Do they believe you are meeting your curriculum objectives? Do they know what these are? These are all important questions that might help shape what you offer, and therefore also the experiences of students within your school.

Completing face to face interviews with students, or conducting online surveys, are useful ways in which you can get a good feel as to the climate surrounding PE. Never feed individual negative comments back to staff, but always relay the positive. Handle and present the results of your findings carefully, and ensure, once any changes have been made to your curriculum following student feedback, that you let them know they helped shaped their own learning.

Physical Education Leader and Youth Sport Trust PE CatalYST, Paul Beeson, offered his experiences when moving to change PE within his school. 'We felt that the old National Curriculum levels and GCSE grading only really helped the more able students, and didn't reflect fairly on the work/efforts that all pupils were putting in. We also felt there was more to PE than just performance, and that this should be reflected in our curriculum and assessment as well. The key thing for us was to really put the students at the heart of our curriculum/assessment and ensure that all students could feel like valued members of the class that can still contribute and progress regardless of their practical ability.

It took a lot of research, two years of trial and error of new structures and models, and lots of leadership-level discussions, and then whole department discussions to ensure we were implementing something that we felt was best for our students, but also that staff were excited to teach. We trialled it first with a couple of classes, then got feedback from the teachers and students. Then we reviewed it, tweaked it, and repeated the process. After this, we implemented it with all KS3 classes, continued to update it, and now run it through all years 7-11. Each year we review it by getting feedback from all staff and students and the PE leadership team, then look at this feedback and discuss all of it, and apply any changes/consideration that we feel would benefit the students.'

The process of listening to the opinions of students was a key component when developing and evolving his PE offering. He went on to discuss the impact that this change has had: 'Feedback from staff and students has been positive. Students feel like they don't need to be good at sport to still feel like they are making progress in the lessons, whilst the more able, county and national standard athletes, still feel like they are being stretched practically and cognitively.'

Whilst the impact of the change was positive, Paul spoke of the need to re-train teachers in order to focus on concepts and not performance: 'For existing teachers, we held regular meetings and training sessions on what it might look like to run our new curriculum/assessment. We also created a bank of resources and objectives to give an idea of what it might look like. We then modelled it with some classes and allowed staff to observe us. Throughout the whole process, the key thing was that we were and are always looking to evolve. It is a fluid system that is constantly changing to suit staff and students, to the stage that it even changes from year group to year group to match them personally, rather than a one size fits all model.'

Developing a sports council or student PE leadership team is a great way to promote your subject to the student body, and also to gauge how students feel. Do be aware, however, that the students most likely to sign up to this initiative will be your sport enthusiasts, and therefore might not give you the sample of opinions you require, though these students will do a great job at promoting your subject in assemblies and representing you at open evenings.

Even simple changes, such as a department's approach to sanctioning, can have a big impact on culture and students' perceptions of our subject.

Taz Malhi reflected on his time in two secondary schools, and the impact PE had on engaging the disengaged. Malhi spoke of the unique intake of students at Wodensborough Ormiston Academy in Sandwell, with a Pupil Premium intake of over 50%: 'The majority of the students did not participate in any form of sport or fitness-based activities outside of school; therefore, the time in school was vital.'

The school followed the 1-9 levelling structure in all subjects and, although students were making some progress, it was clear that this was due to teacher inflation and not student improvement. Malhi opted to move to a concept-driven approach, looking at life skills over sport specific performance. The feedback provided through assessment was also personalised and focused on character building rather than sporting ability.

Malhi said, 'We still taught sports, but the focus was on the key skills concepts. As a result, of the personalised feedback, we could now interact the 14% EAL students, as the feedback comments could be translated, and the students could respond in their own language.' Malhi reflects on the impact the new concept-driven approach had: 'We went from averaging 30 students a day refusing to do PE, down to two-five.'

Malhi then left to take over as a PE second in department at Blue Coat Academy in Coventry. 'When I arrived, the PE delivery culture was sport-driven. Teaching-focused on coaching skills and levels 1-9 very similar to Wodensborough. Students did not enjoy PE, but with a strong behaviour policy they would turn up, though with little engagement. 'As the other 6 staff had never worked in another school, their understanding and pedagogical approach to PE was limited.

They struggled to comprehend the adaptations needed to support student engagement. They had used the same PE kit policy for 15 years, even though the catchment area of students had changed, and we had a bigger influx of deprived students. My first approach was to bring in spare PE kit with no punishment, as a result, we reduced the number of detentions and students' engagement levels increased.'

Malhi moved away from sanctions in order to create a more positive culture. Students would not associate PE with negativity and grow to further resent the subject through detentions. Whilst this transition is still on-going, behaviour issues have improved, students are far more engaged, and student feedback was positive. These once disengaged students have now embraced PE again.

In a very different context, Stewart Orton from Blessed George Napier School in Oxfordshire, attributed the increase in engagement and enjoyment in PE to moving to a concept-driven curriculum from one that focused purely on sport.

'It used to break my heart going into schools and looking at their PE assessment – a load of tick box sport specific skills and a curriculum/lessons totally designed to enable the teacher to assess them. Assessment was all sport skill specific – overhead clear, lay-up, top spin or forehand. We taught sports with lessons designed for us, not the pupils, so we could tick off our objectives – we called them teaching objectives, but they weren't – they were coaching objectives.'

Orton continued, 'Coaches might as well have been employed. The few students excellent at a broad range of sports did well and enjoyed it, but we were ignoring the majority. At the time, we were governed a 'this is how it's always been done' attitude. So many disillusioned pupils, especially girls, avoiding PE at all costs. A few years ago, I started designing 'concept' based curriculums and lessons to enable success and enjoyment. I always measure this against KS4 PE – when you reach the stage of total participation and enjoyment during KS4 lessons, you know you're doing something right! Pupils arriving from primary schools, especially nowadays, are generally enthusiastic, but the old ways would quickly knock the stuffing out of them. Now they realise that PE is for everyone – and all can succeed, be active and enjoy! We are really enthusiastic about sports leadership as well – it forms part of our curriculum from Y7 to Y13. Some of our most outstanding pupils are not the traditional best sports performers, but our sports leaders. Many go on to study PE and sport at University. That is a damn good feeling! Of course, we love our teams and individuals doing well in traditional sports, but we find if we get the enjoyment part right, success follows! I couldn't bear it, couldn't bear the fact that most students were switched off by Y9, especially girls, couldn't bear that if students thought themselves not sporty then PE wasn't for them, couldn't bear seeing excited and enthusiastic Y7's, become disinterested and switched off Y8/9's. So, we planted 'Sports Leadership' at the heart of the curriculum along with 'performance', which is generic: attack, defence, and decision making, not sport specific skills – although they are integrally taught, but not the focus. I have added 'Wider Knowledge and H and F and they form our 3 Intentions. Students are taught a wide range of PE topics that come under the 3 intents.'

'We use traditional sports and activities as our delivery vehicles, but we do not judge someone on how well they play football or netball. All students know exactly the key focus for their units (concepts), and understand it is against them that they will be assessed. They are then more relaxed, less anxious, more focused, active and enjoying. We still develop decent performers, both male and female, but this happens as a nice consequence. Most importantly, the large majority enjoy, engage with, access extra-curricular opportunities, and find room for physical activity in their lives. And, we hope, will continue to do so into adulthood.'

The PE Department was even recognised by Ofsted during an inspection, who in their report said, 'The school's work as a former sports college helps pupils develop appropriate attitudes to health and fitness, find a sport of choice, and understand the benefits of teamwork and competition.' Stewart concluded: 'I don't think any of this would be possible without our concept-based curriculum, and removing the pressure and anxiety many pupils feel about being judged on performing sport specific skills. It has raised the enjoyment levels immeasurably.'

If children and young people have positive experiences of physical activity, they are more likely to remain active. Removing the judgement around performance and replacing it with conceptual learning can achieve this aim, as proven by Orton and his Department.

The educational value that conceptual learning can bring to PE was something Kate Thornton-Bousfield wanted to capture when looking to shift from a performance-focused curriculum. Currently working for the Youth Sport Trust as the Head of PE and Achievement, Thornton-Bousfield taught at four schools, fulfilling departmental and pastoral roles. As a leader embarking on change, understanding her 'why' was important in order to realise her vision, and intended direction of travel. 'My mantra was always every child needed to leave school knowing what was going to keep them active – what they enjoyed, but also given the tools through the knowledge and understanding gained to lead a healthy active lifestyle'.

Discussing taking over as Head of Department in one school, Thornton-Bousfield commented: 'I inherited a very traditional department and experienced staff. The curriculum was activity and skills focused, but there was a range of activities on there. I wanted to move to a more in-depth curriculum, longer units, and deeper learning. I wanted to move to a concept-based curriculum, rather than activities. It really was a step-by-step approach. Too much too fast and I would have lost the department. I would trial things with some teachers to get their buy in and support and honesty before we went to full scale adoption of changes to practice and pedagogy. I was fortunate that the National Curriculum changed during my time as Head of Department, so this helped me structure my approach.

Thornton-Bousfield led a move towards more sport specific concepts, as well as practical skills already being delivered: 'We looked at delivering concepts through an area of activity based on what learners needed to know, do and understand. Learning through concepts and skills that were transferable, e.g.: decision making; teamwork; leadership; independent learning; creativity; self-reflection. We would also have a 'skill' through which they would focus on; acquire, develop, identify, apply, analyse, compare and contrast, evaluate etc.'

'The impact over time was significant. Engagement of learners and teachers dramatically improved. Learners became more accomplished, they could transfer skills across activities, and our numbers for accreditation PE went from a class of 21 for GCSE PE to three sets of GCSE and a BTEC group. Our extra-curricular programme flourished, participation tripled.'

Thornton-Bousfield understood her 'why' and the dynamics of her team. By drip-feeding change and working with specific individuals to achieve buy-in, she was able to make impactful change and realise her vision.

Here is a list of suggested questions and considerations Will Swaithes created for subject leaders. Which of these questions jump out as relevant to you and something your offer does (could or should) contribute towards?

2019 Ofsted Inspection Framework (EIF) – Considerations for PE & sport

Quality of education	Behaviour and attitudes
Intent: - Is a clear vision & purpose of PE understood, relevant & meaningful to students? - Are students prepared for their future lives? (health, happiness & employability) - Is social disadvantage addressed? - Are there appropriate pathways? (core, GCSE & vocational) - Is the offer rich, varied and flexible? **Implementation:** - Are individual student needs serviced? - Is feedback given to help students progress? - Is assessment used to inform teaching? - Is teaching engaging, exciting and innovative? **Impact:** - How do you capture holistic learning & progress? - What have students learned? Think beyond national assessments and exams! - What is in place to support most disadvantaged & SEND? - Are students ready for their next stage?	- Is the environment safe, calm & productive - Are clear routines in place? - Are students motivated to learn and engaged? - Is bullying a problem? **Personal development** - Do you support diverse aspects of life? (for example through school trips, visits & clubs) - Do you connect with community clubs? - Do you develop SMSC, Fundamental British values, promote equality & an inclusive environment? - Do you develop character, confidence, resilience and mental health? - Do all students know how to keep physically healthy & maintain an active lifestyle? - Do most students engage in extra-curricular clubs? **Leadership and management** - Is there a culture & ethos of physical activity? - Do staff engage in wellbeing activities? - Do parents and the community support your offer? - Is appropriate safeguarding & risk assessment complete?

(Will Swaithes, 2019)

These changes are not possible without the support and collaboration of an effective team. In order to change practice, teachers must first understand 'why', but must also receive the support and structure to implement and effectively deliver the 'how'. This was something Tom Brush identified when starting a new Head of PE position.

Brush, Head of PE for Nishkam High School, a multi-faith school in Birmingham with a Sikh ethos, has had experience of supporting teachers in their mentality shift. Brush recalls when he first took over the role: 'I did not want to make any changes to begin with, as I wanted to observe and see how things were done.' It wasn't long until Brush knew that changes were needed. 'For every kid that liked sport, there were twice as many who didn't, and the first thing that stood out to me was the performance led assessment.' Brush found Matt Bowler's 'Me in PE' on Twitter and connected with the holistic view on assessment and then looked to implement it with his department. 'We changed the descriptors to meet our school needs, but the first year was very much trial and error. We were unsure how much prominence to give the 'physical me', as some members of the team thought this should be the main focus; however, I felt that all of the elements were equal. So, we tried it a few ways out to see what worked best'.

Brush understood the importance of collaboration, and the involvement of his team in creating and implementing the new model; 'We made assessment an agenda item in every meeting, I delivered training, peer observations, performed joint moderations, even recorded some students so that we could watch and discuss against the performance criteria we were writing.' Collaboration was critical to the success of implementing this change for Tom and his team.

Brush wasn't finished there: 'once staff and students were familiar with the assessment model, I wanted to focus on pedagogy and curriculum.' Sports were previously delivered in 6-week blocks, before moving on to the next activity. 'Even if students had not progressed or could perform the skills required, we would still move on to the next sport. I had to tell my team that there was no rule to say we had to move on. Just because that is how it has always been done, didn't mean we had to continue to do it in that way.'

He had researched various model-based approaches and trialled cooperative learning with a Year 8 class through indoor athletics. Cooperative Learning focuses on students working together in small groups to master subject matter content. Students have the joint responsibility of both learning the content, but also ensuring that their peers learn it as well (Sporticus, 2016).

Brush collected student feedback, and used this to demonstrate the impact to his team. They recognised a new way in which PE could be delivered through the feedback and their own observations. With this new method employed and rolled-out, they also changed from 6- to 12-week blocks, providing more time for students to practice key skills, as well as offering new activities that would support students' ability to meet the success criteria for the newly introduced assessment.

Brush had a vision as to the direction he wanted to take PE, but it was very much a team effort. 'We created everything together, shared resources, discussed what worked and what didn't. We found it tough to begin with, as it was a new way of thinking, but I kept reminding them of the long-term plan. We made the changes bit by bit, and now, after a few years, we have made tremendous progress.'

Through good leadership, this team have developed something that will positively impact students' lives for a long time to come. Though they faced obstacles and doubted themselves on occasion, through collaboration and a clear goal, they have achieved what they set out to do. They have also changed the mindset and habits of the teachers in order to successfully deliver a curriculum of this nature, and Brush commented on the noticeable increase in confidence that his staff demonstrated when delivering model-based approaches and holistic assessment through this work.

Teamwork, and the importance of collaboration, was a recurring theme when talking with PE teachers about their work in creating and implementing change. The issues discussed at the start of this book were not exclusive to the UK, and many discussions with practitioners teaching in international schools further proved this point.

Technological advances and the use of social media platforms such as Twitter have enabled many international schools to share their outstanding practice. One such example is Phil Mathe. After finding himself in a sales and marketing career, Mathe retrained as a PE teacher. He then made the decision to teach abroad and went on to work in schools in Kenya, Egypt, and now works in the UAE as a Director of Sport.

Mathe discussed what he believes to be the current state of our subject: 'PE globally is at a real crossroads. In some ways, it's never been better positioned, but in other ways it's in a real mess. There are more research and evidence-based PE teachers than I can remember at any point in the past. More and more research is being carried out into PE, Sport, Physical literacy and fitness, which is great for driving innovation, but it's leading to an even greater variation in PE teachers' perceptions of what PE is, what it isn't, and how it should be delivered. I think PE really needs to look hard at itself and establish exactly what it is, is not, and what we want it to be in the future. If we want to be seen as the most important subject (that every PE teacher knows it is) then we need to collaborate more, fight a common cause, and really decide what PE is, why PE is important, and what we are trying to instil in our pupils globally.'

In his school, Mathe oversees a concept-based, holistic PE curriculum focusing on health-related fitness, healthy lifestyles, leadership, collaboration, and challenge. This is complemented by a 'Games' curriculum, that is much more like a tradition curriculum, which focuses on skill, tactics and techniques and is built around a game sense approach to PE. 'Add weekly swimming lessons into the mix, and I think we are in a pretty good place'.

'We try to cater for everyone. We have a real mix of local and expat students with varying levels of English, a huge variety of home lives, and very different perspectives on what PE and Sport means and its value. We link our PE and Games curriculums through our assessment structure. We feed the Games curriculum into our Extra-Curricular programme, with a strong 3-tier approach to competitive sport. Internal house competition for all, local sports fixtures for most, and international and representative competition for a few. This provides pathways that build enthusiasm and engagement and replaces the pathway structure that doesn't really exist outside of our school community.'

The expertise that practitioners, like Mathe, and many others, can provide from around the world, as well as the online platforms by which to collaborate, will be another key component to ensuring meaningful change within PE. Every school and every student is different, no matter the country in which it is delivered. The principle of physical literacy is universal, and many of the challenges we are all faced with are the same. Working together, and sharing best practice, will help us unite to provide positive and meaningful PE experiences for all students around the world.

Take Away Reflections

- What are the needs of the students in your school? How do you know?
- Use Grant Huddleston and Angela Whitehouse's SPACE model (specifics, pedagogy, assessment, curriculum and extra-curricular) to reflect on all that is offered by your department.
- What methods could you employ to listen to the views of your students?
- What does your student's engagement during lockdown (2020 or 2021) say about their attitudes and motivation towards physical activity?
- What opportunities are given to your team in order to collaborate?

Assessment

It is vital for students to fully engage and own the assessment model and, more specifically, the feedback taken from it. 'When we plan, we must have a clear idea of what we want students to be able to do at the end of the programme, at the end of a unit, or at the end of a lesson. We share intended learning with pupils, so they are clear on the expectations, and assessment criteria give more detail of the learning expected (Frapwell, 2015, p.31). If the true purpose of assessment is for the teacher to check what has been taught, and for students to know what they need to do to improve, and then receive the opportunity to do that, why in PE do we do it so differently?

We teach a sport, assess at the end of the scheme of work based on the student's ability, and then move on. We do not address misconceptions, re-teach skills not fully acquired, or, most importantly, give the students the chance to improve the areas that have been addressed through the assessment.

In-fact, most of the time, students will not get the opportunity to practice these skills again until that particular sport rolls around on the curriculum the following year. Not to mention the different success criteria that comes with every different activity, making it almost impossible for students to understand what improvement really means in each activity. Where is the purpose in that?

Assessment should be incorporated into the curriculum. It should not change with the sport or activity, and should be accessible for both staff and students, and it should focus on the whole child and not just the physical side of them.

One such example is the 'Me in PE' model, created by Matt Bowler, director of PE at King Alfred's Academy in Wantage. Bowler worked with the Youth Sport Trust as part of the Assessment Without Levels working group and completed a postgraduate degree in Educational Leadership. He then set about reviewing and changing the focus and delivery of the PE curriculum, which in turn involved a dramatic shift in the assessment of the individual students.

Bowler spoke of how each setting is different, and every leader should take their setting into account when leading a change in an area. He asked his department: 'what would we like a King Alfred's student to look like when they leave us?' He wanted to get to understand, after 390 hours of curriculum time over five years, what characteristics, traits and skills were important to each member of the PE team, and that students needed to flourish in be active in their adult lives.

Bowler believes that this part of the process, whereby gaining an insight into his team's 'why' and knowing what was important to them, was vital to piecing together their model; he calls it the 'Ikea effect'. When buying a piece of flat pack furniture from Ikea, it's fairly inexpensive, but once you have invested time building it and you have the finished item, it now holds much more value to you. This is the same as creating something like an assessment model as a team; by building it together, each member has a sense of ownership, and therefore it adds personal value to each member.

Through these team discussions about what was important to them, 'Me in PE' was born. Originally, Bowler and his team agreed on 7 different 'Me's' including:

- Physical Me
- Social Me
- Personal Me
- Leading Me
- Thinking Me
- Healthy Me
- Creative Me

This was then rolled this out, Year 7-11. Each unit of work would focus on 'Physical Me', and one of the other 6 and would then receive a target for each moving into the next unit.

After one year, the team reflected, and felt that there was too much to assess, too much going on, and lots of overlap. Therefore, they removed Social Me and Personal ME as they fell in with Leading Me and Thinking Me, and created Me in PE version 2.0.

This ensured a greater focus with the model and the ability to better meet the team's 'why'. Over 10 blocks, students will cover each Me in PE element twice, still receiving a target at the end of each block. Each lesson has an underlying physical element but, as Bowler said, 'using the example of Rugby, there could be an underlying focus on leadership.' The PE department developed the assessment criteria; when reporting the progress of students, Matt and his team provide an 'attitude grade', and then assign the statements that students have achieved, though only the attitude grade is shared with home.

Bowler highlighted the support that was needed for staff when implementing this model. 'What was clear was that everyone's teaching mode was definitely the physical element. Lots of learning walks, support, and use of curriculum time is definitely needed with that shift towards the teaching of other elements. The sharing of this model, the students' progress, and achievements in line with the assessment was crucial to changing the way people felt about PE'.

Bowler identified that this is particularly pertinent to parents: 'What we need to remember is that we do still have a large section of society that had really bad experiences in PE when they were at school.' Through the sharing of the model,

Bowler and his team were able to change people's mindset around school PE. Finally, it is important to sustain, reflect and review your model, to ensure you continue to offer the best to the students that are in front of you.

Bowler understood the need for change with the way in which he assessed students in PE and, therefore, devised his progressive model, focusing on different concepts and traits he and his team wanted students to acquire by the time they left school. Students that were once assessed based purely on competence were now looking to develop different aspects of themselves, and the assessment provided real meaning to them and PE. They were no longer demotivated by a level or grade, which reinforced their 'lack of ability' or 'no good' at PE perception. Now they were given a meaningful target, with which they could become better people.

Another Physical Education leader that is in the process of re-thinking assessment is Simon Bradbury, Head of Department at Bulmershe School in Reading. Once a specialist sports school, Bulmershe are fortunate to have a number of different sporting facilities on site: Goals Centre, Bulmershe Gymnastics Club, Kingfisher Table Tennis Centre, Bulmershe Leisure Centre, Fitness Suite, Dance Studio, Outdoor Tennis and Netball Courts, as well as acres of field big enough to host cross country events.

When considering the current state of PE, Bradbury said, 'I think PE is at a changing point in terms of how it is seen and valued, and I think this was occurring before Covid. I think that there is a change in emphasis where PE is not just about the physical aspects but taking a more holistic approach. I still feel it is not valued as highly as it could and should be amongst SLT. I feel assessment initiatives like Head, Heart, Hands and ME in PE have been excellent for promoting that PE is not just about the physical, but looks at many more aspects.'

Bradbury discussed the obstacles he has faced in ensuring PE is valued at Bradbury: 'Potentially teaching sports and activities in blocks is now dated, and perhaps we should focus less on the sports and activity and more on the topic we are trying to get across, e.g.: outwitting an opponent. I feel our subject is valued by some, but certainly not all, and many have no idea of the lengths that we go to ensure the best experience for our learners. When I started at Bulmershe, students in KS4 would have 2 hours a week of PE lessons; now they get 1 hour a week. Our year 9s used to get 2 hours a week of PE, and now they get 3 hours a fortnight. Year 11s would often be taken out of core PE lessons to do some intervention in another subject, but this has now stopped, as I think it is so important that students still have their PE lessons all the way through school.'

The department previously assessed students using a 1-9 GCSE style system, focusing only on practical ability. Bradbury was worried about the message this was sending to students and their parents: 'When in discussion with parents on parents' evening, they would often mention how they were aware their child was 'not sporty', and therefore couldn't achieve in PE, though there are many sports coaches at the highest level that have never been players'. Bradbury wanted to better highlight to students and parents that PE was so much more than just practical ability. His department has worked to change how students are assessed in PE, using the Head, Heart, Hands framework, which would hopefully improve how many perceive PE, and the learning that can take place.

Discussing the shift to the new method of assessment, Bradbury said: 'We now assess students against the Hands (practical ability), Heart (relationships, emotions and behaviour) and Head (knowledge and understanding). We provide assessment grading for Head and Heart based on our observations in lessons. With the Head element of the assessment framework, we provide short 30-question multiple choice forms that focus on the activities and the topics we have covered. Students are provided with immediate feedback as these forms are self-marked, which also reduces teacher workload. We are then able to provide a comprehensive assessment of the students' development in PE. Now, when parents talk to me and mention their children are not sporty, I can refer them to their progress in their knowledge and understanding or their attitude to provide meaningful feedback'.

L			
	Knowledge / Understanding / Analysis / Feedback / Responsibility / Rules (through observation in lessons, questioning as well as quiz assessment at the end of a unit of work)	Communication / Leadership / Respect / Resilience / Effort / Confidence (through observation in lessons)	Physical Ability / Fitness Levels / Competitive / Technique / Tactics / Problem Solving (through observation in lessons)
9	a. Critically evaluate own and others' performances, giving detailed feedback using extensive technical and tactical understanding. b. Analyse how the components of fitness, principles of training and training methods can improve performance.	a. Consistently show exceptional leadership qualities when leading large groups in lessons and after-school clubs. b. Demonstrate outstanding confidence, authority and respect when officiating, leading, and participating.	a. Demonstrate, with outstanding precision, control and fluency, an extensive range of appropriate skills and techniques in exceptionally challenging activities. b. Consistently make outstanding decisions and apply a range of tactics, often with creativity, in challenging situations.

8	a. Evaluate the quality of own and others' performance across different activities b. Have detailed knowledge of different training methods and use this to provide accuracy feedback to the performer.	a. Show outstanding leadership qualities in lessons and after school clubs. b. Be a positive role model who is inspiring to others.	a. Demonstrate , with consistent precision, control and fluency, an extensive range of appropriate skills and techniques in very challenging activities. b. Consistently make effective decisions and apply a range of tactics in challenging activities.
7	a. Analyse performance of yourself and peers in order to improve skills, techniques and/or fitness levels. b. Accurately explain the advantages of following a healthy active lifestyle.	a. Show good leadership qualities in lessons and after school clubs. b. Be respected, respectful and have developed positive working relationships with staff and students across the school.	a. Demonstrate, with precision, control and fluency, an extensive range of appropriate skills and techniques in challenging activities. b. Make effective decisions and apply a range of tactics in challenging activities.
6	a. Identify problems with peers' or own technique and give feedback to correct mistakes. b. Explain short and long-term effects of exercise on physical, mental and social well-being.	a. Be confident and competent when leading large groups. b. Often inspire others to participate and progress in sporting activity.	a. Demonstrate, with consistent accuracy and success, a range of appropriate skills and techniques in challenging activities. b. Apply complex tactics to activities.

5	a. Have a good knowledge of rules and tactics of several different sports and be able to give some feedback to peers and teams on overall performance. b. Explain the importance of taking part in regular physical activity (i.e.: physical / social / mental)	a. With some success, lead a large group of people in a variety of roles e.g.: official, coach and captain). b. Demonstrate empathy and respect for peers and support them to improve performance.	a. Demonstrate, with consistent accuracy and success, skills and techniques across a variety of sports in competitive activities. b. Apply tactics in competitive activities with success.
4	a. Have a good knowledge of skills and techniques, which improves own and others practical performance. b. Explain the long-term benefits of regular exercise upon the body.	a. Often volunteer to lead large group warm ups and activities. b. Develop respectful relationships with peers.	a. Demonstrate, with some accuracy and success, skills and techniques across a variety of sports in competitive activities. b. Apply tactics across a variety of activities with some success.
3	a. Use knowledge of techniques to improve own performance and give feedback to others. b. Explain short-term effects of exercise upon the body.	a. Show confidence and effective communication within discussions and activities. b. Consistently show respect of equipment and others.	a. Demonstrate, with some accuracy and success, skills and techniques across a variety of activities in high pressured practices. b. Apply tactics with some success.

2	a. Use basic knowledge of techniques to analyse and improve own performance. b. Lead an effective warm up, identifying most relevant major muscles.	a. Lead small group of peers with some confidence. b. Show respect for equipment and others.	a. Demonstrate, with some accuracy and success, skills and techniques across a variety of activities in moderately pressured practices. b. Apply basic tactics in passive practices.
1	a. Have some understanding of techniques, and start to reflect upon own performance. a. Identify some muscles and describe reasons why we need to warm up.	a. Lead and warm up. b. Describe why respect for equipment and others is important.	a. Demonstrate, with some accuracy and success, basic skills and techniques in passive practices. b. Describe basic tactics within an activity.

The difference in the messaging that this model sends to students, and the focus on holistic development, is clear and important. Bradbury also reflected on how this shift in assessment, and in the topics they are now delivering, moving away from delivering only sports, was that he was observing, 'students that had never previously shone really start to flourish in PE. They were starting to see that PE wasn't just competition, but it could include other activities like orienteering'. All students at Bulmershe were really starting to see the value of PE, only available previously to those considered 'sporty'.

Head of Department Natalie Rose, and Deputy Head of Department Sian Mason, collaborated on their own adaptation of the Head, Heart, Hands framework in their department, part of a coeducational secondary school in Leicestershire.

Both leaders struggled with the lack of clarity and guidance that their 'old' assessment model provided. Rose comments: 'There was no real structure to assessment in core PE; to follow it was more on teacher judgement, and was mostly based on skills'. Mason explained further, 'assessment was not effective and teachers would often just put a flightpath down that they 'thought' without clear criteria. I have found this to be similar when doing my teacher training too'.

Rose and Mason were faced with a challenge many PE leaders can sympathise with – the use of target grades based on English or Maths scores from a previous primary school. Mason said, 'We always find great frustration that the majority of the time students' targets grades are based on what they achieved in KS2, and students are set based on English groups, which, as you know, makes no sense in a PE setting! We decided to revisit the assessment, which previously has been mainly skill-focused and linked to flightpaths.'

Calculating their own PE-focused flightpath, Rose and Mason set out their own criteria, based on the three learning domains, and work out an average of the three. This shift has not, however, been without challenge. 'We have already met a barrier with the minimum flightpaths that have been calculated from the recent English and Maths tests. As a Head of Department, I have questioned this, as our new way of calculating the students 'currently working at' flightpath has indicated that PE doesn't follow suit. I have emailed our Senior Leadership Team to see if we are able to change this, whilst informing parents on the new assessment structure in PE, so students and parents fully understand why the flightpath that they have been awarded is below that of the one calculated using English and Maths.'

The Head, Heart, Hands framework stood out to Rose and Mason, who connected with the opportunity to recognise those the previous form of assessment ignored. Rose also recognised a chance to improve qualification uptake by developing a stronger connection between students and PE at an earlier age. 'As Head of Department, I decided to change assessment methods to give a more meaningful purpose to each sport that students took part in during core PE. This will then hopefully lead to a more successful uptake in option PE in year 9. With Head, Heart, Hands, students will begin to see the importance of leadership and respect within sport, which will lead to a more successful leadership programme within the Academy.'

Rose and Mason set about developing their own version of the Head, Heart Hands framework, creating both student-friendly and teacher support versions. As seen below in the student-friendly version of the assessment criteria, students' progress up the framework based on the consistency of the required attribute demonstrated.

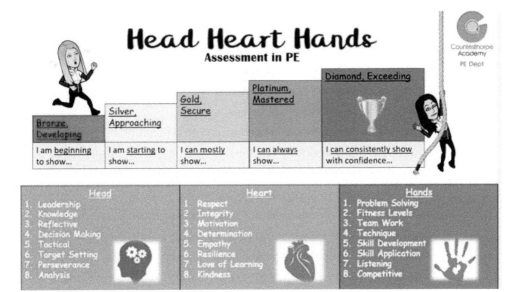

Teachers are supported to deliver the above consistently by referring to the teacher assessment criteria as shown below with examples of the Head, Heart, Hands bronze developing and diamond exceeding phases.

Bronze, Developing

Head

- I am beginning to show an ability to lead limited elements of warm-ups and cool downs to a partner in one curriculum-based activity.
- I struggle to use appropriate terminology to describe and reflect on my own and other performances in team and individual activities. I can offer vague feedback to recognise strengths and areas in need of future development.
- I am beginning to understand how to make decisions in many team and individual activities successfully and how tactical knowledge is applied appropriately to many activities to outwit opponents.
- My knowledge of the activity is limited, however I often persevere at the set task to ensure I understand the basic skills and rules to achieve my best.
- I am able to a set target with the help from peers to achieve my best in each lesson.

Heart

- My love of learning in the curriculum activities I like is limited, although this is inconsistent across the range undertaken. I have shown little interest in extracurricular sport and on occasion applied some effort in curriculum activities.
- I show signs of giving up when faced with difficult or challenging situations in many sporting activities. I need have more resilience and be willing to take failure more positively, understanding that failure is the first steps to success.
- I demonstrate little motivation to succeed in practical activities. On occasions I have shown some determination in activities I like.
- I have shown little empathy and respect for others when sharing ideas and need to improve on my mind to be kind so everyone is able to work more effectively within a team.
- My participation and kit record has room for improvement as I have forgotten my kit numerous times.

Hands

- I am beginning to show an understanding of how skills should be performed, although I struggle to maintain techniques within many isolated and progressive drills. I am starting to demonstrate these skills with some fluidity.
- I need to improve on working within a team and sharing ideas with my peers to successfully achieve the outcome of the lesson.
- I find physically demanding tasks difficult, resulting in flaws in performance as a result of a lack of physical fitness.
- I apply some basic skills into isolated drills, although I fail to maintain the appropriate technique in progressive drills.
- When face with competitive situations, my technique deteriorates over a range of both individual and team activities
- I struggle to listen to key information from the teacher or peer which results in me making mistakes.

Diamond, Exceeding

Head

- I consistently apply maximum effort in all curriculum and extra-curricular activities regardless of their nature. I act as a role model to my class peers, demonstrating a determination to succeed in all practical activities. I demonstrate a high degree of empathy towards my class peers, providing support and encouragement to others, regardless of their ability.
- I understand and demonstrate that success takes hard work and time to achieve. I take setbacks and failures maturely, using my experiences, feedback and attitude to demonstrate progression in all activities.
- I consistently demonstrate the school's motto of care and respect for everyone in all practical activities I undertake. I celebrate and embrace diversity in PE, encouraging others to participate in extra-curricular activities.
- I always support the teachers or coaches in handling, maintaining and transporting equipment at the start and conclusion of the activity.
- I maintain, demonstrate and promote high levels of motivation in a wide range of curriculum and extra-curricular sporting activities.
- I am proud to represent my school in many extra-curricular sporting activities. I remain committed to demonstrating the best version of myself and maintain an exemplary participation and attendance record.

Heart
- I consistently apply maximum effort in all curriculum and extra-curricular activities regardless of their nature. I act as a role model to my class peers, demonstrating a determination to succeed in all practical activities. I demonstrate a high degree of empathy towards my class peers, providing support and encouragement to others, regardless of their ability.
- I understand and demonstrate that success takes hard work and time to achieve. I take setbacks and failures maturely, using my experiences, feedback and attitude to demonstrate progression in all activities.
- I consistently demonstrate the school's motto of care and respect for everyone in all practical activities I undertake. I celebrate and embrace diversity in PE, encouraging others to participate in extracurricular activities. I always support the teachers or coaches in handling, maintaining and transporting equipment at the start and conclusion of the activity.
- I maintain, demonstrate and promote high levels of motivation in a wide range of curriculum and extra-curricular sporting activities.
- I am proud to represent my school in many extra-curricular sporting activities. I remain committed to demonstrating the best version of myself and maintain an exemplary participation and attendance record.

Hands

- I consistently demonstrate advanced skill technique within both isolated and progressive drills. Skills are performed with few errors and I adapt when faced with progressively challenging situations.
- I demonstrate outstanding levels of physical fitness over a broad range of activities.
- I can successfully apply complex skills into both isolated and progressive drills. My technique is maintained throughout many activities when faced with more advanced competitive situations. My skills are consistently applied with fluency, control and confidence.
- I demonstrate advanced technique and application of skill in competitive activities over a range of both individual and team sports.
- I can acquire and develop complex skills consistently well to a broad range of both team and individual activities.

This form of assessment is currently in its infancy, as it is being trialled with Year 7 (aged 11-12), before hopefully being rolled out to other years – another strong example of how assessment has shifted away from just physical ability and more towards holistic development. Despite the challenges facing PE leaders, as seen with Rose and Mason, meaningful change in assessment methods is occurring.

Whilst there is much consensus regarding the use of holistic assessment the methods of delivery are varied, even within the same framework, following the same Head, Heart, Hands approach, Liam Durr implements the framework differently. A former Senior Leader, Durr now works as a Head of PE at St Oscar Romero Secondary School in West Sussex.

Durr spoke of his struggles to find the right form of assessment that works within his school, whilst fitting with the requirements place on him. 'I find assessment difficult. The fact that it is now so open and varied across the country is something I struggle with. Always looking for ways to better our own system means I struggle to embed. We have changed our assessment framework multiple times since assessment without levels was introduced. We have always been required to create a system with levels within our school system. Some have been disasters, and some have been successful. We had a complex whole school system that made assessment in PE difficult (i.e.: 1, 1.25, 1.5, 1.75, 2...etc.). Students struggled to understand the sublevel logic, let alone the criteria we were attaching to these sublevels.'

Directed to keep some form of levelling, Durr has adapted the holistic method of assessment to meet the needs of his school. 'We have three sublevels (+ = -). This works well as it allows for a more holistic assessment when compared to old National Curriculum levels. Currently we use an average across the three domains to provide one grade.

Durr and his department use the assessment to create the individual lessons' learning outcomes. When researching how some schools implemented the framework, he noted that many focused on one strand per lesson/scheme of work. However, Durr prefers to focus on all three strands each lesson. Whilst too early to assess impact, Durr reflected, 'Each KS3 student has a tracking card that we log/assess twice per unit. We look for evidence from at least two activities to tick off a statement. These are still at very early stages, although students did seem to have a greater understanding of their attainment in PE and what they needed to do to improve'. An example of the student tracking cards can be seen below.

LEVEL	HEAD — The cognitive domain refers to (a) performance analysis and (b) application of theoretical knowledge.
9	(a) Critically evaluate own and others' work, showing understanding of how skills, tactics and fitness impact the quality and originality of performance. ☐☐
	(b) Critically evaluate how the components of fitness, principles of training and training methods can be used to improve own and others' performance. ☐☐
8	(a) Evaluate own and others' work, showing understanding of how skills, tactics and fitness impact performance. ☐☐
	(b) Discuss training principles and how these should be used to optimise exercise. ☐☐
7	(a) Analyse own and others' work showing understanding of how skills, tactics and fitness relate to performance. ☐☐
	(b) Discuss training methods and how these could be used to improve own and others' performance. ☐☐
6	(a) Analyse how skills, techniques and ideas have been used in own and others' work, and suggest ways to improve. ☐☐
	(b) Discuss the importance of fitness components and how they impact own and others' performance. ☐☐
5	(a) Analyse skills and techniques and how these are applied in own and others' work. ☐☐
	(b) Explain the link between regular physical activity and health (i.e. physical / mental / social). ☐☐
4	(a) Compare how skills, techniques and ideas have been used in own and others' work, and use this to improve. ☐☐
	(b) Explain the long-term benefits of regular exercise upon the body. ☐☐
3	(a) Discuss differences between own and others' performances and use this to improve. ☐☐
	(b) Explain the short-term / immediate effects of exercise upon the body. ☐☐
2	(a) Explain differences between own and others' performances and suggest ways to improve. ☐☐
	(b) Complete effective warm up and cool-down, explaining the importance of both. ☐☐
1	(a) Describe and comment on own and others' actions. ☐☐
	(b) Complete basic warm up and cool-down, describing the importance of both. ☐☐

LEVEL	HEART — The affective domain refers to (a) leadership behaviours / qualities and (b) attitudes and relationships.
9	(a) Consistently show exceptional leadership qualities when leading large groups in lessons and after-school clubs. ☐☐
	(b) Demonstrate outstanding confidence, authority and respect when officiating, leading and/or participating. ☐☐
8	(a) Show outstanding leadership qualities in lessons and after-school clubs. ☐☐
	(b) A positive role model who is inspiring to others from across the school community. ☐☐
7	(a) Show good leadership qualities in lessons and after-school clubs. ☐☐
	(b) Respected, respectful and have developed positive working relationships with staff and students across the school. ☐☐
6	(a) You are confident and competent when leading large groups. ☐☐
	(b) Inspire others to participate and progress in sporting activity. ☐☐
5	(a) Lead large group in variety of roles (e.g. official, coach and captain). ☐☐
	(b) Demonstrate empathy and respect for peers and support them to improve. ☐☐
4	(a) Often volunteer to lead large group warm-ups / cool-downs or activities. ☐☐
	(b) Eagerly accept challenges and develop respectful relationships with peers and staff. ☐☐
3	(a) Show confidence and effective communication within discussions and activities. ☐☐
	(b) Consistently show respect, effort and resilience during challenging tasks. ☐☐
2	(a) Lead small group with some confidence. ☐☐
	(b) Often show respect, resilience and effort. ☐☐
1	(a) Lead own warm up and / or cool-down. ☐☐
	(b) Demonstrate basic respect, resilience and effort. ☐☐

LEVEL	HANDS — The physical domain refers to (a) physical literacy / development and (b) tactical application.
9	(a) Consistently select, combine and apply advanced skills, showing high levels of precision, control, fluency and originality. ☐☐
	(b) Consistently apply advanced tactics with proficiency, flair and originality. ☐☐
8	(a) Consistently select, combine and apply advanced skills, often showing creativity. ☐☐
	(b) Apply advanced tactics with proficiency and flair. ☐☐
7	(a) Consistently select, combine and apply advanced skills, adapting them appropriately. ☐☐
	(b) Apply advanced tactics. ☐☐
6	(a) Select, combine and apply advanced skills. ☐☐
	(b) Apply tactics in response to changing circumstances and own / others' strengths and weaknesses. ☐☐
5	(a) Consistently select, combine and apply fundamental skills. ☐☐
	(b) Adapt tactics during performance. ☐☐
4	(a) Select, combine and apply fundamental skills. ☐☐
	(b) Apply tactics in different activities. ☐☐
3	(a) Link and apply fundamental skills. ☐☐
	(b) Apply a simple tactic. ☐☐
2	(a) Use, vary and link simple skills. ☐☐
	(b) Explain a simple tactic. ☐☐
1	(a) Explore and vary simple skills. ☐☐
	(b) Describe a simple tactic. ☐☐

Durr has shared an example of how PE leaders are overcoming the challenges placed on them, in terms of how assessment should be recorded, still seeking new and innovative ways to make assessment holistic and meaningful.

Planning Assessment

Learning is transformative and therefore assessment should be on-going to reveal what we need to know about a pupil's achievement and how it can be improved. Secondly, assessment of learning refers to the clear alignment between our aims and our application of assessment.

The AfPE have outlined their 3 principles to assessment (2015) as: assessment for learning, assessment of learning and assessment as learning. Assessment for learning identifies that the primary purpose of PE assessment is to improve pupil progress and attainment. We should use assessment for learning as a key driver to improve ways of doing things for our learners.

A clear understanding of what students are expected to achieve, and the criteria in which success is measured, should be incorporated. Our assessment criteria should be effectively communicated to students, so they fully understand what is required in order to progress. Assessment as learning relates to how we design our methods of assessment. When planning we must consider how teachers will assess, and the nature of the assessments students will take (Frapwell, 2015).

Peter Scullion is a Head of Department in Brighton who has adopted the Head-Heart-Hands approach to assessment. Scullion spoke of his desire to engage all in PE: 'I did not want two 'sporty' students dominating lessons while the rest of the class were on the margins. I wanted to celebrate these students who were passionate about the subject but make lessons more inclusive and try to create a love of PE for all, and promote physical activity for life. I was inspired by webinars hosted by the AfPE, where I was introduced to research on a 'Health Based' curriculum by Dr Sammon and Dr Bowler.' Following this, he read Andrew Frapwell's work on life without levels, and was motivated to employ a similar approach. Scullion and his team set to work creating an assessment model that reflected the learning he has gained.

When implementing the assessment, he did so by demonstrating it alongside current curriculum content. 'I had planned a basketball scheme of learning that I would practically deliver to all staff during a September inset. Staff would take part in the lesson and experience the activities, expectations and forms of assessment. We would then discuss and reflect upon the activities as a team and look at areas to improve and develop the assessment. Frapwell suggested a buddy system, so staff would then develop and discuss their scheme of learning in relation to the assessment with their buddy.'

Though much has been said about the reasons a teacher should assess, it is vital for students to fully engage and own the assessment model and, more specifically, the feedback taken from it. A student should not only understand where they are now, what they have demonstrated in order to have achieved that, but what they need to do in order to progress.

They should be able to identify key skills or techniques from the assessment rubric in order to gain some meaningful insight into how to develop areas of themselves further. This feedback and reflection stage are critical, and, without it, the assessment serves little purpose, only supporting the teacher. The use of assessment booklets supports this process, with students being able to reflect often during a scheme of work, reviewing the rubric against their progress in individual lessons. Class discussions and plenary reflections will also serve to embed the assessment, and permit students to own their learning.

Oliver Bishop, from Upton Court Grammar School, discusses his vision for how assessment in his school would be accessed by students: 'As part of our previous form of holistic assessment, we used reflection booklets in which students had to complete lengthy self-reflection boxes, whereby they would state the current stage of learning they were at, why they believed this to be true (cross references the assessment model), and then identify what they should do to improve further and access the next stage. However, this would often take up practical lesson time, and students saw it as more of a chore than a genuine opportunity for reflection. We wanted to maximise practical time in lessons, using the assessment model as a tool for reflection and development. Therefore, with the help of the team, and taking inspiration from other departments' best practices, I put together the following:

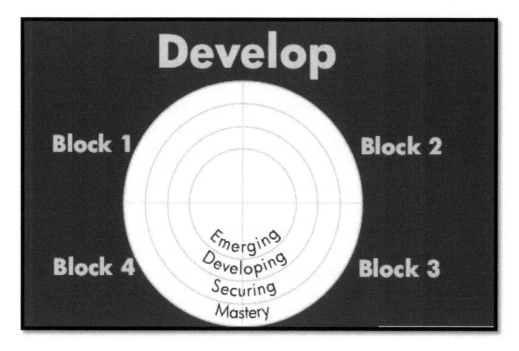

As can be seen above, the students' planners include a simple reflection wheel that should be completed at key points within a scheme of work. Students will colour in the stage of learning they believe they are working at in each of our four curriculum objectives (develop, educate, engage and prepare). Over the course of the year, they can see how they have progressed in different aspects of their learning. We found that using this simple visual reflection tool offered students tangible evidence of progress and enabled them to easily identify areas of learning they needed to focus on next. This provided as much reflection opportunity and took up much lesson time than our previous form of writing and justifying current levels of learning.

Bishop understood the power of visual representation when employing assessment in PE, and the impact of this tool was evident in conversations with students. They were better able to articulate their strengths and weaknesses, whilst often referring to these reflection wheels to evidence their points.

Exam Results

Just because we have introduced key concepts into our curriculum does not mean we are no longer under pressure to deliver examination results. The pressure and the need to focus on skills and techniques to ensure progress was made is a huge concern for a lot of our colleagues. These skills, the sports, and the opportunity to develop the examination student's competence, will not be lost by transitioning to a concept-based approach.

Teachers are still welcome to use the lesson to instruct students on key techniques, address skill misconceptions, demonstrate best practice, and support skill specific learning. We are now more interested in the concept, the student's ability to link this concept to the wider world, and transfer that knowledge to new contexts. The most able will continue to thrive, their performance will not drop, nor their progress plateau. I hope you feel more reassured that it doesn't have to be one or the other; you can achieve both good results and concept development.

Take Away Reflections

- What are you assessing?
- When and how often are you currently assessing?
- Where is the assessment best being used in your department?
- Why do you assess?
- How effective is your current form of assessment at developing the learning you would like the students to leave with?
- How do students use the information gained from assessment?
- How effective is this?

Strategies for Leading Change

It is vital that, as a leader, you describe an opportunity that will inspire your team. This opportunity won't exist forever, so you need to act now.

You have your own 'why', and the team now have theirs. You have your mission statement, and have communicated your curriculum intent. Now we are ready to truly improve PE at your school.

In order to effectively support the process of implementing change, I suggest we follow Dr Kotter's 8 Step Process for Leading Change. Kotter's work on leading change has influenced businesses around the world to follow his process, and ensure change is executed effectively. As the title suggests, Kotter has outlined eight separate steps for a leader or organisation to follow.

The steps are:
1. Create a sense of urgency.
2. Build a coalition.
3. Form a strategic vision and initiatives.
4. Enlist a volunteer army.
5. Enable action by removing barriers.
6. Generate short-term win.
7. Sustain acceleration and finally.
8. Institute change.

I will apply this process, along with other research, supported guidance and examples, to provide you with the tools to drive change.

Step 1 – Create a Sense of Urgency

'Establishing a sense of urgency is crucial in gaining needed cooperation' (Kotter, 2012, p.37). The pandemic has created an opportunity for change.

It is vital that, as a leader, you describe an opportunity that will inspire your team. This opportunity won't exist forever, so you need to act now. The Covid virus, although horrific, has permitted reflection time and made people think about pedagogy, and doing what is right for students.

Many sports were not deemed 'Covid-secure', and curriculums had to adapt in order to continue to provide meaningful PE. This forced many people to change their current practices and leave their comfort zones with the desire to deliver a safe curriculum. New activities were considered, and many traditional sports were temporarily scrapped. Many physical educators had the opportunity to re-align the current practice with their, 'why'.

'Creating a strong sense of urgency usually demands bold or even risky actions that we normally associate with good leadership' (Kotter, 2012, p.45). A subject in dire need of change was afforded an opportunity for its leaders to reflect, review, learn and collaborate. Though this time is limited as, now restrictions are fully lifted, the expectation for normality and indeed the easy option will be to go back as it was before.

Once you have your vision, ensure you effectively plan and communicate the need for change now. Let your team know what success looks like and the impact that the suggested change could have. By creating this need to act, and sharing the importance of the change, they will feel inspired and will voluntarily support this process. Providing your team with evidence will serve to support your vision.

- Offering some reading from this, or other, books might help your case, as well as gathering some national, local and student voice data.
- Setting your students an optional survey that focuses solely on the curriculum and their opinions of it could highlight why change is needed. The results should be presented anonymously, so that no teacher feels targeted – this is not about the teacher, it is about the curriculum.

Public Health England's *What works in schools and colleges to increase physical activity?* publication discusses the importance of engaging student voice when planning a curriculum; by giving students a voice, you enhance their ownership of the PE delivery and ensure that activities are appropriately tailored to their needs and support participation (Public Health England, 2019).

Helping them to discover the problem for themselves with carefully planned tasks will enable you to create a shared understanding as to why they should act now. One method to highlight the issue is to conduct a SWOT analysis. Either individually, or as a team, you could ask them to, on an A4 piece of paper, write down the strengths, weaknesses, opportunities and threats of a particular topic such as: 'Our sport-driven curriculum's ability to meet the needs of all students' or 'the capability of the current curriculum to teach life skills'.

This will hopefully highlight that sport is not the only thing PE can offer and it does not meet the needs of some students. A SWOT analysis helps to open up discussion and allow everyone to contribute, whilst also understanding there are things to improve (Cope, 2016, p.82). Collate everyone's responses and link with your vision for change accordingly.

See below a SWOT analysis template that can be used to support the overall performance of the Department.

PE Department SWOT Analysis

Strengths

- What does the Department do really well?
- What expert knowledge/unique skills do we have in the department?
- What experience do we have?
- In what areas do we lead the school?

Weaknesses

- In what areas do the department need to improve?
- What resources do we lack?
- Where do we need further education/experience?
- What costs us the most time/money?

SWOT

Opportunities

- What goals should we be working towards?
- What resources might we gain access to?
- Are there changes to the school that will support us?
- What other opportunities are available to us?

Threats

- What obstacles do we face?
- What are others doing that we are not?
- What is happening in the school/education that might affect us?

Step 2 – Build a Guiding Coalition

Your team understands the need for change, so it's time for you to build your 'guiding coalition'. The aim is to build a connection between the coalition and your vision. Displaying your mission statement and communicating your vision is all well and good, but if people don't believe in it, then it means nothing. You must inspire them to believe in what you believe. Ideally, you would like a diverse group of people that include SLT and teachers. Realistically, it is more likely to be your team that form this group to begin with, though you will need to get everyone on board.

'There are only two ways to influence human behaviour: you can manipulate it, or you can inspire it,' (Sinek, 2009). In all honesty, on occasions, you might need to do both. For those staff that buy-in to a CDC, and are inspired by your pitch for difference, simply involving them in the planning of the implementation will be enough.

If there is someone in your team that, even after sharing their 'why', still can't understand the need for change, you have a couple of options. Meet with them individually before every team meeting. Let them know what you will be doing in that meeting in relation to the curriculum, ask for their feedback before the meeting and, if needed, go back to them with a solution or a decision prior to the meeting taking place. This might seem long winded, but they will feel their opinion is valued and are less likely to input negativity during the actual meeting.

Another option is to make them a big part of the change. By meeting with them again individually and asking them to support with certain elements of planning, they will feel a sense of ownership and are more likely to buy-in to your vision. They can even lead on and share their contributions in the team meetings.

PE teachers have long had to advocate the importance of PE to school senior leaders. An alarmingly high number of schools opt to cut PE in a drive to improve results in other subjects. This is not new ground for us, though this time we have some serious weight behind our argument. Firstly, we have the backing of Ofsted. In their *Education Inspection Framework* released in 2019, Ofsted purposefully include the school's ability to support personal development as part of their inspection overview. More specifically, the inspectors will look closely at, and make judgements on, the extent to which a curriculum supports the personal development of learners.

The Framework explicitly mentions a curriculums ability to develop students' character – including resilience, confidence, and independence, as well as helping students keep physically and mentally fit. Tick, tick and tick!

No doubt, there will come a time when you will be asked to justify this change to SLT, or a line manager. When preparing for this meeting, ensure you can clearly communicate your curriculum intent and how your sport-driven curriculum was not meeting its desired purpose. Ensure your vision and what change could look like are well-defined. Match your 'why' with the mission or priorities of the school if possible. Apply your vision to the current issues that the students in your school are facing. Any evidence that you can provide will only support your case.

The use of student voice results is a prime example that can demonstrate where you are now and why change is needed. Finally, back yourself. If you fully believe that this is the right move, then have confidence in your vision.

When it comes to the parents, you might not have as much of a fight on your hands as you might expect. A survey led by the Youth Sport Trust reported that 64% agreed that the well-being of pupils was more important when choosing a school than academic grades (48%). Furthermore, 81% agreed that cuts to PE, sport and break times were likely to have a negative impact on students' well-being (YST, 2021). A gentle reminder of the issues facing young people, that sport is not lost in a concept-based curriculum, and the most able can still thrive, should support your decision.

Step 3: Form a Strategic Vision and Initiatives

Kotter (2012) believes that targeted and coordinated activities, if executed effectively, will make your vision a reality. This stage will provide the action plan of your vision and motivate people to take action. It provides the clarity. Without strategic vision, your team will not know what to do, not take ownership of any particular role in executing the change, or ensure arrangements are coordinated. To be clear, this process could cover a term, a year, or a few years, if the change is extensive.

Agreeing responsibilities and setting dates for tasks to be completed is an important step. This can be agreed upon in one-on-one meetings or as a team. Minutes should be kept and distributed after each meeting to ensure all details are recorded, and members of the team can go back and remind themselves of what needs to be done. Follow-ups should occur in the next meeting, and support should be given to those who need it. This is not a way to hold people to account, it is simply a way of keeping track of who is to do what.

If you're looking for a more personal method of achieving this strategic vision then you could, as Cope (2012) calls it, give your team a 'HUGG' or a Huge Unbelievably Great Goal. You and your team can establish the aim of the 'what' you would like to achieve. In this case, to implement a concept-driven curriculum. Then break down this huge goal into smaller jobs or tangible actions that will ensure you achieve it. The model is often used when implementing personal changes such as 'giving up smoking' but can perform just as well in an organisational setting too.

Step 4: Enlist a Volunteer Army

'Leading is not the same as being the leader. Leading means that others willingly follow you – not because they have to, not because they are paid to, but because they want to' (Sinek, 2011).

Once in stage 4, you are looking to engage and inspire others to join your vision. Leading or offering training for your staff is also a good way to build your volunteer army and share your passion for the future of this subject. Now you know what needs to be done and how it will happen, you are looking to give others a reason to join your movement.

Whilst sharing your vision internally is the obvious priority, it is worthwhile considering communicating it externally too. Something that we as physical educators have now that most before us did not is social media, particularly Twitter. Sound advice to any trainee teacher is to create a Twitter account and follow the many other teachers online that are looking to share ideas, resources and collaborate. Chances are, whatever your vision for PE or change you are undertaking, someone else has had similar thoughts or experiences. Any opportunity to collaborate is worthwhile, however social media really has enabled a plethora of networking opportunities. A majority of the contributions in this book, as well as the actual opportunity to edit and publish it were found online. Other leaders around the world are willing to support a great idea and meaningful change, it is certainly worth sharing any ideas externally for others to comment on, improve or even share any workload. If they have tried something before, imagine the time you might save by learning from their failures or applying what they have created to your context.

Step 5: Enable Action by Removing Barriers

Put simply, by removing obstacles, leaders provide the freedom needed for their team to create real impact. Barriers that might negatively impact success could include, but are not limited to, pressure to perform, workload, fear of failure, rules or procedures, lack of time, lack of opportunity for collaboration, or narrow mindedness.

A leader should be a good listener and ensure they understand the needs of the team. Unnecessary pressure should be removed, and a risk-taking culture built. The idea of removing learning walks, or formal observations for a period of time, and replacing them with by peer observations, in which colleagues are encouraged to try something new could be considered.

Talk openly about failures and share best practice. As we are going to teach the students, we must embrace failure as a part of the learning process. Tackle any conflicts as soon as they arise, and ensure enough time is given to enable collaboration both within the team and with others outside of it. Provide scaffolding or models that will support the planning of conceptual learning.

One idea that could be used to tackle individual concerns within a group setting is a consultancy approach. Each member has the opportunity to share something that is worrying them. The group will then decide on one of these issues to discuss. The group will have a set time in which to ask questions to gain a deeper understanding of the issue, and then will be given a new set time in which to discuss solutions to it. The person with the concern should only listen during this time. After having listened to the solutions offered by the group the individual can state which solution they intend to action. This solution-focused approach creates unity within the team and provides a further opportunity for collaboration.

Another successful method in which teams can positively lead change is the use of the Appreciative Inquiry (AI) method. It is used to implement change by focusing on the team or organisation's strengths rather than weaknesses. This approach-focuses on the 4-D cycle (Discovery, Dream, Design and Destiny). Put simply, the first step of discovery poses the questions of when have we been at our best or what currently works really well?

Related to a PE department looking to implement a concept-driven approach, this might be to look at a time or a lesson that students most enjoyed in PE. The second stage of the cycle is dream, and here we consider what is it that the school or our students need, or the how the team envisions what might be. Design is the next stage, and here the team discuss what action they would need to take in order to deliver this change. The final stage of the cycle is destiny – here the team go about leading the change. The use of this approach can ensure a team are positively focused on implementing big changes to the way things have been done.

Step 6: Generate Quick Wins and Celebrate Success

It is so important that you and your team collectively celebrate any successes that come with implementing this change. This could be from a job being completed to communicating improved student voice feedback. Celebrating each and every success is critical to maintaining motivation and continuing to progress towards the final huge goal.

At the start of each team meeting, recognising and appreciating good work, embracing failure, demonstrating the right values, and taking positive steps towards the goal are all important ways of celebrating quick wins. A bar of chocolate or a thank you note go a long way too. It is important to create a culture that, if someone does well, we all win and share in the success of that person's work. We all share the same mission and, no matter how big or small any positive contributions to achieving that mission, should be appreciated. Never underestimate the power of positivity. These wins inspire more wins and will only serve to boost morale.

Hold a cake and coffee break-time, during which staff can come along, enjoy a doughnut and network with the pre-set rule that the only conversation can be about conceptualised learning or your new assessment model. This will support staff to share good practice, discuss what did not go well, and create a support network that they can rely on when faced with challenges.

Step 7: Sustain Acceleration

You have achieved some success and your vision is becoming more and more of a re-ality. It is easy when things are going well, and you have celebrated quick wins, mean-ing complacency can start to creep in. Staff can take their foot off the pedal, but this is not the time to take it easy, this is the time to sustain the acceleration of change (Kot-ter, 2020). Much like step one and creating a sense of urgency, your aim is yet to be met, and the opportunity could still pass. Keep the momentum going by revisiting the urgency needed and the impact meeting the end goal will mean for the future of PE.

Revisit your end goal often and refresh your ideas and processes in order to maintain that focus. It's not easy to make a change, but it's often harder to sustain it. Staff members and even leaders could be tempted to move on to the next idea. It is beneficial at this point to review the impact they have already made through student feedback. Remind them they are making an impact, but the mission is not yet complete.

Step 8: Institute

If you have achieved steps 1-7, then now you must institute change by making it part of daily practice. Ultimately, you want to replace the old ways of working with the new curriculum, pedagogy and assessment that you have implemented. This is where you become the manager of day-to-day practice. Continue to encourage collaborative planning and sharing successes and failures. The new practices now must be deeply rooted in order to replace old practices.

Linking the delivery of a concept-driven curriculum, or the development and application of a holistic PE assessment model with performance management or appraisal objectives, is a worthwhile way to ensure habitual practice. It is important that you continue to link the work of your team to the overall success of your department. This will also provide some individual accountability to the overall improvement of your team's performance and delivery. This does not replace gaining true 'buy-in' from your team but can certainly support it from a performance measurement perspective.

Summary

We have covered a lot in this section and provided practical tips and experiences from teachers that I believe are leading the way. I hope this will enable you to make the change required. Please remember that this change takes time – be patient, but relentless.

The importance of reflecting on what drives you and establishing your 'why' was discussed. Then, use this to create unity and focus to support your team to discover their own 'why'. Communicating your department intent is a vital component when students come to communicate why PE exists in their school.

We have highlighted innovative ideas around the planning and delivery of a PE curriculum, that involve conceptualised learning and understanding personalities. We focused on the importance of pedagogy in delivering the positive experiences we want to provide, and how we might go about changing the mindsets of our teachers to shift from a performance focus to a more holistic approach.

Assessment, and the need to move to a more developmental methodology, was demonstrated with the ME in PE and Head, Heart, Hands frameworks as prime examples of this approach. Though the assessment alone will not improve outcomes, the feedback, discussions, and reflections following assessments are critical to student progress.

Use this insight and back it up with evidence about why change is needed in PE and why it is needed now. Set out clear objectives and celebrate all the successes along the way. Constantly remind colleagues of your mission and embrace failure.

Finally, believe in yourself. If you truly feel that making this change will benefit the lives of the young people in your school, and transform the delivery of PE for the good, then trust you are doing the right thing.

Take Away Reflections

- Why is change needed and why is it needed now?
- What strategies can you use to ensure others see the urgency for change?
- How will you inspire others to believe in your vision?
- What is your team's huge unbelievable great goal?
- What are the smaller tasks that will need to be completed in order to achieve this goal?
- What obstacles might you have to clear in order to achieve your goal?
- How will you clear these obstacles?
- How will you generate quick wins and celebrate small successes?
- How will you ensure that you achieve your vision and complacency does not creep in?
- How will you ensure your vision becomes part of daily practice?

Case Study: The Infinite Learners

'Can we do better to help students organise their thoughts and knowledge to better understand the concepts around them in an ever-changing world?' Lewis Keens.

Two physical educators leading the way when it comes to conceptual learning and delivering positive PE are Lewis Keens and Alan Dunstan, otherwise known as the Infinite Learners (www.theinfinitelearners.com). Lewis and Alan work in international schools and have been developing and implementing their own vision of a concept-driven approach to curriculum design. It was these two gentlemen that first inspired me to look into the theory and research behind concept-based learning and its potential to fulfil the full potential of PE.

In this chapter, Lewis and Alan have collaborated to share their thoughts and experiences on developing a concept-based approach, how they implemented it, and how it can impact the future of PE.

Learning That Transfers in PE and Sport - Keens and Dunstan's First Interactions with Concept-Based Learning

We first became aware of Concept-Based Learning a decade or so ago. Erickson's approach struck us both as very relevant and appropriate to 'real-life'. We didn't know it then, but we had both read and liked the idea of creating links across topics and exploring relationships between different concepts, that we would work on together for years to come.

Ten years ago, based on different continents, we were ill-prepared to unpack, understand and apply a new approach to learning into our daily practice. Like a lot of young teachers, we were working hard to make an impact in middle leadership roles we had been thrust into, with the hope of our enthusiasm making a difference. Concept-Based Learning was an excellent idea, but we were too busy ensuring that students were doing what we had asked them to do. We were ready, planner-in-hand, to apply a school disciplinary procedure if they dared disagree with 'a teacher'.

Like so many in our profession, Keens and Dunstan were trying to find their way, whilst attempting to develop their practice and fit into the culture of their school. When speaking with them, they both believed strongly in PE and its ability to deliver more than just sport. They continued to discuss how they realised the impact conceptual learning could have.

Fast forward through a few years, and we were reintroduced to the concept-based style of learning by Stern. During what was a mind-bending couple of days, Stern visited the British School Manila (BSM). She shared with us videos of squirrels navigating obstacle courses, people jailed for trying to recycle computers, and children trying to vertical jump onto a stool.

The videos were entertaining, but the real power, the mind-bending part, was the fact that students could learn how the messages within these videos could help them organise and recognise relationships to create learning transfer both in simple and complex terms. We certainly didn't cover this at University, and we had never seen it in any school we had worked in before. Well out of our comfort zones, we found ourselves in classic fight or flight mode!

We worked hard to find relationships between squirrels, computers and jumping on a stool, but struggled at first. This whole approach seemed much more abstract than anything we'd ever seen before. As others around us seemed to 'get it', we found ourselves laughing out loud as we tried to piece together the message Stern was sharing. We were working hard to ask the question – how on earth would this help us in PE?

In today's world, what do you do when you don't really know or understand something? You Google it. Unfortunately, there was not a great deal under 'Concept-Based Learning in PE'!

We both enjoy learning, and we are the kind of people that will ask if we don't understand something, so off we went reading and researching and, once we knew a bit more, we started asking questions, lots of questions. Stern was generous with her time and made considerable effort to create PE examples and take into account our curriculum and content.

It became clear that some of the answers were right under our nose, and we just needed to find a way of simplifying the language to a level that everybody could understand.

This helped facilitate discussions in our department as we slowly pulled PE-related concepts out of our units of work across primary and secondary schools. It turns out this approach could help us in PE, and it would for years to come.

It was clear to Keens and Dunstan that, although at that time they did not fully understand how to apply concepts to Physical Education, it had the potential to make PE relevant and impactful. Once they decided that this was something they wanted to pursue, they set about creating their vision.

How We Have Used Learning That Transfers

A good PE curriculum will be made up of many moving parts, including but not limited to:

-    Physical Activity

- Sport
- Exercise
- Physical Literacy
- Play
- Health
- Well-Being
- Learning Skills
- Values
- Physiology

Unfortunately, even in 2020, many traditional curriculums ignore many of those parts, and focus solely on Physical Activity and Sport. Whatever your curriculum looks like, concept transfer can be a part of it.

Across a 7-year journey at BSM, our PE department 'leaned in' despite knowing the workload this may entail. We aimed to think bigger than PE lessons, to consider how learning in PE can be applied to school, relationships and, generally speaking, life.

We didn't fully understand how to embed concepts and drive learning transfer, so we started with small changes to units to include transferable skills. We stopped slotting sports into tidy half-term blocks. 'Tennis' changed to 'net games', as we started to look more broadly at the principles included in being an influential performer. Lessons were structured to enhance the learning, linking and transference of skills from one context to another.

Our invasion games topic allowed us to teach a multitude of activities with opportunities to link concepts. 'Attacking', 'defending', and 'creating space' were focuses of a strategies-based approach, commonly used in the *Teaching Games for Understanding* model, advocated by Bunker and Thorpe back in 1982.

BSM was a forward-thinking school and, at that point, had several multidisciplinary skills initiatives in use. We had a version of Claxton's *Learning Power*, the IB learner profile, now approaches to learning skills. We had just introduced Global Citizenship, previously internationalism. A lot of the multidisciplinary skills are 'hidden' below the surface, and we felt if we could bring these to the forefront of our learning, we would be preparing students for life after BSM.

According to The UN charter for Physical Education & Sport on the UNESCO website:

'Sport has the power to provide a universal framework for learning

values, thus contributing to the development of soft skills needed for responsible citizenship'.

These learning values are known as the term 'Sports-personship'. It's a term that we are all familiar with, but what does it mean? At BSM we broke down 'Sports-personship' to create our own set of BSM sporting values for our After-School Sport Programmes.

BSM SPORTING VALUE	BSM DEFINITION
RESPECT	Recognising diversity and difference through effective communication. Having a sense of belonging and wearing the uniform with pride.
HUMILITY	Appreciating the performance of self/others and acknowledge these contributions. Listening and acting on effective feedback.
COMPETE	To participate to the best of ability showing resilience. Can reflect upon performance, learn from mistakes, and set targets.
FAIR PLAY	Sticking to agreed rules and displaying appropriate sporting etiquette.
GRATITUDE	Displaying a growth mindset, being thankful and appreciative of oneself and others.
DIGNITY	To lift other people and lead with confidence.

These values are taught intrinsically through Health and Well-Being lessons, and within the sports programme at BSM. In lessons, we aim to deliver these values through the students experiencing the concept of:

- **Think** – What we think?
- **Feel** – What we feel, emotional engagement?
- **Act** – What we do, long-term transfer goal?
- **Reflect** – How did that impact you/others?

The 6 BSM sporting values are linked with our 6 Learning Power skills and our Health & Well-Being units of work.

The 6 BSM sporting values are linked with our 6 Learning Power skills and our Health & Well-Being units of work.

These values and skills were embedded into our Understanding by Design (UbD) plans for PE, with the explicit transfer goal that we wanted students to take away from the unit. We linked a BSM Sporting Value with a Learning Power skill:

- Communication with Respect
- Thinking with Humility
- Reflective with Competition
- Inquiry with Fair play
- Independent with Gratitude
- Collaborative with Dignity

We allocated these values and skills concepts to units. Invasion Games was linked with Communication and Respect. Lessons were based around those concepts rather than focusing on acquiring the 'physical' skills for that game. The transfer goals became more about the 'real-life skills' that students needed to develop. For example, working as part of a team and respecting differences, rather than being skills-focused on the physical outcome. Is your lay-up shot technique important on a day-to-day basis?

The introduction of the BSM well-being framework then moved us onto the next level, and the challenge of creating units based around five strands:

1. Self-Acceptance
2. An Active and Balanced Lifestyle
3. Ability to Self-Regulate
4. Sense of Belonging
5. Capacity for Growth and Resilience

We then took the step to reframe our Key Stage 3 units to embrace the Learning that Transfer model in full.

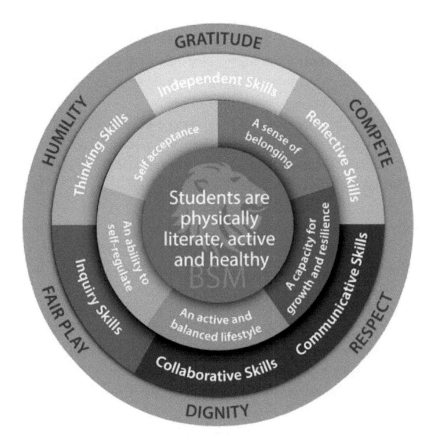

We created the BSM Learning Wheel and have experimented with a PE, Health & well-being curriculum at KS3. It is very much a journey, and we don't know the answers, but we are giving it a go and seeing where it takes us!

Our invasion Games unit, formerly 'Football' or 'Rugby', became a unit exploring the concept of 'belonging', using the Acquire – Connect – Transfer model.

We used the inclusive and fun game of Tchoukball as the vehicle in this unit of work. The specific rules and skills were delivered alongside the concepts, but the 'focus' wasn't on skill development; instead, the spotlight was on 'belonging', and the concepts that can impact a 'sense of belonging'. There are, of course, a whole host of different concepts that impact belonging including identity, collaboration, and self-acceptance. We focused on two key concepts:

- Communication
- Confidence

Acquire

For any team, class, or group of people to be effective over more than a short period, there will need to be a sense of belonging amongst them. To understand what belonging is, we first address knowledge acquisition. In other words, we didn't assume that students know what the word 'belonging' means.

Using definitions, examples, and non-examples we unpicked belonging, communication, and confidence to start and rebuild students' understanding with practical and theoretical models. To do this, we incorporated flipped-classroom and student leadership strategies.

Connect

To start connecting these concepts, we explored how conceptual questions can be used to analyse how one concept can impact/interact with another. Examples of conceptual questions include:

- What is the relationship between communication and confidence?
- How does effective communication help create a sense of belonging?
- How does a sense of belonging affect self-confidence?
- Can communication affect confidence in others?

Using practical examples and scenarios, students could think about and feel the relationships between the concepts, allowing them to begin organising their thoughts and understandings, to lead towards transferring their knowledge to a new and different context.

Transfer

The transfer phase came through modified games, creating appropriately challenging situations to test their understandings.

Our broad offering of extra-curricular sport enhanced this area of the learning process. We crunched data to identify children accessing our programmes, including sport, and looked to increase the opportunities for transfer by creating more programmes across critical categories of learning and student interests.

We began focusing less on extrinsic rewards within our programmes. Instead, our celebrations were often based around values, and the transferable concepts students were learning in PE, and also other subjects within the school.

Student Voice

Our 'new' way of PE teaching was a real chance to move the dial at BSM and step away from a traditional games-based approach. Through student surveys in Key Stage 3/4, we asked for feedback and received some interesting comments, which we took on board.

Generally, students loved the lessons focusing on 'real-life skills' and a move away from sports, understanding that, if they wanted to play specific sports, they could still access these as part of our After-School Sport Programmes. We also found lower ability students were happier and more engaged in lessons.

We always learned something that will likely shape our practice forever. There is no 'right way' to group students – the only consensus was that they wanted some element of choice.

Keens and Dunstan saw an opportunity and, through insightful research, constructive conversations, and trial and error, were able to develop something meaningful. They were able to successfully deliver real world lessons through physical activity and sport. Both have been able to apply the Learning Transfer Mental Model to support the delivery of the concept in a PE context.

The Future of Education

We know we are educating children for a future of which we have very little knowledge. Learning needs to be 'future-proof', and wider than learning specific skills for the sake of exams and assessments. Can we do better to help students organise their thoughts and knowledge to better understand the concepts around them in an ever-changing world?

We could ask – What is the relationship between organising concepts, education, and the future?

If you are still wondering how the squirrels, the computer recycling and the little girl jumping onto the stool are linked – the concepts were resilience, perseverance and risk-taking, but you already knew that, right!?

Keens and Dunstan have developed their own concept-driven curriculum, and their students are now thriving in Physical Education within their schools. Not much existed regarding conceptual learning within a PE setting when they both set out, so it is fair to say that their work has inspired other departments, including my own, to try something similar. With this methodology, alongside the inclusive pedagogy and holistic assessment, Keens and Dunstan will achieve a positive and meaningful PE experience, as set out in my model. Both have now gone on separate paths to new schools and contexts to build these experiences for students once again. In the next section, we explore how you and your school can lead a similar change, in order to truly meet the needs of your students.

Take Away Reflections

- Using the experiences of Keens and Dunstan, what changes to your PE offering would you like to make?
- How do you intend to make these changes?
- What impact could this have on the students you teach, and your ability to create positive and meaningful PE experiences for all?

6

Closing Thoughts

Positive and Meaningful Physical Education

Creating positive and meaningful PE is the future for our subject. As physical educators, we need to fully embrace the power of PE, and ensure that we fulfil its full potential for every child. Much like the popular myth that a human only uses 10% of their brain, a sport-focused curriculum was only accessing a small percentage of what PE is truly capable of.

PE has the power to change lives for the better, to create lifelong physically active and resilient individuals. PE can prepare students for life outside of school and give them the knowledge to deal with many different situations.

For PE to succeed in creating physically literate students that enjoy PE and perform in examination subjects, we must create a positive PE experience – one in which students can fail, and learn from their failures, understand how to progress, receive the praise for demonstrating a positive attitudes and participate in activities planned for their needs.

The curriculum, pedagogy and assessment must all unify in providing these positive experiences. When these three elements of education work together with the same vision, PE can be truly game changing.

Providing positive and meaningful PE experiences is the future for our subject. It feels like PE has remained unchanged for so long and has lost sight of the reason we are here. A subject that has, in recent times, failed to meet the needs of its students, and become a miserable experience for so many. A subject that is doing more harm than good in tackling the issues in our society.

Positive and meaningful PE can change that. Student-centred learning in PE serves as the foundation for a lifetime of healthy decision making. It is what all of us depend on for future well-being. We need people to understand that a healthy citizenry drives economic progress and human vitality' (Ennis, 2014).

In this book you have been introduced to the need for change in PE and considered the implementation of a concept-driven and personalised curriculum, inclusive pedagogy, and holistic approach to assessment. Together, these changes will enable a more positive experience for all in PE.

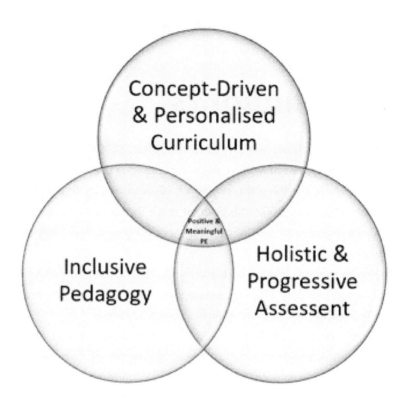

In summary, to achieve positive and meaningful PE, we should:

- Reflect on your 'why'. Knowing and sharing your 'why' is an important first step in realising what drives you. It forms the values that you live by and, as a leader, it can support your decision making too. It will allow you to reflect on your current practice and whether it aligns with your motivation. Once you know your 'why', you can really make a difference.
- Curriculum intent is not just a term from Ofsted; it is knowing what you hope to achieve with your subject. What do you want students to learn? It's important to communicate this to everyone. It creates a connection between the individual and your subject and will support everyone in articulating why PE is so important in your school.
- A shift in focus is needed when curriculum planning. The sport-driven model is turning many off physical activity and fails to meet all students'

needs. A concept-driven approach provides relevant learning to all students, learning that can be transferred in different and unfamiliar concepts.

- A curriculum can be designed to provide autonomy and personalisation. The use of personality types, motivations, and attitudes toward physical activity can be incorporated to better meet student needs, whilst providing students with an opportunity to shape their own curriculum can encourage engagement.

- Provide a range of sports and activities in your curriculum to meet the different needs of your students. The activities offered should meet the requirements of the National Curriculum and the movements needed to achieve competence in physical literacy. Traditional sports can be included, but alternative activities, including Yoga and fun fitness, could be offered to provide real breadth.

- Teachers should shift from fitness for performance to fitness for life (Harris and Cale, 2019). No longer should the attention only go to the most able and the reward to the winners. We must, in order to build motivation in our learners, use praise and encouragement and always remain positive. Teachers can best support the positive environment in which students progress and enjoyment thrives. Reward attitude and progress over performance and ability.

- Educate staff on the physical literacy principle. Understand how your current offering might be impacting the ability to truly nurture physical literacy. Consider the PE environment you provide and its ability to develop and nurture physical literacy.

- The Acquire, Connect and Transfer principle (Stern et al., 2021) can be employed to assist the delivery of key concepts.

- Performance related assessment which focuses only on sport specific skills should be scrapped. They are no longer fit for purpose and provide the wrong message to most that physical literacy is unattainable. A holistic and progressive approach to assessment is needed.

- Formative and summative assessment should be used together when implementing your assessment system.

- Feedback provided from the assessment is more important than the assessment model itself; it should be positive and constructive. Students should be able to clearly understand what they need to do to progress and have the opportunity to build on it.

- Listen to your students. They will give you the best indication whether you are truly meeting your department mission statement or not. Use their feedback to shape your planning and provide staff with positive feedback.
- Collaborate. No one can provide positive and meaningful PE on their own. Work together. Team members will feel a sense of ownership if they have been part of the creation. Share best practice and failures in order to improve. Have a clear action plan and celebrate every step towards achieving your goal. Remind your team of the vision and manage the day-to-day practice in order to institutionalise the change.

Our Legacy

I spoke at the start of this book about the New Zealand All Blacks rugby team philosophy of 'leaving the jersey in a better place.' I hope this book and the work I do in school helps me do that for PE. The idea translates into our ability to create a legacy and understand the higher purpose of what we do every day, content in the knowledge that, when we pass the jersey on to the next generation of PE teachers, we are handing it over in a much better position than when we were handed it.

That's not to say that those before have done a bad job – it's saying that times have changed and now, so must we. If, during our time as leaders, we created positive and meaningful PE experiences for all by implementing a concept-driven curriculum, inclusive pedagogy and holistic assessment, then what a legacy that would be.

We will have better nurtured physical literacy and promoted lifelong engagement, results and enjoyment will have increased, and students would have felt better prepared for life though engaging physical activity.

I want to end this book by answering two questions I started it with. Firstly, is PE in crisis? Hopefully, after reading this book, chapters 4, 5 and 6 have proven that not only is change possible, but that change is happening, now! There are so many amazing physical educators who have taken it upon themselves to move away from the dominant and failing sport-focused delivery for something that better represents everything that PE can be.

The second question I asked was, what will be your PE legacy? I believe that if we create positive and meaningful PE experiences during our time in charge of this great subject, we can hold our heads high. For we truly will have built a remarkable legacy and left the subject and profession in a better place.

Take Away Reflections

- What will be your PE legacy?

References

AIESEP (2020). AIESEP Position Statement on Physical Education Assessment. [Online] Accessed at: https://aiesep.org/wp-content/uploads/2020/06/AIESEP-Position-Statement-on-PE-Assessment-FINAL1.pdf [Accessed 8 August 2020].

Association for PE (2015) AfPE's position on fitness testing for school aged pupils. [Online] Accessed at: https://www.afpe.org.uk/physical-education/fitness-testing/ [Accessed 13 January 2021].

Bailey, S. and Vamplew, W. (1999) *100 Years of Physical Education 1899-1999*. Warwick Printing Company Limited.

Baumeister, R., Bratslavsky, E. and Finkenauer, C. (2001) *Bad is Stronger than Good*. Sage Journals

Caldwell, H.A.T., Di Crisofara, Natascja, A., Cairney, J., Bray, S.R., MacDonald, M.J. and Timmons, B.W. (2020) *Physical Literacy, Physical Activity, and Health Indicators in School-Age Children*. [Online] Available at: https://www.mdpi.com/1660-4601/17/15/5367 [Accessed 26 July 2020].

Casey, A. and Kirk, D. (2021). *Models-Based Practice in Physical Education*. Routledge.

Centre for Creative Leadership (circa 2018) *Developing Talent? You're Probably Missing Vertical Development*. [Online] Accessed at: https://www.ccl.org/articles/leading-effectively-articles/developing-talent-what-youre-probably-missing/ [Accessed 16 July 2020].

Chambers, F., Aldous, D. and Bryant, A. (2021). *Threshold Concepts in Physical Education: A Design Thinking Approach*. Routledge.

Christodoulou, D. (2016) *Making Good Progress? The Future of Assessment for Learning*. Oxford University Press.

Cope, A. and Whittaker, A. (2012) *The Art of Being Brilliant*. Capstone.

Department for Education (2013) Statutory guidance: National Curriculum in England: Physical Education programmes of study. [Online] Access at: https://www.gov.uk/government/publications/national-curriculum-in-england-physical-education-programmes-of-study/national-curriculum-in-england-physical-education-programmes-of-study [Accessed on 1 June 2020].

Department for Education (2019) *School Sport and Activity Action Plan*. [Online] Available at: https://assets.publishing.service.gov.uk/government/uploads/system/uploads/attachment_data/file/848082/School_sport_and_activity_action_plan.pdf [Accessed on 1 August 2020].

Department of National Heritage (1995) *Sport: Raising the Game.*

Donarski, S. and Bennett, T. (2020) *The Research Ed Guide to Assessment: An Evidence-Informed Guide for Teachers.* John Catt

Dowling, S. (2021) *Pivot, Flex, Adapt: Physical Education Through the 2020 Pandemic.* United Learning.

Durden-Myers, E.J. (2018). *Physical Literacy: A Guide for Educators.* Scholary.

Durden-Myers, E. J. (2020) *Operationalising physical literacy within Physical Education teaching practice through professional development.* PhD Thesis. The University of Bedfordshire.

Durden-Myers, E. J., Whitehead, M . (2021) *Lifetime Contributions in Physical Education: Celebrating the Work of Len Almond (1938-2017) and Joy Butler (1957-2019).* Scholary.

Education Endowment Foundation (2011) *Metacognition and Self-Regulated Learning: Guidance Report.* Education Endowment Foundation.

Education Scotland (2017) *Benchmarks: Physical Education.* [Online] Available at: https://education.gov.scot/nih/Documents/HWBPhysicalEducation-BenchmarksPDF.pdf [Accessed on 20 January 2021].

Ekkekakis, P., Ladwig, M. and Vazou, S (2018) *My best memory is when I was done with it: PE memories are associated with adult sedentary behaviour.* [Online] Available at: https://www.researchgate.net/publication/327118352_My_best_memory_is_when_I_was_done_with_it_PE_memories_are_associated_with_adult_sedentary_behavior [Accessed on 22 March 2021].

Ennis, C. D. (2006) *Curriculum: Forming and Reshaping the Vision of Physical Education in a High Need, Low Demand World of Schools.* Quest, 58(1), pp. 41-59.

Ennis, C. D. (2014) *What goes around comes around... or does it? Disrupting the cycle of traditional, sport-based Physical Education.* Kinesiology Review.

Erickson, H. Lynn. (2007). *Concept-Based Curriculum and Instruction for the Thinking Classroom.* Corwin.

Fletcher, T. (2021) *Pedagogical principles that support the prioritisation of meaningful experiences in Physical Education: conceptual and practical considerations* [Online] Available at: https://www.tandfonline.com/doi/ful

I/10.1080/17408989.2021.1884672 [Accessed on 22 February 2021].

Frapwell, A. and Caldecott, S. (2011) *In Deep: Learning to Learn*. Coachwise.

Frapwell, A. (2015) *A Practical Guide to Assessing Without Levels: Supporting and Safeguarding High Quality Achievement in Physical Education*. Coachwise.

Green, K. (2005). *Examinations: a 'new orthodoxy' in physical education*. In Physical education: essential issues. K. Green and K. Hardman (Eds), pp. 143-160. London, Sage.

Harris, J. and Cale, L. (2019) *Promoting Active Lifestyles in Schools*. Human Kinetics.

Huddleston, G. and Whitehouse, A. (2020) *Reflecting on Your Curriculum: Using SPACE as a Reflective Framework*. Physical Educations Matters, Association for PE.

International Physical Literacy Association (2020) *Choosing Physical Activity for Life: Be Your Best*. PE Scholar.

Johnson, S. (1999) *Who Moved My Cheese: An Amazing Way to Deal with Change in Your Work and in Your Life*. Vermilion.

Kerr, J. (2013). *Legacy*. Constable.

Kirk, D. (2010) *Physical Education futures*. Routledge.

Kotter, J.P. (2020) *8 Steps to Accelerate Change in your Organisation*. [Online] Accessed at: https://aiesep.org/wp-content/uploads/2020/06/AIESEP-Position-Statement-on-PE-Assessment-FINAL1.pdf [Accessed 8 August 2020].

Kotter, J.P. (2012) *Leading Change*. Harvard Business Review Press.

McCuaig, L., Marino, M., Gobbi, E., and Macdonald, D. (2015) *Taught not Caught: Values based education through Physical Education and School Sport: Literature Review*. AIESEP Partners for WADA, ICSSPE, IOC, Fairplay & UNESCO.

Meyer, J.H.F and Land, R. (2005) *Threshold concepts and troublesome knowledge (2): Epistemological considerations and a conceptual framework for teaching and learning*. Springer Link.

Mental Health Foundation (2016) *Fundamental Facts about Mental Health 2016*. [Online] Available at: https://www.mentalhealth.org.uk/publications/fundamental-facts-about-mental-health-2016 [Accessed 23 February 2021].

Murphy, A. (2017) *A Quick Guide to Concept-Based Learning and Curriculum*. [Online] Accessed at: https://www.onatlas.com/blog/concept-based-learning-curriculum [Accessed 29 May 2020].

Myatt, M. (2018) *The Curriculum Gallimaufry to Coherence*. John Catt.

National College for Teaching and Leadership (2014) *Beyond Levels: Altering Assessment Approaches Developed By Teaching Schools*. [Online] Accessed at: https://assets.publishing.service.gov.uk/government/uploads/system/uploads/attachment_data/file/349266/beyond-levels-alternative-assessment-approaches-developed-by-teaching-schools.pdf [Accessed 3 August 2020].

Ofsted (2019) *The Education Inspection Framework*. [Online] Accessed at: https://assets.publishing.service.gov.uk/government/uploads/system/uploads/attachment_data/file/801429/Education_inspection_framework.pdf [Access 20 June 2020].

Penney, D., Brooker, R., Hay, P. and Gillespie, L. (2009) *Education and Society*. Routledge.

Petrie, N. (2014) *Vertical Leadership Development–Part 1 Developing Leaders for a Complex World*. The Centre for Creative Leadership.

Royal College of Paediatrics and Child Health (Circa 2018) *About Childhood Obesity*. [Online] Available at: https://www.rcpch.ac.uk/key-topics/nutrition-obesity/about-childhood-obesity [Accessed 3 August 2020].

Sealy, C., and Bennett, T. (2020) *The Research Ed Guide to the Curriculum: An Evidence-Informed Guide for Teachers*. John Catt.

Sinek, S. (2009) *Start with Why*. Penguin.

Sport England (2014) *Under the Skin*. [Online] Accessed at: https://sportengland-production-files.s3.eu-west-2.amazonaws.com/s3fs-public/youth-insight_under-the-skin.pdf?Rhi.oCS5QHjLCQfUtGBn6F7eXg9qDyX1 [Accessed 16 August 2020].

Sport England (2019) *Active Lives Children and Young People Survey*. [Online] Available at: https://sportengland-production-files.s3.eu-west-2.amazonaws.com/s3fs-public/2021-01/Active%20Lives%20Children%20Survey%20Academic%20Year%2019-20%20report.pdf?4Ti_0V0m9sYy-5HwQjSiJN7Xj.VlnpjV6 [Accessed 21 January 2021]

Sport England. (2021). *Active Lives Children and Young People Survey*. [Online] Available at: https://sportengland-production-files.s3.eu-west-2.amazonaws.com/s3fs-public/2020-01/active-lives-children-survey-academic-year-18-19.pdf?cVMsdnpBoqROViY61iUjpQY6WcRyhtGs [Accessed 29 July 2020].

Sporticus (2016) *A Models Based Approach to PE: Cooperative Learn-*

ing. [Online] Accessed at:https://drowningintheshallow.wordpress. com/2016/07/17/a-models-based-approach-to-pe-cooperative-learning/ [Accessed on April 20 2020].

Sporticus (2020) *At Arm's Length.* [Online] Accessed at: https://drown- ingintheshallow.wordpress.com/2020/08/23/at-arms-length/ [Accessed on 23 August 2020].

Stern, J., Ferraro, K. and Mohnkern, J. (2017) *Tools for Teaching Conceptual Understanding: Designing Lessons and Assessments for Deep Learning.* Corwin.

Stern, J., Ferraro, K., Duncan, K. and Aleo, T. (2021) *Learning That Transfers: Designing Curriculum for a Chagning World.* Corwin.

Swaithes, W. (2015) *10 Steps to a World Leading Physical Education Depart- ment.* [Online] Accessed at: https://www.youthsporttrust.org/want-world- leading-pe-department [Accessed 25 July 2020].

Thorburn, M. (2007). *Achieving conceptual and curriculum coherence in high- stakes school examinations in Physical Education.* Physical Education and Sport Pedagogy. 12(2), pp. 163-184.

Toward, G., Henley, C. and Cope, A. (2016) *The Art of Being a Brilliant Middle Leader.* Crown House Publishing.

UNESCO (2015) *Quality Physical Education (QPE), Guideline for Policy Makers.* [Online] Accessed at: https://en.unesco.org/inclusivepolicylab/sites/de- fault/files/learning/document/2017/1/231101E.pdf [Accessed 12 January 2021].

Vuca-World (2020) *What does VUCA mean for your Leadership and your strat- egies?* [Online] Accessed at: https://www.vuca-world.org [Accessed 18 July 2020].

Youth Sport Trust (2018) *Improving Wellbeing Through Secondary Physical Education.* [Online] Accessed at: https://www.youthsporttrust.org/sys- tem/files/resources/documents/Improving-Wellbeing-Through-PE.pdf [Accessed 17 June 2020].

Whitehead, M. (2010) *Physical Literacy Throughout the Lifecourse.* Routledge.

Willingham, D.T. (2009) *Why Don't Students Like School?* Jossey-Bass.

Wiliam, D. (2011) *Embedded Formative Assessment.* Solution Tree Press

World Health Organisation. (2018). *A vision for a more active World.* [Online] Accessed at: https://apps.who.int/iris/bitstream/hand le/10665/272722/9789241514187-eng.pdf [Accessed 20 August 2020].

World Health Organisation (2020) *Obesity and Overweight.* [Online] Accessed at: https://www.who.int/news-room/fact-sheets/detail/obesity-and-over-weight [Accessed 23 February 2021].

World Health Organisation (2020) *Physical Activity*. [Online] Accessed at: https://www.who.int/news-room/fact-sheets/detail/physical-activity#:~:-text=Levels%20of%20physical%20activity%20globally&text=World-wide%2C%20around%201%20in%203,physical%20activity%20to%20stay%20healthy.&text=Insufficient%20activity%20increased%20by%205,countries%20between%202001%20and%202016. [Accessed 23 February 2021].

Youth Sport Trust (2014) *The Power of PE: The Future of Physical Education*. [Online] Accessed at: https://sportengland-production-files.s3.eu-west-2.amazonaws.com/s3fs-public/youth-insight_under-the-skin.pdf?Rhi.oCS5QHjLCQfUtGBn6F7eXg9qDyX1 [Accessed 3 July 2020].

Youth Sport Trust (2018) *PE provision in secondary schools 2018: Survey Research Report*. [Online] Accessed at: https://www.youthsporttrust.org/system/files/resources/documents/PE%20provision%20in%20second-ary%20schools%202018%20-%20Survey%20Research%20Report_0.pdf [Accessed 28 June 2020].

Youth Sport Trust (2018) *Research finds whistle being blown on Secondary PE*. [Online] Accessed at: https://www.youthsporttrust.org/news/research-finds-whistle-being-blown-secondary-pe [Accessed 1 July 2020].

Youth Sport Trust (2019) *Assessing without Levels in Physical Education*. [Online] Accessed at: https://www.youthsporttrust.org/system/files/resources/documents/Assessing_Without_Levels.pdf [Accessed 1 July 2020].

Youth Sport Trust (2021) *Parents want wellbeing prioritised in schools as pandemic hits home*. [Online] Accessed at: https://www.youthsporttrust.org/news/parents-want-wellbeing-prioritised-schools-pandemic-hits-home [Accessed 12 March 2021].

Lightning Source UK Ltd.
Milton Keynes UK
UKHW050856060322
399626UK00004B/334